An OPUS Book

Law and Modern So...

SECOND EDITION

P. S. Atiyah was for over thirty years a teacher and writer on law. He taught at universities in four continents, including Australia and the United States, where he spent a year as a Visiting Professor at Harvard. He was Professor of English Law at Oxford from 1977 until 1988 when he retired. His publications include *The Rise and Fall of Freedom of Contract* and *Accidents, Compensation and the Law*.

Law and Modern Society

SECOND EDITION

P. S. Atiyah

Oxford   New York

OXFORD UNIVERSITY PRESS

1995

Oxford University Press, Walton Street, Oxford OX2 6DP

Oxford New York
Athens Auckland Bangkok Bombay
Calcutta Cape Town Dar es Salaam Delhi
Florence Hong Kong Istanbul Karachi
Kuala Lumpur Madras Madrid Melbourne
Mexico City Nairobi Paris Singapore
Taipei Tokyo Toronto

and associated companies in
Berlin Ibadan

Oxford is a trade mark of Oxford University Press

First published by Oxford University Press 1983
Second edition first issued as an Oxford University Press paperback 1995

British Library Cataloguing in Publication Data
Data available

Library of Congress Cataloging-in-Publication Data
Atiyah, P. S.
    Law and modern society / P. S. Atiyah. — 2nd ed.
    Includes bibliographical references and index.
    1. Law—Great Britain.   2. Lawyers—Great Britain.   3. Courts—
Great Britain.   I. Title.
    KD662.A86 1995   349.41—dc20   [344.1]   95–13064
    ISBN 0–19–289267–3

10 9 8 7 6 5 4 3 2 1

Typeset by Graphicraft Typesetters Ltd., Hong Kong

Printed in Great Britain
by Biddles Ltd.,
Guildford and King's Lynn

Preface

In the twelve years since this book was first published many major changes have occurred in our laws, our legal institutions, and the subjects of most current interest and importance. This edition has been extensively revised to shift the focus to these areas of greater relevance and topicality. In particular, I have given much greater emphasis to the effect of membership of the European Community on our law. It is surprising how few members of the general public appear to be aware that it has become clear in the past few years that, for all practical purposes, the sovereignty of Parliament is now subject to the laws of the European Community. Even in a book designed primarily for laymen this has seemed such a remarkable change in the foundations of our legal system as to justify a full account of what has happened and how it has happened. I have also explored briefly the possibility of the creation of a federal Europe. In addition I have greatly expanded the account of the European Convention on Human Rights, and its effects on our law. Other subjects dealt with more fully in this edition include recent controversy over the independence of the judiciary, problems arising from the cost of legal services and legal aid, the Mackay reforms which have changed the relationship between the two parts of the legal profession, the many appalling miscarriages of justice which have disfigured the legal system in the past decade, and the effect of recent changes in the law on the 'right to silence'.

I am much indebted for research assistance in preparing this edition to Mr Craig Arnott.

P. S. ATIYAH

Contents

1 Law in the courts

Courts and the legal system

When the ordinary person thinks of 'the law' he may tend to think of the police. It is often thought that in popular underworld parlance the police are actually spoken of as though they *were* the law ('Here comes the law'). But in other contexts, we often associate 'the law' more strongly with courts, judges, and magistrates. When we speak of the law's delays, or complain that the law is old-fashioned, we are often thinking of the courts and the legal system rather than of the rules of law themselves. This association between the law and the legal process, between the rules of law and the courts, is one which lawyers are particularly prone to make. To a lawyer, the courts are the very heart and centre of the law. A modern lawyer would find it impossible to conceive of a legal system which contained rules of law, but no courts. In fact he would probably find it less difficult to imagine a society which contained courts but no rules of law.

Why should this be so? It might seem that logically speaking laws come first, and that courts are merely secondary. After all, in modern society it is the primary function of the courts to apply and enforce the law which actually exists. And anyhow courts and judges are themselves creatures who owe their status, their authority, and in a sense their very existence to the law. It is the law itself which tells us that this elderly gentleman sitting on this dais in that Victorian building in the Strand known as the Royal Courts of Justice, is a judge of the High Court, and that while he sits there he actually *is* the court.

Moreover, anyone who looks at the whole machinery of government in the broadest sense might find it odd that lawyers should place the courts at the centre of their legal universe. Isn't that a bit like pre-Copernican astronomy? Isn't Parliament the real sun round which the law revolves? Acts of Parliament after all are very real laws, as lawyers would unhesitatingly agree. And Acts of Parliament have a very tangible 'existence'. They are often quite solid documents running to a hundred pages or more. You can buy them, and bind them into volumes, as lawyers do. In them you will find all sorts of rules which often say very little or nothing about the courts or judges who are to enforce them.

Then again, it must be admitted that there are some laws—sometimes extensive and complex bodies of law—which are rarely handled by ordinary courts and judges at all. This is particularly true of modern welfare state legislation, such as the law relating to social security. This enormous mass of law defines the conditions under which people are entitled to a wide variety of welfare benefits, and how these benefits are to be calculated in particular cases. There is a great deal of this law and it is complex and difficult to find. But the point is that it is not generally administered or applied by ordinary courts, judges, or magistrates. For the most part it is administered by civil servants working in the Department of Social Security—the DSS. People who want to claim benefits go to their local DSS office and fill in a form. The form is processed by the officials. It is true that a special system of tribunals exists to which the citizen can appeal if he is not satisfied by the initial decisions of the officials. And these tribunals hear cases and decide them according to the law, in much the same way (though with far less formality) as ordinary courts. But lawyers rarely penetrate into these tribunals, and they certainly would not think of them, as they think of the ordinary courts, as being at the very centre of the legal system.

So it may seem curious that lawyers tend to identify 'the law' so heavily with courts and judges. But there are reasons for it, some historical, some practical, and others perhaps less easy to classify.

Among the historical reasons for the modern lawyer's pre-Copernican perception of the legal universe we can identify two factors in particular. The first is that it is not true, in a historical sense, to say that laws came before courts. The central court of the modern English legal system—the High Court of Justice—is the direct descendant of a number of old courts, some of them dating back to the twelfth century, which were never created by a deliberate act of law-making. These courts grew up gradually as offshoots of the authority of the King and, as the very word 'court' indicates, these courts of justice were originally a part of the royal court. They were not created by law in order to administer pre-existing laws. They were created, or grew up, in order to solve pressing practical questions—to dispose of arguments, to solve disputes, and to suppress violence and theft. As they developed into what we would today recognize as courts of law, they actually created the law as they went along. Eventually their decisions began to fall into regular and predictable patterns, people began to take notes of what the judges were deciding, and in due course there emerged the modern 'law reports'. A substantial body of English law was created in this way, and much of it remains in force to this day, modified and modernized in all sorts of respects both by more recent judicial decisions and by Acts of Parliament. This part of the law, usually known as the 'common law', was thus created by the courts in the very process of deciding cases before them.

So when the modern lawyer thinks of the common law it is not surprising if he still tends to think of the courts as in some sense primary, and the law as secondary, rather than the other way around. What is more, the old common law remains in a sense the more fundamental part even of modern English law. In sheer bulk modern legislation is no doubt outstripping the common law, but naturally enough the common law tended to deal with more essential and basic legal issues than much modern legislation. The common law was the *first* part of the law to be created, and the first part of the law in any society must necessarily deal with essentials. Naturally the common law evolved the basic principles of the criminal law— it was the common law which first prohibited murder, violence, theft, and rape. Similarly, much of our basic property law was first laid down by common law courts, and so was the law of civil liability. The law of contract and the law of torts (or civil wrongs) were very largely created by the courts out of the simplest of ideas—that it is wrong to harm or injure others. Although much of this law has been amended and qualified in all manner of ways in modern times, there is a sense in which the modern lawyer tends still to see the common law as the central repository of legal ideas and principles. Given the very basic values and interests recognized by the common law, this is hardly surprising, and this also helps to explain why courts are still so very central to the way lawyers think about law.

The second historical factor which helps to explain the lawyer's perspective on these matters is that until quite recent times the courts were, relatively speaking, a far more important part of the whole machinery of government than they are today. In modern times the day-to-day administration of government lies in the hands of vast armies of officials in central and local government, including in particular the police; and at the central level, the authority of Parliament is generally undisputed and can readily be used to overturn rules of law laid down by the courts which do not find favour with the government. So in one sense the courts are today a small, though important, part of a very extensive machine. But in historical terms this is all a fairly recent development. Until the eighteenth century the machinery of government was very weak, at both central and local levels. Parliament's law-making activities were confined within fairly narrow limits in practice, and so the role of the courts was then relatively far more important than it is today. Indeed, it is widely thought by historians that the early common law courts were deliberately used as one of the main instruments by which royal authority was extended over the whole country in the twelfth century and onwards. It is from these, and perhaps even earlier, days that the custom began of sending judges out on assize, travelling from town to town, hearing cases, helping to create a body of uniform law across the country, and at the same time, showing the people that the authority of the King extended to every corner of his realm.

Now it may of course be said that all this is old history, and it is surely high time that lawyers recognized the Copernican revolution. The law does not revolve round the courts today, whatever may have been the position 200 years ago or more. Why are lawyers so historically minded? Is this just another illustration of their conservatism? I shall later have something to say on these and similar issues, but for the present it will suffice to admit that lawyers do tend to be somewhat historically minded, at least in the sense that they often tend to perceive the world, the law, and the legal system in ways which other people would regard as old-fashioned or even obsolete. But this is hardly surprising. English law today is the product of continuous development extending over 800 or 900 years, unbroken by revolutions or similar cataclysms. Changes and modernizations of the law often take the form of imposing new layers of law over the old layers, but frequently in such a way that bits and pieces of the old layers survive; even when sweeping legal changes are introduced the new law is built on the foundations of the old. It is thus very difficult to learn, or teach, English law without acquiring some understanding of its history. The system of precedent, about which I shall have to say something later, also tends to make the lawyer rather backward-looking, but enough has been said to show why it is part of the historical culture which an English lawyer acquires to see courts as the centre-piece in the law.

There are, in addition, other very practical reasons why lawyers tend to have such a court-oriented view of law. One of them is the simple fact that the courts are where the lawyer goes, on behalf of his clients, when disputes arise which cannot be settled amicably. Just as the civil servant doubtless tends to have a government-oriented vision of law and regulation, because most problems that he deals with tend to get settled within or by governments and government departments, so, for similar reasons, the lawyer sees the courts as the focus of the system of dispute settlement in which he is involved.

A related factor is that when disputes arise it is frequently the case that both the facts and the law applicable to those facts may be unclear. When this happens, a lawyer tends to take a severely practical approach to the question of legal rights and duties: he asks himself what a court is likely to decide if the case comes before it. Indeed, this can quite often be a necessary exercise even where the facts appear clear enough to the client and the lawyer, but there is great difficulty about proving them. To the lawyer, a fact is really a provable fact or it is nothing. Similarly, where the law is uncertain, or where its application is uncertain in particular cases, the lawyer's main concern is with the available lines of argument—he knows that some forms of legal argument are acceptable and others less so—and with the probable outcome. He is in fact interested in *predicting* what a court is likely to do. This does not, of course, mean that all law is nothing more than a series of predictions about how judges and other officials of the legal system are likely to behave in certain circumstances. It is absurd to suggest that the law prohibiting murder is really just a prediction that anybody who commits murder and is brought before the courts will be sent to gaol for life, or until the Home Secretary chooses to release him. But it is nevertheless a fact of life that practising lawyers, when faced with legal problems, habitually ask themselves: If I had to argue this in court, how would I present the case? How would the judge be likely to react? It is also a fact that making predictions of this kind is not always something that can easily be done by merely looking the law up in books. The lawyer needs a 'feel' for how a judge is likely to react to his case, and this is something which can normally be acquired only by actually practising in the courts and appearing regularly before the judges.

It is this which gives some truth to the aphorism, 'the law is what the court says it is'. Snappy sayings like this can be misleading if pressed too far (for instance, judges themselves do not think the law is merely what they say it is), but there is undoubtedly some truth in them. In the last analysis it doesn't matter what is in the books, the law reports, even Acts of Parliament. If a judge sentences someone to gaol, then to gaol he will assuredly go. The judge may have got it wrong, he may even be perverse, but the immediate result is the same. Of course there may be the possibility of an appeal. But the decision of the appeal court may be equally wrong or perverse. Then what *that* court decides is what matters. Perhaps it is wrong to suggest that this is what counts 'in the last analysis', because obviously if judges habitually flouted Acts of Parliament or established precedents, they would be removed from office. But that is to enter the realms of fantasy. It is because judges don't behave in these extreme ways that one can safely assert that in the last analysis what they decide is the law.

Finally, there are other factors of a less readily identifiable nature which tend to make the lawyer think of courts as the centre of the law. In particular, the leaders of the legal profession tend to be seen, both by the public and also by the profession, as the judges, particularly the high court and appeal court judges. Most able barristers see judicial appointment as the apex of a successful career at the Bar. Judges actually decide cases over which lawyers have pondered and argued. So naturally lawyers are encouraged in their tendency to think of the law as something almost wholly associated with, or even dependent upon, the courts. We shall in the next chapter also have to say something of two new developments in our legal system which promise to make courts even more central and important than they have hitherto been, because these developments are beginning to give some courts powers of decision which are in a sense even superior to those of Parliament and government. And when this happens—as the American experience vividly shows —judges sometimes become more important than politicians.

The superior courts

The English legal system has certain élitist characteristics. One of its most striking features is that it has only a few superior courts, presided over by senior judges of great authority and prestige, who hear a very small number of cases; and a lot of lower courts, presided over by less senior judges or magistrates, who hear a very large number of cases. Of course, the superior courts tend to deal with the more important cases, while the lower courts deal with the less important. But the distinction between important and less important cases is not necessarily an uncontentious one. Many small cases may be desperately important to those involved in them; even magistrates have the power to send offenders to gaol for periods of (normally) up to twelve months, which is no light matter for the accused. And some cases which go on appeal to superior courts are only important because of their potential public repercussions rather than because they raise crucially important issues between the actual litigants themselves. For example, a decision in a tax case may involve a few hundred pounds for the particular taxpayer, but if the decision turns upon the interpretation to be given to an important section of a taxing Act, the result may determine thousands of similar cases in which many millions of pounds may be involved.

We cannot here set out in detail a full account of all the courts and the relationships between them. A thumb-nail sketch of the system will suffice, though rather more will then be said about the professionals who operate it. Of the superior civil courts, the central court is the High Court of Justice. The High Court is based in the Royal Courts of Justice in the Strand, and most of its work is done there. But a small number of High Court cases are heard by judges in twenty-four provincial centres distributed throughout the country.

The High Court is divided into three divisions—the Queen's Bench Division, the Chancery Division, and the Family Division—and each judge on appointment to the High Court is allocated to one of the three divisions. The High Court is a civil court which hears no criminal cases at all, though the *judges* of the High Court may and often do hear the most important criminal cases—but they do that in the capacity of judges of the Crown Court.

The different divisions of the High Court deal with all the civil litigation in the country which involves claims of more than £50,000, as well as other litigation which is important because of the issues rather than the amount which is at stake. The largest division is the Queen's Bench Division, which deals with the great bulk of ordinary civil cases which find their way to the High Court—for example, claims for damages for serious personal injuries, commercial claims, say on insurance policies, or arising out of international contracts between business men, shipping claims arising out of collisions at sea, or claims by cargo owners for damage to goods at sea, and so forth. This division also deals with many claims against governmental and other public authorities where it is alleged that they have acted beyond their powers or in some other unauthorized or illegal manner. The Chancery Division is the descendant of a distinct court formerly called the Court of Chancery which was in its earliest days a one-judge court in which the Lord Chancellor sat. Today this division deals mainly with claims arising out of trusts, the administration of estates of deceased persons, and actions arising out of contracts relating to land; it also exercises certain supervisory powers over companies. The Family Division, as its name implies (and it alone is a very new creation), deals with applications for divorce, and with matters relating to family property such as claims for maintenance or claims arising from the division of family assets on divorce.

It also deals with matters relating to children, such as custody and guardianship disputes, and it can make adoption orders. (The jurisdiction of the courts in family cases often overlaps, so some of these matters are also sometimes dealt with by other courts.) The old Probate, Divorce, and Admiralty Division of the High Court was abolished in 1971 and its work transferred to the present three divisions named above.

Neither the High Court nor the separate divisions of the High Court actually sit as courts in the ordinary sense. Nearly all their work is done by single high court judges, sitting alone. A judge who sits as a judge of any of the divisions of the High Court is in law *the* High Court while he sits, and has the full powers of the High Court. In a few cases only, two or three judges sit together as a 'divisional court' of one or other of the divisions. In the Queen's Bench Division, the most important sort of cases heard in this way are petitions for a review of the legality of governmental acts of various kinds.

From a decision of the High Court it is possible to appeal to the Court of Appeal. This court also sits in divisions, but there is no formal separation between the divisions, so they would be more appropriately called panels. Usually three judges sit in one panel. In rare cases it is possible to carry a further appeal to the House of Lords, which is the apex of the judicial system, not only of England and Wales (with which alone this book is strictly concerned) but also of Scotland and Northern Ireland, which in all other respects have their own legal systems and judges. Historically, of course, the House of Lords which was the final Court of Appeal of the English legal system was the ordinary House of Lords which is still one of the Houses of Parliament—though it is now the House of Lords of the whole United Kingdom. But today, when sitting as a court, the House of Lords bears very little relationship to the legislative body of the same name. Only senior judges, known as Lords of Appeal, sit when the House of Lords deals with legal appeals, though they are also sometimes joined by other senior judges such as the Lord Chancellor and former Lord Chancellors. Usually five judges sit in appeals to the House of Lords. Needless to say, when sitting to hear appeals the House of Lords is bound like any other court to apply the law as it is, and does not behave as it does when sitting as a branch of the legislature when (in conjunction with the House of Commons) it has power to *change* the law. Labour party proposals to reform the legislative House of Lords if it wins the next election, by abolishing the right of hereditary peers to sit and vote, will, presumably, not affect the powers of the House of Lords as a court.

As I have previously mentioned, these great courts only deal with a relatively small number of cases—indeed, a tiny number of cases compared to the total volume of litigation, or measured against the country's population. In 1993, for instance, the total number of cases heard in the High Court (excluding cases in the Family Division) was 1,781, the total number of civil appeals disposed of by the Court of Appeal was 1,045, and the number of appeals heard in the House of Lords was a minuscule 84. But despite this, most lawyers tend to think of these courts as the 'ordinary' courts, and much law teaching concentrates on them at the expense of the lower courts. There are several reasons for this.

First, and obviously, these courts do deal with most of the big litigation where really large sums, or vital issues, are at stake. Secondly, the appeal courts hear appeals (though not in all cases) from the lower courts as well as from the High Court, so that they do have the final say in the small numbers of cases they deal with. Thirdly, the High Court is the only court of *general* jurisdiction as opposed to courts of limited or special jurisdiction; so cases which raise novel points or which do not fall within the competence of other special bodies or lower courts—residuary cases, in other words—must go before the High Court. Fourthly, the peculiar prestige and status of the judges of the High Court and above tend to make them and their decisions of more interest and importance both to the legal profession and the public at large; and finally, it is only these judges whose decisions create 'precedents' which are reported and so help to make new law. I shall enlarge briefly on these last two points.

The judges

The élitist characteristics of the English legal system are most apparent in its different treatment of the judges of its courts. Judges of the High Court and above have immense prestige and status. They are invariably knighted on appointment to the Bench (ladies are made Dames of the British Empire). In court they are addressed as 'my lord' or 'your lordship' (or, 'my lady' or 'your ladyship') even though they are not actually peers or peeresses; officially they become Mr Justice Smith or Lord (or Lady) Justice Brown. They are paid substantially more than Cabinet ministers. They always become (if they are not already) members of the governing body of their Inns of Court—benchers. The most senior of all—the Lord Chief Justice, the Master of the Rolls (who is President of the Court of Appeal), the Lords of Appeal—are nearly always made life peers; indeed, the Lords of Appeal have to be, in order to sit in the House of Lords. Socially and even politically, much deference is paid to them. The press is ready to report almost any comment they make, and (for example) criticism of a government department or other public body made by a high court judge in the course of a case before him nearly always produces a flurry of activity in the appropriate quarters. It might even lead to an inquiry, and at the least it often produces apologies or ministerial statements. These superior court judges are also much in demand for non-judicial tasks. Governments frequently turn to them to head Royal Commissions, and other inquiries of all kinds. For instance, the inquiry into the Matrix Churchill affair was held by Lord Justice Scott, and the inquiry set up in 1994 to inquire into standards in public life is being chaired by Lord Nolan, a lord of appeal. Judges have even been used as arbitrators to settle major industrial disputes, though that practice has largely fallen into disuse since Lady Thatcher first became Prime Minister.

There are other respects in which the position of superior court judges does not differ markedly from that of some of the lower court judges. For example, they are expected to refrain from open political partisanship. They are not allowed to stand for Parliament. They are not expected to resign their judicial positions in order to take up other paid employment, and only one such case has occurred in living memory. And within their own court-rooms, circuit judges enjoy nearly (though not quite) as much power and deference as superior court judges. In their background, and traditions too, there is little difference between superior and lower court judges.

Judges tend to be middle-aged to elderly. Superior court judges have hitherto invariably been appointed from the ranks of practising barristers, though it seems unlikely that opening the judiciary to solicitors will have much impact on the age at which appointments tend to be made. It is rare for a person to be made a high court judge unless he has had at least fifteen years' experience at the Bar. Most have had much more. Nowadays it is unusual for anybody to be appointed to the Court of Appeal who has not previously served a stint as a high court judge and, similarly, Lords of Appeal are usually appointed from the ranks of the Court of Appeal judges. All this means that judges are unlikely to be young, and the more senior the judges, the older the average age tends to be. Few high court judges are under 50, few judges in the Court of Appeal under 55, and few Lords of Appeal under 60. Many, in all three courts, are much older than this. By contrast, John Major was 49 when he became Prime Minister and Tony Blair just 41 when he became Leader of the Opposition.

Senior judges also tend to come overwhelmingly from the professional and managerial classes. It is still the case that a high proportion of them (probably over three-quarters) have been to public schools and thereafter to Oxford or Cambridge. In 1987 a survey found that twenty-nine out of thirty-four law lords and lord justices of appeal had attended public school and Oxford or Cambridge. Very few judges come from working-class backgrounds. Politically, it is probable (though judges do not parade their political views) that the overwhelming majority of judges are somewhat conservative, though it seems likely that their conservatism is of the kind which was more popular before the arrival of Mrs Thatcher as Prime Minister. However, too much can be made of these facts. Senior barristers and judges lead a more 'ordinary' life than would have been common fifty or a hundred years ago. Undoubtedly they are among the wealthier sections of the community, but they are not all aristocrats who have no contact with the 'common man'. Certainly, there is no reason why judges today should not have a pretty clear idea of how the 'common man' thinks and works and lives, even if it is going a little far to claim, as Lord Devlin has done, that judges think of themselves, in some sense, as representing the common man. On the other hand it probably is true, as Lord Devlin has also said, that the problem (if it is a problem) of the 'politics of the judges' is common to nearly all those in senior positions in our society. In all institutions—the civil service, the political parties, the professions, the armed forces—those who reach the top posts are usually 'mature, safe and orthodox men'.

Minorities are not well represented in the judiciary. No woman has ever been appointed a lord of appeal, and in 1994 there was only one lady justice of appeal and three female high court judges. No black judge sits on the High Court or above, though there is one black circuit judge. The Lord Chancellor insists that there is no discrimination in making judicial appointments, and claims with some justice that the pool of suitably qualified applicants today reflects the fact that there were few women or black barristers twenty-five or thirty years ago, the age cohort from which present-day judges must expect to be found. Today there are plenty of women barristers and barristers from ethnic minorities. The Bar Council also claims that the social mix among law students and young barristers grows wider every year, so that in due course this fact may expect to be mirrored in the composition of the judiciary—but it may be a long while before the change is very noticeable. Unfortunately, there are still many allegations that barristers from the ethnic minorities, and perhaps women also, are the subject of adverse discrimination which prevents them gaining the experience which would qualify them to become QCs and ultimately judges.

In many of these respects, the position of the superior judges probably differs little from that of the lower court judges. They too are nearly all drawn from the Bar, although there are now a few circuit judges who were formerly solicitors. Possibly lower court judges are less likely to be from the public schools/Oxbridge mould, but little research has been done into the comparative social origins of the different grades of judges. On the other hand, in the various respects referred to earlier (prestige, status, and so forth) the position of the superior court judges is unique.

The independence of the judiciary

The superior court judges enjoy many statutory protections designed to guarantee their independence and immunity from governmental pressure. Of course, the days are long past when the government or the Crown attempted to browbeat or persuade judges to decide in their favour in important public cases. Indeed, it was just because the Stuart kings had regularly done this that the Act of Settlement in 1701 gave the superior judges their present conditions of tenure, as a result of which they cannot be dismissed during good behaviour. Thus they are virtually irremovable (except by the almost unprecedented procedure of an address to the Crown by a vote of both Houses of Parliament); and their salaries are 'charged on the consolidated fund', which means that they do not have to be voted every year by Parliament like ordinary departmental budgets, and so the judges are not exposed to the risk of annual criticism. There are also procedural rules in the House of Commons designed to protect the judges from criticism with regard to their conduct in individual cases.

Despite the fact that a government would not generally dare to tamper with the independence of the judiciary in any blatant way, our system is not foolproof in its attempt to insulate the judges from governmental power. For instance, we now have a well-recognized promotional ladder, whereby judges from the High Court are generally the only candidates for appointment to the Court of Appeal, and likewise, judges from that Court are normally the only people who are likely to be appointed as Lords of Appeal. This means that a government can reward judges it favours by promoting them, perhaps out of turn, and punish those it dislikes by holding them back. It is widely believed that Sir John Donaldson was in this way 'punished' by the Labour Prime Ministers Harold Wilson and James Callaghan, who refused to promote him to the Court of Appeal in 1974–9, as a mark of their disapproval of the fact that he had been President of the ill-fated Industrial Relations Court set up by the Heath Government in 1971, but detested by the Labour party and boycotted by the trade-union movement. Conversely, Margaret Thatcher is thought to have been motivated by precisely the opposite considerations when she promoted Sir John to be Master of the Rolls in 1982. But it is very difficult indeed to guarantee that judges will never be badly treated by politicians who disapprove of the things they have done. Even in the United States, where the independence of the federal judiciary is constitutionally guaranteed, Congress has sometimes shown its disapproval of judicial behaviour by refusing to increase federal judicial salaries in line with inflation.

As all this shows, the independence of the judiciary is not just a matter of constitutional law. There are other factors which have long been just as important as the law itself. For instance, the fact that the superior court judges have always been drawn from the Bar has greatly contributed to the long tradition of sturdy independence. At the Bar, they will have constantly appeared for one side or the other in much common litigation. One day a barrister may appear for the Inland Revenue in a tax case, the next day he may appear for a taxpayer in a similar case; one day he may be prosecuting in a criminal case, the next day appearing for the defence; one day he may be briefed by an insurance company to defend in a personal injury claim, the next day he may appear for the plaintiff in such a case. Barristers do not confine their work to one side or the other in such cases, and nothing strengthens the tradition of judicial independence and impartiality more than having regularly appeared for different sides in situations of recurrent conflict. It is regrettable, though perhaps inevitable, that this will change in the future, now that solicitors can obtain rights of audience in the superior court, and so qualify themselves for appointment as judges. Solicitors may be just as competent and just as well qualified as barristers, but solicitors often work in firms which specialize in litigation on behalf of one side or another in regularly conflicting situations. For instance, one firm may regularly represent insurance companies, while another firm works on behalf of trade unionists suing their employers for injuries where the claim is in reality against these very insurance companies. Solicitors who only have experience of one or other side in such common types of litigation may lack the experience which helps barristers to maintain their independence and impartiality.

Another factor which in the past has helped to maintain the independence of the judiciary from government is that the judges have traditionally had a powerful friend in the government in the person of the Lord Chancellor. The Lord Chancellor is always drawn from the Bar, and that has usually meant the English Bar, though the present Lord Chancellor, Lord Mackay, comes from the Scots Bar.

As a former barrister, the Lord Chancellor will share the traditions and ideals of the Bar, and has in the past been a powerful voice on behalf of the Bar and of the judiciary within the corridors of White-hall and indeed in the Cabinet counsels.

It must be said that in these respects recent years have seen some unhappy changes, and these changes have had a lot to do with the changing role of the Lord Chancellor. In modern times the Lord Chancellor has become the head of a very large administrative de-partment, because he is responsible for the system of legal aid, whose costs have soared to such a degree that the Treasury has become justifiably concerned about the efficiency of the whole legal system. Added to the fortuitous fact that Lord Mackay (who by 1994 had filled this post for some seven years) is from the Scots Bar, and has brought a degree of detachment to his position, the result has been that relations between the Bar and Bench on the one hand, and the Lord Chancellor and government on the other hand, had by 1994 reached a very low ebb. For present purposes, the importance of this lies in the fact that the judiciary fear that their independence is being eroded, and that the Lord Chancellor, at the behest of the Treasury, is the person responsible for this.

These fears centre round the fact that control of the *administrative* side of the judicial system has largely been taken out of the hands of the judges and placed in the hands of the Lord Chancellor and his civil servants. The administrative aspects of the judicial system relate to such matters as the actual court-rooms where the judges sit, the provision of facilities, like computers and video cameras, the listing of cases, the allocation of appeal cases to different panels of the appeal courts, the appointment of enough judges to do the work entrusted to them, the provision of adequate accommodation in the traditional judges' lodgings, when the judges have to sit away from their home towns, and so on. Some of the current controversy may be resolved by the recent decision of the Lord Chancellor to hand over control of the more mundane aspects of judicial administration (especially the provision of court-rooms and their facilities) to an independent agency, into which the judges will be able to make some input.

However, other aspects of the administration of the judicial system will not be handled by this agency, but will remain under the control of the Lord Chancellor. Everybody agrees that administrative matters must have some bearing, even if indirectly, on the way judges work, and that is where the difficulty lies. To take one example, if there are not enough judges to do the work which has to be done, a backlog of cases will build up. If the backlog becomes serious enough, eventually it must have some impact on the way the judges work. They may decide to speed up certain hearings, or to hold appeals in two-judge Appeal Courts rather than the usual three-judge courts, or insist on curtailing the length of legal arguments, and so on. A more disturbing example concerns the power of allocating appeal cases to differing panels in the Court of Appeal, or even in the House of Lords. The power to choose (in effect) which judges will hear which cases is plainly one which can be misused, because it will often be known that a certain judge has at least a prima-facie view on the point of law to be decided on the appeal.

Another problem is that as the required number of high court judges never keeps pace with the volume of work, more and more high court litigation is being conducted before barristers who sit as temporary judges, appointed for a particular case or a short period of time. In fact the Lord Chancellor is attached to this procedure because it gives him the opportunity of allowing prospective trial judges a probationary period, in which their performance as judges can be observed. While this may be desirable in itself, and may help to preserve the high quality of the judiciary by weeding out unsuitable candidates before they are given permanent appointments, it obviously poses potential threats to the independence of the judiciary. Nobody would suggest that the Lord Chancellor actually studies the record of temporary judges to see if they are deciding cases in a way which is displeasing to the government; but the whole point of guaranteed judicial tenure is to prevent the very possibility of this kind of thing happening. But with so many cases being decided by temporary judges it cannot now be said that it is impossible.

Because the Lord Chancellor continues to stress his own commitment to the principle of the independence of the judiciary—and plainly nobody for a moment would expect him to try to influence the way a judge should actually decide a case—the current dispute is largely confined to legal circles, and is carried on in relatively restrained language in addresses to legal audiences or articles in legal journals. It has not yet erupted into public consciousness, but there is no doubt that considerable anxiety and even anger is building up in certain quarters of the judiciary.

On the other hand, it needs to be said that the Lord Chancellor, and even the Treasury, have a case on these matters. Although the Lord Chancellor and the government have (it is hoped) no desire to influence the way judges decide cases from a legal point of view, they do have a legitimate interest in ensuring that the legal system is as efficient as is compatible with the proper administration of justice. If, for instance, Judge A is slow and takes two days to decide a simple case which Judge B can hear in a morning, there may be some legitimate public interest in the disparity. The public pays the costs of the legal system, and the salaries of the judges. A public (and Treasury) interest in the efficiency of the way judges work is just as likely to develop as a public and Treasury interest in the efficiency of surgeons in a hospital. Of course judges, like surgeons, do not wish to have their efficiency tested by outsiders, and certainly the public has an interest in having a judiciary whose members feel independent and unpressurized as they work. But the public also has an interest in an efficient legal system.

It may be that the time has come, also, when the conditions of tenure of judges below the level of the High Court need to be reconsidered. As the volume of judicial work constantly increases, and as the number of high court judges does not keep pace with this increase, more and more serious litigation is now being conducted in County courts before circuit judges. But circuit judges do not have the tenure rights of high court judges. They can be dismissed by the Lord Chancellor, and although nobody has suggested that the Lord Chancellor is likely to dismiss a circuit judge because of the way he has decided a case, it may be right to recognize that the independence of the judiciary requires a more formal dismissal procedure to be adopted. The position of temporary high court judges may also need to be regularized in some way, though this may involve some change to the method of appointment to the high court bench, a point which is considered again below.

Law-making by the judges

There is one other respect in which the position of the senior judges is unique. It is only judges of the superior courts who have the power to create new law by deciding new points in such a way that their decisions become precedents. Decisions of lower court judges, and even of magistrates, may sometimes involve quite new points of law, to which there is no clear answer; and when this happens, the point must be decided. But it would be unusual for lengthy reasons for such a decision to be given (almost never would it happen in a magistrates' court), and in any event the reasons would not be published in any series of law reports nor would they constitute a binding precedent. But decisions of high court judges and, still more, of the appeal judges on novel points of law are likely to be reported, that is, published in one or more law reports. Such decisions *bind* lower courts to follow them, so that these judges have a quasi-legislative function which is interwoven with their primary function of actually deciding the case in front of them. This quasi-legislative function is not usually of great importance in cases in the High Court, partly because a decision of a single judge does not carry much weight as a precedent, but mainly because decisions at this level rarely involve novel points of law. But the law-making functions of the Court of Appeal and the House of Lords can be very important. Much of the work of these courts involves deciding new points which have never arisen (or been litigated) in quite the same way before. Moreover, decisions of these courts are powerful precedents. A decision of the House of Lords binds all the other courts in the country—indeed, it binds everybody else too, including (for example) the government. If the government dislikes a judicial decision of the House of Lords sufficiently strongly, it can introduce a Bill to change the law as thus laid down. But, short of that extreme response, governments, like everyone else, accept that what the House of Lords says is the law, *is* the law. Decisions of the Court of Appeal are not ultimately authoritative in the same way. They can be appealed to the House of Lords, or they can be overruled by the Lords in a subsequent decision, but so long as they remain unappealed and not overruled, they too bind everybody in the sense that the law as thus laid down must be accepted as correct. The precise workings of the system of precedent are considered further in Chapter 6; here I am concerned with the general nature and the legitimacy of the doctrine.

It is worth stressing that the binding force of judicial precedents is not something that is only relevant in other cases which arise in court. Most disputes involving legal rights and obligations are not litigated in court at all. They are settled more or less amicably between parties, with or without lawyers or other advisers. When lawyers (or other advisers with some knowledge of the law) are involved in attempting to settle such disputes, they rely upon judicial precedents in the same way that lawyers do in court. For instance, if a person who has been involved in a road accident is attempting to negotiate a settlement of his claim with the other driver's insurance company, his lawyer may refer to a decision of a court which establishes that the claimant is entitled to damages for a certain sort of loss—for example, the cost of hiring another car while his own is being repaired. The insurance company's advisers would accept that such a decision *is the law*, though they might, of course, argue that it is not relevant for this or that reason. Or again, a person arguing with his Inspector of Taxes might claim that the interpretation of a particular section of the Taxing Act has been determined by a decision of the House of Lords which settles the matter in his favour. If that was indeed the case it would be unhesitatingly accepted by the tax authorities. They might argue (for instance) that the decision is not relevant because the two cases are not wholly the same, but they would never argue that the decision was wrong, or not binding on them, or that they preferred to interpret the section in a different way.

So the principle of the binding force of precedents is not a rule of interest only to lawyers. It is a constitutional principle which is accepted by the government and all other bodies exercising authority. It must be stressed that the law-making power of the judges is, in the aggregate, a very small part of their functions. We have already seen that it is only the superior court judges who wield the power at all, and it is only to a limited extent that high court judges do so. The great bulk of judicial work takes place in lower courts which have no law-making power; in any event, most court cases do not involve arguments about what the law is, but are about pure questions of fact. It is also true, as we shall see later, that the judicial law-making power is hemmed around in all sorts of ways—it is of course far less extensive than the legislative powers of Parliament. Nevertheless, it is an important and undeniable fact that the superior court judges do make law, and this has given rise to a great deal of discussion among jurists and political theorists. In particular, it inevitably gives rise, in a democracy, to questions of legitimacy and accountability. The judges (at least in Britain) are not elected by the people, nor are they formally accountable to anybody (other than appeal courts) for their decisions; moreover, as previously suggested, they are as a group almost certainly politically right of centre. So is there something undemocratic or undesirable about this law-making function? Would it, in fact, be better if judges were more politically representative of public opinion, or perhaps even elected? Before attempting any sort of answer to questions like this, it may be useful to give a couple of illustrations of recent judicial decisions which made new law, and of the sort of issues that arose in them.

In 1975 a case came before the Court of Appeal which is known (as usual) by the names of the parties involved in it, *Congreve* v. *Home Office*. The case is reported in the law reports in the 1976 volume of the Queen's Bench Reports at p. 629. The official reference is written thus: [1976] QB 629. Mr Congreve was a solicitor with a colour television set. His licence was due to expire on 31 March 1976. On 29 January the Home Secretary announced that the price of a colour television licence was to be increased on 1 April 1976 from £12 to £18. Acting under statutory authority he made the necessary order to come into force on that date. He also instructed post office clerks to refuse to renew television licences due to expire on or after 31 March before they had in fact expired. But the instructions were not well observed. Mr Congreve (and over 24,000 others) renewed their licences before they had expired, thereby getting them for only £12 at the cost of a few days' loss of validity. The Home Office reacted angrily to this, and wrote to Mr Congreve (and all the others) threatening to revoke their licences unless they paid the extra £6. The Home Secretary had the power under the Wireless Telegraphy Act to revoke licences, but the Act said nothing about the grounds on which licences could or could not be revoked. Mr Congreve sued the Home Office, claiming that it would be illegal of the Home Secretary to revoke his licence, and the Court of Appeal upheld his claim. The point in one sense was a novel one: no previous case raised the precise point about revocation of licences under the Wireless Telegraphy Act. But the judges reasoned that the power to revoke licences under the Act must be read subject to various restrictions. In particular, the minister could only revoke the licence for some 'proper' reason. Here he was threatening to revoke it to obtain £6 from Mr Congreve. But he had no right to do that, because Mr Congreve had validly bought a renewal of his licence at a time when the old charge still applied. In addition, a threat to revoke a licence in order to raise money had to be particularly scrutinized having regard to the Bill of Rights of 1689 which had finally established that revenue could only be raised by the government with parliamentary authorization. Here the parliamentary authorization did not extend to the period prior to 1 April when Mr Congreve had renewed his licence. So the court held that the threat to revoke the licence was unlawful, and Mr Congreve won his case.

The Home Secretary could have appealed, or sought to have the law changed by Act of Parliament; although in this sort of case no British government would have tried to change the law *retrospectively*, it could easily have been changed for the future. In fact the Home Secretary accepted the decision, the threats were withdrawn, and those who had paid the extra £6 had their money refunded. But the Home Office decided that, in future, television licence-fee increases would come into force on the same day they were announced, thus preventing a recurrence of the precise situation—although the practice has since changed again. All this was the immediate effect of the decision. But the case is also a precedent concerning the power of the Home Secretary to revoke television licences. Thanks to this case, it is now clear law that this power is only available in special circumstances, and cannot be used to raise extra money or for other 'improper' purposes.

This decision involved the application of general legal principles to a statutory power; an illustration of a common law type of decision is also worth looking at. *Smith* v. *Eric S. Bush* [1990] 1 AC 831 was an appeal to the House of Lords in which two cases, raising virtually the identical point, were heard together. One of them was the eponymous case, which is usually just called *Smith* v. *Bush*; the second was *Harris* v. *Wyre Forest District Council (D.C.)*. Each case involved questions about the liability of a surveyor who surveys a house and carelessly fails to spot serious defects in the property, so that the buyer, who has bought the house with a mortgage, is ultimately landed with a large repair bill, or even with a house which is uninhabitable. In *Smith* v. *Bush* the building society involved sent the plaintiff a copy of the surveyor's report which stated that no essential repairs were necessary, but the mortgage application form which the plaintiff filled in contained a disclaimer of liability for the accuracy of the report and a recommendation that the plaintiff should obtain independent advice on the soundness of the house. In fact there were structural defects in the property which the surveyor ought to have discovered if he had done his work competently. The second case, *Harris* v. *Wyre Forest D.C.*, was similar, but here the surveyor's report was not even shown to the plaintiffs even though they paid his fee indirectly through the Council from whom they were buying the property. Again, the mortgage application said that no responsibility was accepted for the accuracy of the surveyor's report, which was intended solely (so it was said) for the benefit of the Council. But the plaintiffs obviously knew that the survey was not unfavourable otherwise they would not have been granted the 95 per cent mortgage which they were given.

Two important legal questions were involved in these two appeals. The first was whether—even leaving aside disclaimers—a surveyor is liable to a buyer in this kind of situation for defects in the property which he has negligently failed to discover and mention in his report. This was a difficult point of law largely because the buyer does not himself engage and contract with the surveyor. Although he pays the fee, it is channelled through the building society, or (as in the *Harris* case) through the Council selling the house. Because there is no contract between the buyer and the surveyor, the buyer has to rely upon a general duty of care in the law of civil liability, the law of tort, as lawyers call it. In the law of tort many people who negligently cause injury or harm to others are liable for their negligence without proof of any contract, simply because the law insists that there is a general duty of care, regardless of contract. Such general duties of care are very widespread in cases of physical injury or damage. For instance, every user of the road owes a general duty of care to avoid injuring others by his negligence. But in these two appeals the problem was that the damage or loss suffered by the plaintiffs was not really physical damage. It was financial. The houses they had bought needed repairs, or were even uninhabitable, but the surveyors had not themselves actually damaged the houses. Nevertheless, the House of Lords held the surveyors liable in both cases. The crucial point was that it was well known that buyers rarely commissioned their own independent surveys, and surveyors knew perfectly well that buyers would rely on their reports, even if they did not actually see them. Surveyors are professional people, and they are paid for their work, even if the money does not come directly from the buyer. They know that buyers will rely on their judgment in making very important decisions, namely, whether to go ahead with their purchase. To some extent the decisions were an extension of earlier precedents; and to some extent they made new law altogether.

The second important point involved in the appeals was whether the disclaimers were valid. Even if the surveyors might prima facie have been liable, they argued that they had explicitly stated that they were not willing to assume responsibility for their reports to the buyers. On this point, everything hinged on the effects of a statute, the Unfair Contract Terms Act 1977, which declares that disclaimers of this kind are only valid if they are 'reasonable'. The House of Lords decided that these disclaimers were not reasonable. Surveyors can insure against their liabilities, and so are not threatened by catastrophic losses if they commit professional negligence in this sort of case. But the buyer of a house could be financially overwhelmed by the loss if his house turned out to be seriously defective, so it seems much more reasonable that the disclaimer should not be valid. Of course, surveyors will have to pay for their insurance protection, and they may need to add something to their bills to cover this additional cost, but that seems a small price for buyers to pay for the protection that they get.

This decision of the House of Lords is of considerable importance. Regrettably, the facts of these two cases are only too commonplace. Claims against surveyors in this kind of situation are by no means infrequent, and this decision has settled the law on the point. It will be followed in any other case of this kind. It may also contribute to still further extensions of the law of professional liability in other sorts of cases.

Now that some notion has been given of the kinds of decisions that judges have to make on the law, and the way in which such decisions can be used as binding precedents, it is time to return to the question of the legitimacy of this sort of law-making and the accountability of the people who make it. Basically, there are two views about this, if we can discount altogether the now-discredited fiction that judges don't make law at all, but merely declare it or 'find' it. On the one side, it is said that judges must make law, that much of the time they are dealing with issues that Parliament is not very interested in (or perhaps not very good at) and therefore they should not hesitate to be active in the pursuit of justice as they see it. On the other hand, it is said that there is danger in this, because justice is sometimes a controversial and value-ridden concept; what seems just to judges may not always seem just to others, and conservative-minded judges may be inclined to uphold values and ideals which may seem old-fashioned to many people. So (it is argued) courts should be chary of using their law-making powers very extensively, especially where there is no obvious consensus about the issues.

The appointment of judges

The worries about the legitimacy of judge-made law, and the powers of an unaccountable judiciary, are to some degree aggravated by the fact that the appointing process is, in practice, almost entirely in the hands of one person—the Lord Chancellor. In theory, high court and appeal court judges and lords of appeal are appointed by the Queen, though of course she always acts on advice. In the case of appeal court judges and lords of appeal it is the Prime Minister who is nominally responsible for that advice, in the case of high court judges it is the Lord Chancellor, but in practice it is hard to believe that he does not also have the major say in the nomination of the appeal judges as well, simply because the Prime Minister is unlikely to know much, or even to care much* about the candidates for appointment. The Lord Chancellor also appoints all circuit judges and magistrates. Until recently there was something of a mystique about judicial appointments, which were often thought to be decided upon in back-rooms by senior judges having a quiet word with the Lord Chancellor, perhaps blackballing this candidate, and favouring that one. In the last few years Lord Mackay has done what he can to get rid of this mystique. He has published a booklet setting out the practice of his department in relation to appointments below that of the high court bench, and indeed in 1994, for the first time in history, public advertisements were published in the press for the position of circuit judge. The appointment process of high court judges and above remains a very confidential business, and in some quarters there is now a demand for a more formalized appointing procedure, with an advisory committee perhaps being constituted by statute. It seems unlikely that any changes of this kind would have much effect upon the sort of people who are appointed to these positions, though they might help to eliminate a possible sense of unfairness which may today rankle with disappointed would-be judges.

There are also other, more extreme views; for instance, that judges ought to be elected, because this is the only way of ensuring that the judge's sense of justice keeps in touch with the popular sense of justice. In America some states have elected judges, and though there is evidence that they decide some sorts of cases rather differently from the (non-elected) federal judges, or other non-elected state judges, conventions have grown up which generally keep judges from getting seriously involved in electioneering, or partisan politics. For instance, once elected, they are usually returned unopposed at subsequent elections. In England there would be little support for, and much opposition to, the idea of elected judges. For one thing, it is difficult to see what guarantee there would be of getting competent lawyers on the Bench if judges were elected. But it is also

* Although there have sometimes been exceptions to this, see above, p. 14.

arguable that one of the functions of an independent judiciary is to protect minorities from the majority, and it seems unlikely that this would be well done by judges who had to submit themselves for election.

If we put aside extreme suggestions like that of electing judges, it is not easy to offer any solution to the problem involved in law-making by unrepresentative judges. The fact is, as Professor John Griffith suggests in his stimulating book, *The Politics of the Judiciary*, that it is almost inevitable that judges will tend to be upholders of authority and the *status quo* and traditional values. One cannot expect English judges to be revolutionaries, or perhaps even radical reformers. Griffith tends to attribute this to the role which judges play as upholders of law and order and the forces of authority; but this does not seem a complete explanation. The truer explanation may be twofold. First, the long years at the Bar which every senior judge must undergo before appointment tend to mould a person into a certain image. Those who resist the moulding are unlikely to be candidates for high judicial office. In other words, a judge (like the Pope) tends to be a certain type of person because, on the whole, only that type of person becomes a judge (or Pope). But secondly, and relatedly, the kind of work which barristers and judges do, and the way in which the English legal system works, tend to heighten the importance of many traditional values which some people would regard as associated with conservative (or perhaps more strictly, liberal) political ideologies. The law and the legal system, in other words, encourage a belief in individualism rather than collectivism or socialism. Further, the high prestige and status of the senior judges do not encourage an attitude of humility on the Bench. Because judges have the last word on the cases they decide (subject only to appeals to their more highly placed colleagues), judges may be encouraged to see themselves as infallible oracles. They may see no reason to search their minds for signs of unconscious bias, or to study the ideas of theorists or intellectuals for other possible approaches to the problems they have to deal with. Nor are judges accustomed to challenge their own preconceptions about what fairness or justice may demand by asking about (or reading about) the ideas of fairness or justice of other groups in society. Even on matters of pure fact, judges are often inclined to act on intuition or instinct about what is generally thought to be the case, without apparent awareness that their intuitions and instincts may be faulty.

These weaknesses in the English judiciary are accentuated by the fact that the senior judges are so homogeneous as a social group. Not only are they nearly all middle-aged or elderly men; they have all served the same sort of apprenticeship in a profession which has (as we shall see more fully later) a strongly conformist tradition. Of course this homogeneity is also part of the judiciary's strength. Because judges tend to think alike, the judiciary presents a more solid front in which dissent is relatively unusual, and seriously aberrant views are rare indeed. (In this respect the former Master of the Rolls, Lord Denning, was a quite exceptional and unrepresentative figure; there has probably never been another judge like him on the English Bench.)

It is for these and similar reasons that niggling (or even serious) doubts may remain about the English judiciary, and especially its law-making powers. On the other hand, it must also be remembered that the judiciary has great strengths which tend to be taken for granted, and some of these may also be partly due to its homogeneity. For instance, standards of integrity are of the very highest, and so, in general, are standards of competence. So too, the judges undoubtedly have a very strong commitment to principles of 'due process' (a concept I examine more fully later in this chapter), which among other things means that the conduct of proceedings in court must be, and appear to be, fair. Further, the competence and experience of English judges means that most of them are strong personalities well able to maintain the dignity of their courts and control the behaviour of counsel. This helps to maintain high standards of integrity at the Bar, as well as on the Bench itself. These are all virtues of the present system, too lightly prized by those who have no experience of other systems in which judges may be more representative of the popular will, but have perhaps lower standards of competence or even integrity.

It is perhaps worth adding also that the common complaint that judges are not accountable in respect of their decisions is only true in a formal sense. It is true that a judge cannot be rapped over the knuckles (except by an appeal court) for the way he decides a case. But there is another sense in which judges *are* accountable for their decisions. A judge is always expected to give *detailed reasons* for his decisions, and in cases of any importance these reasons will be published in the law reports. In many cases the reasons will be scrutinized and commented on, and perhaps criticized by academic lawyers, and sometimes by other practising lawyers, and of course by judges in later cases. To be sure, judicial reasoning is often technical, and not accessible to the man in the street. At the same time it is no light thing for a judge to know that his reasoning will have to be exposed, and that if it is to pass muster, it will have to be acceptable by the standards of the profession.

Nevertheless, it cannot be denied that difficulty will remain in justifying the judicial law-making powers so long as the judiciary appears to continue to reflect the views of those who are politically right of centre. In particular, it cannot be denied that judges generally sympathize more with individuals than with collective aspirations of a group or class. The Bar is a highly individualistic profession, and the legal system as a whole tends to exist for the vindication of individual and not collective rights. Courts and lawyers are not the chief instruments used for the implementation of collective goals in our society. This is a question which I shall return to in Chapter 4, when I shall offer an explanation, and perhaps part justification, for this state of affairs.

So far I have been talking mainly of civil courts and the civil law, but there are parallel courts dealing with the criminal law, and here also there are marked differences between superior courts trying a small number of serious cases and lower courts trying huge numbers of less serious cases. Broadly, the distinction between more and less serious criminal cases is reflected by the fact that serious cases are triable on indictment before a jury, while less serious cases are tried by magistrates without a jury. Even among indictable crimes there are further distinctions, the most serious of all being tried by a high court judge with a jury, and slightly less serious ones being tried by a circuit judge with a jury. All indictable criminal cases are now tried in the Crown Court. The Crown Court is notionally only one court, but of course it sits in a great many places throughout the country. Appeals from jury trials go before a special division of the Court of Appeal, known as the Criminal Division, and in rare cases further appeals go before the House of Lords as in civil cases.

Juries

Everybody knows that serious criminal cases are tried before a jury, though it is probably not widely known that until the 1930s the jury was also extensively used in ordinary civil actions too. In the United States it still is, but in England a jury is only rarely used in civil cases today. In cases like libel and fraud juries are sometimes still used, but otherwise the civil jury has all but vanished.

The jury consists of twelve persons who are selected at random from the jury list, which is in fact the ordinary electoral role, with the exclusion only of persons over 65 years of age. Various classes of person are also disqualified from sitting on juries (for example, those with serious criminal convictions) and others are entitled to claim exemption if they wish. Lawyers are rigorously excluded from juries.

Jury-rigging would of course be plainly illegal. The jury must be selected at random, and even the judge has no power to direct that (for instance) in a case with racial overtones the jury should be racially mixed, or that in a sexual case there should be a balance of the sexes. Nor do the police have any right, on their own authority, to indulge in any form of 'jury-vetting'. But the courts have accepted that, under the direction of the Attorney-General, and in accordance with guide-lines issued by him, some checks may be made, for example, to ensure that disqualified persons do not sit on a jury, especially in sensitive cases involving questions of national security. It has been argued that the practice of jury-vetting can come close to jury-rigging, which is obviously inconsistent with the whole idea of the jury as a random cross-section of the public. But the courts have pointed out that in the absence of some jury-vetting there is simply no way of discovering whether disqualified persons may be sitting on juries; and they have accordingly refused to rule the practice illegal, so long as the Attorney-General's guide-lines are adhered to.

In theory a jury is only the arbiter of the *facts*, while the judge remains responsible for decisions on the *law*. The judge also, of course, controls the trial and directs the jury, and sentencing is exclusively within his province in the event of a conviction. In practice, because the jury is ultimately required to render a verdict on the whole case, guilty or not guilty, a jury is able, if it wishes, to disregard a judge's directions on the law and acquit an accused even though, on the facts as it finds them, he is incontrovertibly guilty of the offence. It can less easily do the reverse, that is, convict someone as a result of disregarding a judge's instructions on the law, because the probability is that the judge himself will instruct a verdict of not guilty to be returned, and a jury simply cannot disregard such an instruction. Alternatively, a verdict of guilty given in the teeth of a judicial direction favourable to the accused is likely to be quashed on appeal.

How valuable is the jury in modern times? This is a very controversial question. On one side the jury has much ancient history behind it (though some have argued it is more mythology than true history) as a bastion of the liberty of the subject against repressive governments. To a minor degree the jury can, and occasionally still does, play this role. A perverse acquittal is undoubtedly rendered from time to time as a gesture of defiance against an oppressive prosecution. The last well-known case of this kind was probably the acquittal of Mr Clive Ponting in 1985 on charges under the Official Secrets Act. Mr Ponting, a senior civil servant, did not deny the substance of the charges against him, which were based on the fact that he had sent official documents to a Member of Parliament which were claimed to show that ministers had misled the House of Commons. On the admitted facts Mr Ponting was undoubtedly guilty, and the judge directed the jury to this effect, but the jury acquitted in the teeth of this direction. It probably felt that the prosecution was oppressive, and that if there was any truth in the allegations it was only right and proper that Parliament should see the documents anyhow. In a sense the jury's behaviour in this case was vindicated by amendments later made to the Official Secrets Act, as a result of which Mr Ponting's behaviour would no longer be a crime. Cases of this kind are certainly rare.

Some lawyers believe that the jury remains a valuable safeguard in other cases involving public authorities, for instance, a civil case of wrongful arrest brought against the police, where a jury may still be ordered. It is widely believed that judges are much more likely to believe the police witnesses in litigation of this kind, while juries may be more sceptical of police evidence. On the other hand, it must be said that in the large number of serious miscarriages of justice in recent years (which are discussed later) the accused were all convicted by juries. So it cannot be said that juries are always capable of ferreting out false allegations, police lies, or other injustices if the evidence before them does not reveal the reality behind the case. Moreover, it must be remembered that only a tiny fraction of criminal cases are tried by juries anyhow. In recent years, for instance, magistrates have dealt with about 2 million cases annually, while juries have tried about 26,000.

There are also worries in some quarters that many cases of serious fraud, involving very complicated financial dealings, are incapable of being followed by juries. Sometimes prosecutions may simply not be brought because counsel believe the case is too complex to explain to any jury; in other cases, a prosecution may be brought, but nobody knows whether the jury really understands it. When Mr George Walker (of Brent Walker fame) was acquitted by a jury in 1994 of financial malpractices in connection with his company dealings, he declared to the press that he himself had not understood the charges against him, and he did not believe the jury could have done so either. On the other hand, it must be said that the survey conducted among jurors by the Royal Commission on Criminal Justice which reported in 1993 did not lend any support to these worries. Overwhelmingly, jurors who took part in this survey claimed, not only that they felt they understood the issues and the evidence (which is perhaps not surprising), but also that they felt other members of the jury did so too.

Many people undoubtedly believe that the jury remains a potentially valuable control over the powers of established authority. If lawyers, police, and the prosecuting authorities get too much out of touch with public opinion in certain spheres, the jury is a constant reminder that government by consent is no empty phrase. In recent years the growing liberality of juries in obscenity prosecutions has virtually brought such prosecutions to a complete halt, as the prosecuting authorities have been unable to secure convictions except perhaps in cases of plain hard-core pornography. There are, moreover, many lawyers (especially those who regularly appear in magistrates' court) who feel that it is only before a jury that an accused has any serious chance of an acquittal in certain types of case. Where an accused has a right to elect for trial by jury rather than by magistrates, many accused persons elect for jury trial simply because they believe that the chances of an acquittal by a jury are substantially higher. They are almost certainly right, too. There are, in particular, some types of case in which every lawyer knows that the prospects of acquittal by magistrates' court are very much lower: serious motoring offences, for instance; charges of shop-lifting in which the accused admits that he took the goods but denies that he did so dishonestly; and more generally, any offence in which the accused's state of mind is seriously controverted. Juries seem far more willing to accept that a person may have made a genuine mistake, or acted in a fit of absent-mindedness; magistrates are much more jaundiced about such defences and sometimes appear to assume that everything said by an accused in his own defence must be dismissed as not even raising a reasonable doubt. Another class of case in which juries are notoriously more willing to acquit than magistrates are cases in which everything hinges upon a conflict between the evidence of police witnesses and of the accused. There have been suggestions that the last decade or so has seen a great increase in jury willingness to give the accused the benefit of the doubt in cases of this kind; perhaps an increasing number of jurors have themselves had dealings with the police which have left them somewhat sceptical of police evidence. It is, of course, not easy to say whether differing acquittal rates in magistrates' courts and jury trials reflect the fact that magistrates convict too readily, or that juries acquit too readily.

But it is undeniable that there is disenchantment with juries in certain quarters. Some years ago the former Chief Commissioner of Police, Sir Robert Mark, created something of a storm by protesting that juries acquitted too many who were guilty of serious crime; and it is true that acquittal rates for trials on indictment can be very high—for some offences it is over 50 per cent. But it does not follow that these acquittals are unjustified. Such assertions are difficult to test by research since there is no way of discovering for certain what proportion of acquitted people are in fact guilty. But attempts have been made to analyse acquittals by questioning those participating in the proceedings, and research of this character continues to produce highly controversial results. Much more alarming is some research, now a few years old, suggesting that there is a significant number of jury *convictions* which neutral participants in the trial would characterize as perverse. But even findings of this character may not be what they seem. Lawyers often say that a conviction is perverse because of the state of the evidence, or because, for some technical legal reason, they feel an acquittal is the correct legal answer: the accused may nevertheless well be guilty. It is a difficult question whether the conviction of a guilty person ought to be regarded as a miscarriage of justice, merely because, according to the legal rules, he should have been acquitted.

Other reasons for dissatisfaction with jury trials centre on the inability of an average jury to grasp complex questions, whether of fact or of law. The problems arising out of highly complex fraud cases have already been mentioned. Sometimes also the law is complicated and judges are expected to direct juries in ways which they probably do not understand, or are in practice incapable of acting upon. One common illustration of this sort of difficulty may be worth giving. A and B are, let it be supposed, jointly charged with a serious offence. A has made a statement to a witness in which he indicated that he and B committed the crime. If this witness gives evidence in court of A's statement, the judge must tell the jury that the statement is *evidence against* A but *not against* B. It is evidence against A because a statement of this character alleged to have been made by the accused himself is thought to carry a high degree of plausibility. But it is not evidence against B, because as against B it is simply hearsay: it is a statement of what someone else (A) said out of court. The law is clear enough, but it would be a remarkable jury which was capable both of understanding and acting on the judge's direction. The result is that in some cases of this character the judge's directions to the jury become, to some extent, a sort of ritual which must be strictly complied with, but whose efficacy is impossible to evaluate and may well be minimal. This can give jury trial an air of unreality in which the jury is treated like a *deus ex machina*, a sort of black box or computer whose answers must be accepted provided only that the correct questions are fed into the machine, although we have no idea whether the machine is working properly.

Even putting aside these exceptional problems, it is probably true that juries are simply less competent than judges at their principal function, namely, deciding issues of fact in a controverted case. The judge necessarily has far greater experience of the problem of weighing evidence, of distinguishing between perjury and sheer mistake or confusion, and of evaluating conflicting evidence of rival witnesses. So if the only question was the selection of the most efficient fact-finding tribunal, it is unlikely that the jury would win many votes. It is basically this which has led to the virtual disappearance of juries in civil cases, for in these cases the legal profession unquestionably prefers the more rational, if less dramatic, trial by judge than trial by jury.

It does need to be stressed again that these difficulties affect a very small number of cases. The vast majority of criminal cases are dealt with by magistrates; the great majority even of those who are charged on indictment plead guilty anyhow, so there is no trial and hence no jury—merely a sentence. And of those cases tried by a jury, probably the large majority are relatively straightforward cases in which the jury acts responsibly and satisfactorily. But it is of course true that the importance of an institution like the jury may depend on its potential in rare cases, rather than its routine performance in everyday cases.

In a sense the jury performs in the legal process a function not dissimilar to that performed by the back-bench Member of Parliament in the political process. Both of them represent the lay element in an increasingly professionalized process—the law on one hand, the administration of government on the other. Both of them can bring into their respective processes bigotry and prejudice as well as sheer incompetence; both of them generally co-operate with and are controlled by the professionals around them—judges on the one side, ministers and civil servants on the other. But in the last resort both have the power to demonstrate to the professionals that there are some things the public simply will not tolerate.

The lower courts

There are a great many lower courts in the English legal system, especially if one includes under that term the variety of tribunals which have statutory power to inquire into or decide disputes of a particular nature.

The lower courts, more strictly speaking, consist, so far as the civil law is concerned, chiefly of the County courts, now staffed by circuit judges, and, for certain classes of cases (particularly matrimonial cases), the magistrates' courts. County courts have a general jurisdiction, with listed exceptions, for all claims involving no more than £50,000, but for claims between £25,000 and £50,000, their jurisdiction overlaps with that of the High Court. Magistrates' courts do not have any general civil jurisdiction, though they do hear a number of minor and miscellaneous cases, such as some minor matrimonial cases and claims for council tax. County courts, as already indicated, hear a great many more cases than high court judges, but the status of the judges who sit in them is significantly lower than that of high court judges. They are removable for misbehaviour by the Lord Chancellor, they do not receive knighthoods, their salaries are lower, and in court they are addressed as 'Your honour' rather than 'Your lordship'. Nevertheless, the judges who sit in the County courts must all be lawyers of considerable practical experience. Many County courts also have attached to them district judges who act rather like deputy circuit judges, and hear minor cases, as well as procedural issues involved in more complex cases.

Magistrates' courts are a very different matter altogether. They handle a huge volume of minor, and not always so minor, criminal cases, in addition to their jurisdiction over small matrimonial claims, and a great variety of other semi-administrative duties such as granting licences for the sale of alcohol. At one time even serious criminal cases always began in magistrates' courts, from where the accused would be 'committed for trial' at the Crown Court; but these committal proceedings became more and more of a formality, and the Criminal Justice Act 1994 has abolished them altogether. The only functions of magistrates in relation to indictable crimes which will be tried in the Crown Court are nowadays to consider questions of bail and legal aid. In some cases (which are said to be 'triable either way') a case can be tried either on indictment in the Crown Court or summarily by magistrates, but in many of these cases, and in all summary cases, the trial will start and finish in the magistrates' court. Magistrates are not normally qualified lawyers (though in London and some other large cities, stipendiary—that is, salaried—magistrates who are experienced lawyers are appointed) but they do have a clerk to advise them. The clerk is a qualified solicitor, and is now usually a full-time appointment. In busy magistrates' courts there may be several clerks. Lay magistrates must normally sit in panels of at least two, though stipendiary magistrates sit alone. Magistrates are not paid for their time except, again, in the case of stipendiaries, for whom the post is a full-time appointment. At one time lay magistrates were selected almost exclusively for their political party affiliations, but today the net is cast quite widely, and they can come from all walks of life. The main limiting factor is, of course, that the eligible class is largely confined to those whose normal life enables them to sit in court for a few days per month. There are today about fifty metropolitan and thirty-three provincial stipendiaries, and some 30,000 lay magistrates all told, of whom very nearly half are women.

Although magistrates have no power to deal with the most serious criminal cases, they do have considerable sentencing powers. For offences which in principle carry sentences of imprisonment, magistrates can impose sentences of up to six months' imprisonment for one charge, and sometimes up to twelve months' in total; their powers to fine are normally specified in the particular Acts of Parliament under which a charge is brought, but it is quite common for magistrates to have power to impose fines of up to £5,000 for a single offence. They also have power to make a 'compensation order' where a person has been convicted of a crime as a result of which someone has suffered damage, loss, or injury; and a compensation order can be made for up to £1,000 in addition to any fine which may be imposed. Further, magistrates have very wide powers to grant or refuse bail when a person is first brought before them, and the case has to be adjourned to a later date. Parliamentary policy on matters of bail has varied a lot in the past two decades. For example, the Bail Act 1976 limited the grounds on which magistrates could *refuse* bail, but more recent legislation actually prohibits them from granting bail for certain serious offences where the accused has already been convicted of a similar offence in the past, or where he has previously committed offences while on bail.

The quality of justice administered in magistrates' courts is a matter of some controversy. There is no doubt that it is a great deal higher than it was before the Second World War; magistrates are more carefully selected, and they are today required to undergo a modest amount of training. Magistrates' clerks are also more aware of their responsibilities, and much of the advice they give to the magistrates is no doubt responsible and competent. Nevertheless, many lawyers who practise widely in magistrates' courts are disenchanted, not to say cynical, about the basic adequacy of magistrates as fact-finding tribunals. It is widely complained that, contrary to the fundamental principles of the criminal law, the accused in a magistrates' court is in practice not presumed innocent until proved guilty, but precisely the reverse. It is still thought that many magistrates are too disinclined to reject police evidence, however implausible, perhaps for the reason that they feel the police should always be supported as a matter of principle. There are also widespread complaints that magistrates are still far too ready to accept police objections to bail. On the other hand, there is no doubt that, in many respects, things are much better than they were. Magistrates are now much more likely to take trouble to see that the accused is (so far as possible in the circumstances) put at his ease, that he fully understands what is going on, that he is given the opportunity to apply for legal aid, and so on. Any suggestion that lay magistrates should be replaced by stipendiaries (that is, by qualified, salaried lawyers) invariably raises the question of cost. But the fact is that cost does not seem an insuperable objection unless the country is determined to have its justice on the cheap. Probably about 3,000 to 4,000 stipendiaries would be needed for England and Wales. Some 4,000 stipendiaries, earning (say) £50,000 per annum each, together with overheads, would cost around £250 million a year, which is not a large sum in the overall context of government expenditure (the cost of legal aid is now about £1.4 billion every year, and the National Health Service costs over £30 billion a year). More difficult than the cost would be the problem of finding the necessary number of qualified and willing lawyers, for the post of full-time stipendiary magistrate is not a particularly attractive one. Furthermore, not everyone would agree that a single stipendiary magistrate is necessarily better than a panel of two or three lay magistrates. Stipendiaries who sit day in, day out, to hear cases of petty crime, drunkenness, matrimonial squabbles, and the like, can become so cynical that they may cease to believe anything that is said in their courts, and forget how important cases may be to the accused or the litigant. In 1994 a Working Party was appointed by the Lord Chancellor to examine the role of stipendiaries and the lay magistracy, having due regard to the differences between the needs of rural and metropolitan areas.

So far we have been dealing exclusively with bodies which are accounted as courts in the strictest sense. But there are today a great many other bodies exercising quasi-judicial powers which are not regarded strictly speaking as courts, though many of them do perform functions very closely analogous to those of ordinary courts. To give a few examples, there are a large number of tribunals dealing with questions under the social security legislation. There are several tiers of these, with social security commissioners at the apex, who are themselves qualified lawyers, and whose work is almost indistinguishable from that of the ordinary courts, except in being confined to the one area of law. Then there are Industrial Tribunals which hear, for example, claims for unfair dismissal, and sex- and race-discrimination, many thousands of which are now made every year. These tribunals are presided over by lawyers, but they also contain two other members, drawn from panels representing employers' and workers' organizations. A third example is the Lands Tribunal which, among other things, settles disputes about the value of land compulsorily acquired by public bodies for public use.

There are a great number of other tribunals of a similar character, some being more judicial and some more administrative in character.

One of the growing bodies of law at the present day concerns the powers of the superior courts to supervise and control the way in which these tribunals exercise their jurisdiction. In some cases, a statutory right of appeal is given from a tribunal to the High Court, though in general only appeals on questions of law are permitted. It is usually assumed that specialist tribunals ought to be left to find the facts in their own way, and that there is no reason to suppose that an appeal court would be better placed to discover the facts than the tribunal itself. But, as regards questions of law, it is widely felt that the ultimate arbiters must remain the ordinary courts, and so rights of appeal are often expressly conferred. For example, appeals from the income tax commissioners may be taken to the High Court (and, indeed, all the way to the House of Lords) if a question of law is involved. In other cases, special appeal courts are set up, though usually presided over by high court judges; for example, appeals from industrial tribunals on claims for unfair dismissal can be brought to an Employment Appeal Tribunal, which is presided over by a senior judge and behaves very much like an ordinary appeal court, though it also has non-legal members.

In very many cases, however, no provision for appeal is made at all, or appeals are permitted but stop short of the High Court. Even in these cases the High Court (and the appellate courts above it) retain a broad supervisory jurisdiction over tribunals. They cannot actually entertain an appeal if no such appeal is allowed by statute; but they still have a supervisory power to control and regulate, and in many modern cases it has become clear that the line between appeals and supervision is often thin. For instance, the High Court has power to ensure that a tribunal does not exceed its jurisdiction, even without any statutory appellate power. Decisions in excess of jurisdiction may be quashed as *ultra vires*, beyond the power of the tribunal. Recently courts have shown considerable ingenuity in holding that tribunal decisions may be in excess of jurisdiction, even though, to some eyes, this may look like a straight exercise of appellate power. Suppose, for instance, that an Act gives power to a tribunal to fix a rent for 'furnished accommodation'; suppose also that a claim is made to the tribunal by the tenant to fix the rent, but the landlord contends that the accommodation is in fact unfurnished.

There may here be a straightforward argument about the facts—is the accommodation furnished or not? The tribunal may decide that the accommodation is furnished and may then proceed to fix the rent. But if the High Court thinks that the accommodation is unfurnished it may go on to hold that the tribunal had no power, no jurisdiction, to hear the case at all. An essential pre-condition of the tribunal's jurisdiction has not been made out.

Similar powers are exercised by the High Court to ensure that basic procedural requirements of fairness are complied with. A tribunal which refused to hear one of the parties, for instance, or heard evidence from another party without disclosing it to the first, would be acting in a way which violates every instinct of the legal profession. Behaviour of this sort would be quashed by the High Court, acting, not in an appellate, but in a supervisory capacity.

The legal profession

The legal profession in England, as is well known, is divided into two main groups, barristers and solicitors. In addition, lawyers work in a variety of other ways and places. Lawyers are employed in industry and business, in local and central government, and as teachers in universities. The independent practising professions are, however, those parts of the profession which are most in the public eye, and they will be the focus of attention here.

Although solicitors might resent the fact, the relationship between the two parts of the practising profession has at least an appearance of conforming to the élitist pattern which dominates the court structure. For here too we have a very small 'higher' or 'senior' branch of the profession—the Bar—and a much larger 'junior' branch. There were in 1993 fewer than 8,000 barristers in private practice in the whole of England and Wales, while there were some 55,000 solicitors in private practice. Both parts of the profession have been growing very rapidly, and the number of solicitors has more than doubled in the past twenty years or so. Much of this rapid growth is undoubtedly due to the demand for legal services paid for by the State system of legal aid, so the Treasury has to some degree been funding this extraordinary increase in the number of practising lawyers.

In one sense it is correct to regard the Bar as the senior part of the profession. All higher judicial appointments were until very recently open (by statute) only to those with experience of practice at the Bar; and the higher courts were only open to advocates drawn from the Bar, although solicitors have had rights of audience in some lower courts. Although new statutory changes have recently come into force which enable solicitors to obtain rights of audience (and therefore ultimately to become qualified for the judiciary) the long-term impact of these changes remains to be seen. They are discussed further below. The present focus is on the traditional relationship between the two halves of the profession. In their professional relationship, barristers often appear to be treated as the senior profession. Solicitors take counsel's opinion on difficult questions, and usually rely upon the resulting opinion implicitly; they always defer to barristers with regard to the initiation and conduct of legal proceedings. Of course, solicitors may suggest this or that point to counsel in conference, or in their instructions, but the barrister is usually left to decide. Doubtless, a solicitor who is seriously dissatisfied with counsel's advice would seek advice from other counsel, but he is unlikely to reject an opinion without obtaining another.

However, this version of a profession divided into a senior and junior branch can be seriously misleading. For one thing, the Bar is a very young profession: not long ago one survey showed that 70 per cent of practising barristers were under 40 years of age, and doubtless quite a large proportion are under 30. Barristers of tender years and limited experience are unlikely to be professionally more competent than solicitors of greater age and experience. Moreover, this fact is reflected in the remuneration of the members of the two parts of the profession. The findings of the Royal Commission on Legal Services in 1979 showed that (contrary to popular belief) average net earnings at the Bar were lower than average earnings of solicitors in private practice. It is probable—though there are no more up-to-date figures—that this basic situation has not changed. It is true, of course, that the most senior barristers do earn very large incomes—in 1991 it was estimated that the median annual income for QCs in England and Wales was £183,000—but it must also be remembered that a barrister has to pay all his own expenses (the cost of his chambers, etc.) and fund his pension from his own earnings. The senior partners in the top London firms of solicitors may well earn more than these sums, when account is taken of these facts.

There is another popular belief about the distinction between barristers and solicitors which is at best only a half-truth. It is widely thought that solicitors do the paperwork in legal matters and barristers act as advocates in court, but although there is some foundation for this belief, the reality is somewhat different. Most advocacy in magistrates' courts is in fact done by solicitors, and they also have rights of audience which are quite extensively used in County courts and in some crown court cases. Conversely, many barristers, especially junior barristers, spend much of their time on paperwork, giving opinions, drafting pleadings and other documents related to court proceedings, but also drafting contracts, trust deeds, and other formal legal documents which are not immediately connected with litigation.

There are also other important differences between the professions, some of which are less well known to the public. The first is that the Bar is heavily concentrated in London. Only a third of barristers have chambers in the provinces, and most senior barristers practise in London. Since all appeal work is taken in the Court of Appeal or the House of Lords, both of which sit exclusively in London, there is a natural tendency for the leaders of the profession to practise there. Nearly all barristers in London have their chambers in a small part of the town—the Temple, Lincoln's Inn, Gray's Inn, and the surrounding areas. Barristers have to be members of one or other of the four Inns of Court, which are situated in this part of London, and which own the chambers from which most barristers practise. In consequence they tend to become well acquainted with each other, they often lunch together in the Inns of Court, and they develop a camaraderie which is probably unmatched by any other professional group, except perhaps the civil servants. One result of this is to heighten the pressures to conformity which already exist in most professions, a fact which assumes its importance mainly because all senior judges have been drawn from the Bar. It is, however, something of a paradox that the pressures to conformity tend to encourage a continued faith in individualist values. It is also something of a paradox that this individualist-minded profession should now draw a very substantial proportion of its income (estimated at 40 per cent) from public funds, mostly from legal aid.

The solicitors' profession, as mentioned earlier, is very much larger than the Bar; it is also much less concentrated in London, the profession comprising a little over 10,000 firms (or sole solicitors) spread over the country. The spread is, however, uneven. In 1971 there was one solicitors' office for every 2,000 people in Guildford, compared with one for 26,000 in Salford and one for 66,000 in Huyton. Solicitors naturally set up office where there are clients; and, unlike the Bar, the solicitors' profession draws only a small part of its income from legal aid; the Royal Commission on Legal Services in 1979 found that only 6 per cent of gross fees came from public funds, though the proportion has risen a little since then. On the other hand, solicitors do draw a significant part of their total earnings from conveyancing, that is, the buying and selling of houses. They used to have a statutory monopoly of the right to charge for work of this nature which has been broken by the creation of the modest new profession of licensed conveyancers. But the recession in the housing market has probably done more than any institutional change to slash the earnings of solicitors from conveyancing, though the average provincial firm of solicitors still relies heavily on conveyancing work. Nowadays these firms are branching out in new diections, such as processing claims before Industrial Tribunals and advising on many employment matters, in addition to such traditional fare as minor criminal work, matrimonial work, and a miscellany of other matters. In London a small number of very large firms concentrate on commercial and tax work, their clients naturally being mostly companies and business concerns. These 'mega-firms' deal with business involving millions of pounds, and charge fees accordingly. Their own business methods are ultra-modern (with constant use of computers, fax, and other forms of information technology); the Dickensian image has been left far behind.

There is no space here for a detailed account of the nature or work of the legal profession. But two points may be selected for further mention. The first concerns the traditional court dress—the barrister's wig and gown, the judicial ermine, the solicitor's gown. Why does the profession continue with these trappings? Do they serve a useful purpose of any kind? The answer to the first question is almost certainly that the profession continues to wear traditional dress simply because it is customary, and this is a somewhat conservative profession which is, rather more than most professions, attached to its customs and traditions. While it is possible to think up arguments in favour of the custom (for instance, that it lends an air of formality and solemnity to legal proceedings, and perhaps that it makes lawyers more anonymous), it is absurd to imagine that these arguments would ever lead to the adoption of the present court dress if one were starting with a clean slate. On the other hand, few people seem to find the present customs seriously worrying. The survey of jurors undertaken by the Royal Commission on Criminal Justice surprised most people by showing strong support for the traditional costume, and when the present Lord Chief Justice, Lord Taylor, attempted recently to persuade the profession to adopt a more modern court dress he was defeated by the traditionalists.

The second issue is a rather more important question: why should the legal profession be divided in two as it is in England when almost every other country in the world manages with one? Does this division serve the public interest? Once again, the answer to the first question is almost certainly that we have a divided legal profession because of the accidents of history, and that it is exceedingly unlikely that anyone devising a new legal system today would think it necessary to have a split profession. But it does not follow that the accidents of history have produced a result which is unsatisfactory. The weight of professional opinion is heavily in favour of maintaining the division between the two parts of the profession, and this attitude, though certainly stemming partly from attachment to custom, was also upheld by the Royal Commission on Legal Services in 1979. The strongest argument in favour of the present division is probably that it helps to maintain the high quality of the senior judiciary. The Bar is so small (and the number of senior barristers who are serious candidates for judicial appointment is of course quite tiny for a country as large as this) that it is possible for the Lord Chancellor and his senior colleagues to hand-pick every new judge. And—although complacency is not to be encouraged—the results are undeniably impressive. Nobody who is in a position to compare the English judiciary with that of countries overseas (except perhaps for those which closely follow the English practice, such as Australia) can seriously doubt that the quality of the higher judiciary is probably unsurpassed, and perhaps even unmatched in the world. On the other hand, it must be admitted that this high quality is purchased at some price: in particular, as we have already seen, judges, like barristers, tend to be very much alike in their background, their values, and probably also their politics.

Other arguments for and against the split profession, though much canvassed by the Royal Commission in 1979, are probably of little importance by comparison with this basic question. It is, for instance, argued that a single profession would cut legal costs, because a client would only need one lawyer to see his case right through from beginning to end. Few lawyers really believe that this would happen, however, even in a unified profession, because specialists in advocacy would still exist. The client would almost certainly be passed from one partner to another as his problem became a matter for litigation. Perhaps, as has also been argued, a fused profession would mean that the client would actually see and speak to his advocate earlier and more often than he sees counsel in the present system; and that might be a gain. But on the other side, it is also said, and with some justification, that it is actually better for the advocate to have less personal contact with the client—he can bring a more detached mind to the case, and certainly will find it easier to render a better service to the court itself.

As we have noted already, the Lord Chancellor has recently pushed through statutory changes which have opened the door to the possibility of solicitor advocates with rights of audience in the higher courts, and ultimately to the possibility of judicial preferment. These changes (known by some as the Mackay reforms), which were bitterly opposed by the judges and the Bar but (of course) supported by the solicitors' profession, are not necessarily fatal to the division between the professions. But many barristers argued, during the very controversial debates that accompanied these changes, that in the long run they would inevitably lead to the decline of the Bar. Certainly, if one were asked to advise a young person considering entry to the profession today, it would be difficult to think of many reasons why he or she should choose the Bar rather than become a solicitor. A person seeking to qualify as a solicitor can become a trainee solicitor after three years of university legal education and one extra year doing the legal practice course. As a trainee solicitor it is possible to obtain a paid position even before qualifying. Once qualified, a young solicitor is paid a salary, and has the usual security of good employment, such as sick-pay and holidays with pay. If he eventually becomes a partner he has a chance to buy his share in the firm on deferred terms, which means that when he retires he has an asset to sell to boost his pension. If he wants to argue cases in court he may seek rights of advocacy under the new legislation. On the other hand, the young would-be barrister has much less chance of earning anything before he qualifies, must then obtain a seat in chambers from which he can try to build up a practice, knowing that times will probably be hard for a few years. He has none of the security of employment, must meet his own expenses, cover his own holidays and buy his own (very expensive) sick-pay insurance. In return he gets the satisfaction of wearing a wig, and of being self-employed. Doubtless also, being a barrister still sounds a much more glamorous occupation than being a solicitor, for what that is worth. All things considered, therefore, it would not be surprising if the Mackay reforms gradually do lead to the decline of the Bar as an independent profession. However, this has not yet happened in some Australian states which have long permitted solicitors to do advocacy work, so perhaps the sheer innate conservatism of the profession will somehow preserve the *status quo*.

Courts as decision-making bodies

I return now to the courts and to their role in the government of the country in the broadest sense. Courts exercise power by making decisions. But that is also true of many other persons and bodies in the machinery of government, for instance, the police, civil servants, members of local authorities, Cabinet ministers, and many others. How do the decisions made by courts differ from those made by other bodies and institutions? Is it because the nature of the decisions is different, or because the way in which they are made is different? Or might it be, after all, that there are no essential differences between decisions made by courts and by other power-exercising bodies?

Let us begin by looking a little more closely at the sort of questions which courts decide. Lawyers commonly assume that all questions which have to be decided by courts fall into two categories, questions of fact and questions of law. Certainly these two sorts of questions occupy a large part of the time of most courts, though I shall suggest that there are also other kinds of questions which courts habitually have to decide.

Questions of fact are themselves of various kinds. In many legal trials (both civil and criminal) there is a basic disagreement about what actually happened. The prosecution in a criminal case alleges that the accused stole something from a shop, for instance; the accused claims he was in bed and asleep at the time. This is a straightforward factual question—a question of primary fact—which has to be decided by the tribunal of fact, that is, by magistrates or, if the case is tried on indictment, by the jury. Or perhaps in a civil case a plaintiff claims that he lent some money to the defendant, while the defendant point-blank denies it; here the question of fact will have to be decided usually by a circuit judge or high court judge, as the case may be.

Obviously some questions of fact are more complicated and difficult to ascertain. For instance, it is often relevant to decide with what *intention* a particular act has been done. An accused was seen to walk out of a shop carrying an item which he had not paid for. If he is charged with theft he may admit that he took the item, but claim that he did it in a fit of absent-mindedness, and had no intention to steal. This too is a question of fact for, as was once said by an eminent judge, 'the state of a man's mind is as much a fact as the state of his digestion'.

Questions of this kind, difficult though they sometimes may be, are at least in principle capable of definite resolution. Other questions of fact can only be answered according to probabilities. For example, a workman injured in an accident claims that he fell off some scaffolding because his employer negligently failed to provide him with a safety-belt. The employer replies that even if he had supplied the belt the workman would not have worn it, because all previous experience on the site showed that the workers never wore safety-belts even when supplied. The question of fact which the court has to decide is whether the workman would have been injured if the belt had been supplied. Clearly, the question can only be answered on the basis of probabilities, and that is the only answer which the law requires.

Another kind of question which lawyers often call a question of fact is really an *evaluation* of a piece of conduct. For instance, the law often imposes obligations on people which are couched in terms of 'reasonableness'. People must act with reasonable care; they must give this or that notice within a reasonable time; they are entitled to reasonable warning of dangers, and so on. Whether a particular piece of conduct meets the standard of reasonableness required is treated by lawyers as a question of fact for most purposes, but it is obviously a different sort of question of fact from questions of primary fact, discussed above. Standards of reasonableness are evaluative, and involve value-judgments. Is it reasonable to require a cricket club to erect a 15-foot fence around their ground to prevent the odd six being hit into the street or into adjoining gardens? The answer depends on the relative values to be given to the game of cricket, the security of passers-by in the street, and the right to peace and quiet of the occupiers of the houses adjoining the ground.

Of course, to say that decisions like this involve value-judgments is not to say that they are made in a wholly subjective way. Judges may take their value-judgments from the community—in so far as they can ascertain them—rather than from their own personal inclinations. But there is no doubt that this may be psychologically difficult for the judge, and sometimes he may be unable to prevent his own value-systems from entering into decisions of this character. An obvious example concerns the duty of care which employers owe to their employees. Is an employer bound to anticipate that his workmen may behave foolishly or carelessly, neglectful of their own safety, and guard against the risk of accidents from such causes? Common experience shows that such foolishness and carelessness occurs, and a judge with sympathies for injured workmen may say that it is only 'reasonable' for the employer to anticipate and guard against such risks. On the other hand, a judge who believes in the individual's responsibility for his own safety may be less sympathetic to a workman injured in such circumstances, and may say that it is unreasonable to expect an employer to protect workmen from their own folly. There is no doubt that, during the course of the past hundred years and more, judicial attitudes to workers injured in such circumstances have undergone a fundamental change, much of which is disguised by the continued use of the concept of 'reasonableness' to describe the required standard of care. Judges are today far more sympathetic to actions by injured workmen, of which many thousands are brought every year.

Evaluative questions of fact of this kind approach questions of pure law, but they are not generalizable in the way that questions of law are. Of course, some of the most important questions which courts have to decide, especially higher courts, are questions of pure law. We have already noted a couple of examples of such decisions in dealing with the nature of binding precedent, both of which typify many common questions of law in modern times. Is a minister entitled to exercise a statutory power for this or that purpose when that purpose is not expressly stated in the Act of Parliament creating the power (*Congreve* v. *Home Office*, p. 21 above)? Is a surveyor who carelessly fails to spot a defect in a house liable to someone who buys the house in reliance on the survey, even though the buyer does not directly engage the surveyor himself (*Smith* v. *Bush*, p. 22 above)? Many hundreds of new questions of law have to be decided by courts every year, and these, like evaluative questions, often involve an appeal to values. Of course, not all questions of law are like that. Some of them have a clear and precise answer, even though it may be very difficult to track it down. A complex question of tax law may take several hours' research among the statutes and the cases, but the answer, once discovered, may be quite plain and indisputable, though it is unlikely that such a question will in practice be litigated. But sometimes there is no clear legal answer at all. The wording of the Act may be ambiguous, the point may not have been considered by the draftsman, the case may fall on the borderline between two mutually exclusive provisions, there may be conflicting precedents, and so on. The court dealing with the matter must then decide 'what the law is'; but since we have just assumed that there is *no* (settled or clear) law on the point, to 'decide what the law is' really means to make new law, or decide what it ought to be. And that, of course, is an important part of the function of the courts, especially appeal courts.

Deciding questions of fact, and questions of law, and then applying the law to the facts, are usually thought of as the traditional and typical judicial function. But in modern times judges often exercise other functions which involve the extensive use of discretions. Much modern law gives enormous discretionary power to judges. They can, for instance, order 'reasonable' provision to be made out of the estate of a deceased person for the benefit of a dependant of the deceased who has not been 'adequately' provided for; they can order matrimonial property to be divided between husband and wife in the event of divorce in such proportions as they find fair and equitable; they can strike out 'unreasonable' exclusion clauses in many contracts, even between businessmen; they can settle the terms upon which a tenant of business premises is entitled to renew his lease; and so on and so forth. The concept of judicial discretion is certainly not new. Judges have for centuries had discretions about some matters—for instance, the extent of criminal penalties which can be imposed for many offences, whether to award damages for a breach of contract or actually order the defendant to perform his contract, and so on. But in modern times judicial discretions have proliferated greatly, and there is every indication that the process is likely to continue. Much of the trend derives from modern legislation which delegates very extensive powers to the judges to decide various questions as they think fit, or as may seem just and equitable, rather than in accordance with pre-defined and fixed rules of law.

What is perhaps a subclass of these discretionary decisions may be worth a few words separately. Many judicial decisions concern questions of *amount*, for instance, the amount of a fine, the length of a sentence of imprisonment, the amount of damages in a civil case, the amount of an injury for which the plaintiff himself may be reasonably held responsible where he has been guilty of 'contributory negligence', and so on. Questions of this kind obviously differ from many ordinary questions of fact or of law, because there will inevitably be some arbitrariness about the precise figure chosen.

There is no doubt that decisions of the above three classes are the most important and common sorts of decisions made by courts; and there is a natural tendency to assume that such typical cases exhaust the whole class of judicial decisions. But the fact is that there are certain other jobs done by courts which really are of a very different character, and in effect are almost pure matters of administration. Petitions for an order for the winding-up of a company, for instance, of which a large number are heard every Monday in the Chancery Division of the High Court, are often uncontested. In such circumstances the court's function is almost purely administrative. The judge has to be satisfied that the relevant formalities have been complied with (notices served on the company, and the like) and that the papers before him reveal a prima-facie case for the making of a winding-up order. He then makes an order as a matter of course. Many uncontested orders in matrimonial cases are today likewise largely administrative in character. Similarly, in the judicial task of supervising the administration of estates of deceased persons, or of controlling the actions of trustees, judges are called upon to make simple orders which in practice will often be uncontested, and the task is then of an administrative character.

To say that decisions of this type are administrative in character is something that many lawyers would dislike. To the lawyer, administration is a fundamentally different job from judging. Administrators are thought to decide questions on policy grounds, while judges, even when making routine decisions of the kind described above, are thought to be bound by law to make their decisions in a particular way. So to the ordinary lawyer, identifying the kinds of decisions which courts do *not* make (namely, policy decisions) may be just as important to an understanding of the judicial process as identifying the kinds of decisions which courts do make. We enter here on controversial territory, but there is good ground for rejecting this traditional view of the judicial function. It is no doubt true that two *typical* judicial functions are to decide disputed questions of fact and law, and these do differ in many ways from an administrative decision at a level of high policy, taken, for instance, by senior civil servants. But it is simply not true to say that judges do not have to consider policy issues in many of the decisions they make, nor is it true that administrative decisions by administrators are all policy decisions. Judges certainly have to consider policy questions in those important, if not typical, cases in which they actually have to decide new points of law. But they also have to consider policy questions in many routine discretionary sorts of decisions. Whether to send a convicted person to gaol or merely to fine him, for instance, is in part a policy decision. It may not be *wholly* a policy decision, because justice and fairness can never be excluded from consideration in courts.* But a judge may decide to impose a fine or to make a probation order in a case where imprisonment would not be an undeserved sentence, and he may do this because he thinks that imprisonment is more likely to confirm the accused in a life of crime. That seems a clear policy decision.

Furthermore, many administrative decisions made by relatively junior administrators do not involve policy decisions at all. Many officials in central and local government have, for example, the task of examining applications from the public and processing them in accordance with instructions and guide-lines which leave the administrator with little or no discretion. A clerk in the local social security office who approves a claim for unemployment benefit, for instance, may be deciding a question of fact, and applying the law to those facts, just as much as a judge sitting in the High Court in a comparable claim at common law.

So where does all this leave us? Does it mean that the sorts of decisions which judges and courts make don't really differ from the sorts of decisions made by other administrative organs of the State? The answer to that is threefold. First, even if it is largely true that there is no *inherent* distinction between decisions made by courts and decisions made by other organs of the State, there are some decisions which by long tradition and custom have come to be regarded as exclusively within the province of courts, both in this country and elsewhere. In particular, the imposition of serious

* There is scope for argument over whether decisions based on grounds of fairness or justice can be called 'policy decisions'.

...nd above all, punishment involving a deprivation of
. power which in normal peacetime conditions is not
except by courts. Secondly, although other agencies of the
...ay have to make decisions on questions of law in the course
...rying out their duties, their decisions are not final and authori-
ta...ve in the way that court decisions are. It is true, however, that in
some spheres there are special tribunals (such as the social security
commissioners) who have the power to make final and authoritative
decisions on the law within their particular areas. To that extent
these tribunals must be regarded as possessing the attributes of the
ordinary courts.

But thirdly, and in some respects most importantly, decision-making by courts differs from decision-making by other State agencies,
because court *procedures* differ fundamentally from most administrative procedures. There is a sense in which the factor that marks
off the judicial decision from other decisions is not so much what is
decided but *how it is decided and who decides it*. This is a matter
of sufficient importance to deserve a section of its own.

Due process of law

If an attempt is made to compare the way in which a court makes
a decision with the way in which (say) some minister or civil servant
makes a decision, a number of obvious contrasts stand out. First,
courts are very public institutions. All courts sit openly, and members of the public (and of course the press) are permitted to walk in
and out of any court, subject to very rare exceptions where matters
of national security may be in issue, or where (as with youth courts)
there is a particular social policy in maintaining privacy. But not
only are the courts physically open in this way, everything that
happens in them is also orally and publicly presented. Witnesses
give their evidence orally and publicly; arguments are presented
orally and publicly; and judgments are delivered orally and publicly.
Except in magistrates' courts (where reasons for decisions are rarely
given), a judge always gives reasons for what he does, and he also
does that publicly and openly, and often at great length. By contrast,
much administrative decision-making goes on behind closed doors.

It often happens with such decisions that the identity of the decision-maker is not known, nor is it possible always to identify the factors which have influenced the decision. Some administrative decisions are simply announced with the minimum (or even a total absence) of reasoned argumentation. As is well known, there is today much concern over what many people see as the excess of secrecy in the British system of government, and the unwillingness of governments to publish papers and other background material relating to decisions made by or on behalf of the government. That is not a criticism which could be levelled at the judicial process.

But although the judicial process is itself such an open one, it is a little curious that in recent times the judges appear to have become a good deal more sympathetic to claims for secrecy or privacy by other institutions and agencies in society. The very wide view taken of the concept of contempt of court, for instance, which prevents media comment on current and pending litigation, has recently become extremely controversial because of the degree to which it acts as a fetter on the freedom of the press. Legislation has recently been passed which relaxes the rules of contempt somewhat. But in other areas also there is this same sign of judicial willingness to limit public disclosure of information, for example, on the ground that one person has obtained information 'in confidence' and so should not be permitted to publish it. It is paradoxical that judges who are dedicated, in their own courts and judicial process, to the maximum publicity and freedom of disclosure, should nowadays appear so willing to condone, or assist, other agencies and bodies to restrain publication of information which is often a matter of great public interest. Some would see this as a result of the élitist, pro-establishment, nature of the higher judiciary, who may tend to identify more with senior managers or bureaucrats in their desire to avoid the public gaze, and less with the media who claim to act in the public interest. Fortunately, as yet, these recent trends do not appear to have affected the strong traditional belief in open justice so far as court proceedings themselves are concerned.

Of course, there is a price to pay for the public face of justice. It is sometimes embarrassing, even humiliating, to appear publicly in court. Litigants may see no reason why their private quarrels should be opened to the gaze of the curious, witnesses may be reluctant to give evidence in public, and even judges (though they are probably hardened to it) may sometimes wish that they could announce their decisions in sensitive cases without having to give their reasons to the public and the media. But few would argue that this price is not worth paying for the immense benefits which public justice brings.

A second major contrast between judicial and administrative procedures concerns the right to be heard, and the right to confront one's opponents or accusers. It is one of the most fundamental principles of the administration of justice that a party has *a right to be heard*. Every litigant must be afforded the elementary right of putting his case, and furthermore, in nearly all English courts, this is a right to be heard orally. This right encompasses two separate elements: the right to give or adduce evidence, and the right to present arguments. The first must, of course, be done in person, the second can be done through legal representation. Mention of legal representation raises the inevitable question of cost. How does someone put a case if he isn't articulate enough to do it himself, and cannot afford a lawyer to do it for him? This is an important question to which we must return, but it doesn't affect the basic point that no amount of money will help you put a case if you do not have the right to do so, and the decision-maker refuses to hear you.

The right to be heard is so basic that lawyers call it a rule of 'natural justice'. This is in fact a technical term which is applied to the body of rules which the courts have evolved to control the procedures of tribunals and administrative agencies. So there are many such agencies which are today required by the courts to give parties a chance to state their case before decisions adversely affecting their rights are made. However, this does not mean that parties have a right to present their cases orally, and in fact few administrative bodies (as distinct from courts strictly so-called) conduct oral hearings. It is in any event a serious misnomer to call this right a rule of 'natural justice'. There is nothing natural about it at all. Many decision-makers will quite cheerfully make decisions with very serious consequences for others without thinking it necessary to ask them if they have anything to say. Employers will dismiss workers for misconduct, headmasters (and, alas, even universities) may expel or fine students or deprive them of grants or scholarships, all manner of public agencies and authorities will make decisions affecting citizens, and (if they were not advised by lawyers) many of them would do these things without giving the party affected a chance to be heard or put a case. In calling the right to be heard a rule of natural justice, lawyers may have underestimated their own contribution to one of the great principles of liberal societies.

The right to a public confrontation with one's accusers is also one of the inestimable advantages of the openness of legal procedures. Many people are willing to make private complaints, even to send anonymous letters. Those who receive such complaints may be tempted to think there is no smoke without fire, and if action is taken or decisions are made behind closed doors as a result of such information, grave injustice could be done. The right to cross-examine an accuser in open court is a most powerful tool for the prevention of injustice in this way.

Next, a word must be said about the requirement of impartiality and lack of bias on the part of judges. Here too there is often a significant difference between the judicial and the administrative process. Administrators are not expected to be disinterested in the outcome of the process they administer, but it is of the very essence of judicial proceedings that the judge should be impartial and unbiased as between the parties, and as regards the nature of the proceedings. In England this principle is carried so far that no judge will try a case in which he knows any of the parties or witnesses, or in which he may be thought to have any interest, however remote, in the outcome of the case. Judges are, moreover, trained to look at both sides of a case, to try to see each argument from the point of view of both parties. Long years at the Bar teach a lawyer to do this, because if he omits to look for the weak points in his own client's case, or the strong points in his opponent's case, he will soon learn that there is an opposing lawyer paid to do just that. So every lawyer tends to look at his client's case from the viewpoint of a prospective opponent, often probing and questioning the client to this end; hence the often-felt (and sometimes expressed) reaction of many clients: 'Whose side are you on anyway?' This experience helps to make judges fair-minded and impartial, although that is not to say that there are no bad judges, or judges who have bad days. Of course, impartiality does not mean that a judge has no natural leanings, or no policy inclinations. Indeed, it would be absurd to ask for that, because at least a judge must normally have a bias in favour of justice over injustice, right over wrong, good over evil. The fact that sometimes opinions may differ as to which of these is involved in a particular decision does not mean that it is possible or desirable for a judge not to have a strong feeling for justice himself.

The above three factors—the openness of courts, the right to be heard, and the impartiality of the judge—are the essential factors in a satisfactory judicial trial. They reflect the commitment of English law to the famous maxim that justice must not only be done, it must be manifestly seen to be done. Together, they constitute the set of ideas we know as 'due process of law'. In England, this is not a technical legal term. In a purely formal sense Parliament could pass a law abolishing all these requirements of a fair trial, and the result would still be trial by 'due process of law', because it would be a trial by process authorized by a law validly made by Parliament. But to anybody brought up in the Anglo-American system of law it is unthinkable that the concept of 'due process of law' could be swept away like this, and it would certainly be a contravention of the European Convention on Human Rights to which the United Kingdom is a party. The fact is that the concept of 'due process of law' is probably the greatest contribution ever made to modern civilization by lawyers or perhaps any other professional group. In America, this was recognized by the formal entrenchment in the Bill of Rights of the great fifth amendment to the Federal Constitution which declares that: 'No person shall be . . . deprived of life, liberty or property without due process of law.' In the American constitutional system this means that legislation which infringes the basic ideals which American courts believe to be inherent in the concept of due process is invalid.

The importance of the concept of 'due process of law' to lawyers often gives the impression that lawyers are more concerned with procedures than with substance in the administration of the law. An interesting example of the way in which lawyers' values have demonstrated this comes from the law on 'unfair dismissal'. Since

1971 it has generally been the law that an employee who has been 'unfairly dismissed' can claim compensation from an Industrial Tribunal. The Act of Parliament which brought about this change made it clear that the question of 'fairness' was to be decided without technicality, and according to the substantial merits of the case. But no sooner had the case law on the Act begun to build up than it became clear that the courts were holding that unfair dismissals could be of two different kinds: there could be unfairness because the reasons for dismissal were inadequate, and there could be unfairness because the employer had dismissed the employee *in an unfair way*, for example, by not giving him a chance to be heard, or by not following previously announced procedures. The emphasis on the procedural aspects has sometimes led tribunals to hold dismissals to be unfair even where there seems to have been overwhelming justification for the dismissal in substance.

Decisions of this character often lead laymen to think that the law is excessively technical in its stress on following correct procedures. Within limits this criticism may be justified, though it is today rare that a case is definitively disposed of because of some procedural mistake—more usually such mistakes merely lead to extra delay and cost. In general the lawyer's answer to this criticism would be that nothing conduces more effectively to the making of just decisions than the following of just procedures. But it may be a fair criticism of the English legal system that it sometimes appears to treat just procedures as even more important than seeking just outcomes.

Formality in the English legal system

Emphasis on 'due process' and legal procedures in general is characteristic of a rather formal legal system, and there is no doubt that the English legal system is in many respects a very formal one. The concept of a formal legal system is quite a complex one, and has a number of different facets. One facet of this kind of formality is a strong belief in the value and importance of rules *as rules* and of law *as law*, that is, a belief in the value of rules and law, regardless of the reasons underlying them. Bad rules and bad law may need to be reconsidered and reformed, but in a formal legal system they must be respected and enforced until they are changed. Another characteristic of a formal legal system is that great stress is laid on the proprieties on the surface, and there may be a reluctance to dig deep into underlying factual issues. For instance, it is an aspect of the formality of the English legal system that the verdict of a jury is very difficult to upset, *provided only that the jury has been properly instructed on the law by the trial judge, and provided that all other procedural rules have been observed.* So a misdirection by the judge, even on a relatively minor issue, may lead to a verdict being quashed on appeal; on the other hand, a verdict which seems strange and against the weight of the evidence is much more difficult to upset. Appeal judges tend to take the view that, constitutionally, verdicts are entrusted to juries, and that they have no business to overturn jury verdicts except on the strongest possible grounds.

This is one of the main reasons for the appalling string of miscarriages of justice in serious criminal cases which have come to light in the past few years. In case after case—the Guildford Four, the Maguire Seven, the Birmingham Six, and at least half-a-dozen others—convictions which were impeccably arrived at by due process of law, were repeatedly upheld by appeal courts. Only after years of agitation, often by honourable and disinterested lawyers and journalists and other public figures, and repeated re-hearings by the Court of Appeal have the true facts come to light in these cases, and the convictions ultimately been quashed. It must of course be said that quashing a conviction does not necessarily prove that the accused was innocent; it may only show that the conviction was obtained by methods and by evidence which was unsatisfactory. But in all these cases there could be no doubt of the unfairness of the convictions when the facts were fully known. In some cases clear evidence emerged that police witnesses had lied; in others, that scientific evidence was suppressed or flawed; and in others, that confessions were obtained by unfair or oppressive means (often from suspects of abnormally low intelligence or in abnormal psychological states). The difficulty has so often been that appeal courts have looked only at surface issues of due process of law. If there is no reason to believe that police witnesses are lying, if there is no reason to suppose that evidence favourable to the defence has been suppressed or not disclosed by the prosecution, if a confession appears to have been given freely and without use of oppressive methods, then the judges have generally assumed that the guilty verdict has been properly arrived at by the jury and should not be disturbed. The trouble about this approach is that it is based on the fundamental assumption that other participants in the trial process—police, prosecutors, expert witnesses, and so on—have all behaved impeccably. If this assumption is unfounded, then concentrating on surface due process is simply not good enough. Judges appear to be almost instinctively aware of this because they have been very reluctant indeed to believe that police malpractice is widespread; if they once come to believe that police evidence is unreliable in ordinary, everyday criminal cases they seem aware that criminal trials and appeals simply could not be conducted in the traditional way.

This long series of miscarriages of justice seems to have been the main impetus to the establishment of the Royal Commission on Criminal Justice under Lord Runciman which reported in 1993. But the Royal Commission recommendation that a special body should be established to examine cases where a miscarriage of justice is alleged has not yet been implemented. It seems probable that eventually some such reform will be carried out, and indeed the Queen's speech at the opening of the new parliamentary session in 1994 foreshadowed the introduction of a bill for this purpose later in the session. But some people (including the present author) may think it is a deplorable confession of failure that the ordinary courts cannot be trusted to do justice, but have to be rescued from their own failures by a special body outside the ordinary system. Perhaps this only goes to demonstrate that the English legal system is so formal, that when it gets things badly wrong despite having followed due process to the letter, it needs to be rescued by some body outside the system altogether. American lawyers would be amazed and probably also aghast at this, and would regard it as a serious reflection on the failures of the ordinary courts.

The cost of legal services and of litigation

The cost of legal services is well known to be high; and the cost of litigation is so high as to be almost prohibitively expensive for people of ordinary means. Except for a handful of the very rich, litigation is in practice largely indulged in only by corporations, public institutions, and those lucky enough to have the backing of some organization which has a collective interest to maintain or defend, such as a trade union or a voluntary association of some kind. The position is to some degree aggravated by the well-established practice of awarding costs to a winning litigant, so an individual who takes on a large, well-financed institution must not only somehow cover the costs of his own legal expenses, but must also take the risk of paying for the other side's costs if he ultimately loses. In practice this simply means that some legal rights are not really protected at all. For instance, if the BBC chooses to mount a programme designed to show that a well-known public figure has been guilty of corruption or other scandalous behaviour, the law of libel—which is notoriously expensive to invoke—is in practice of very little use to him unless he is very rich indeed or can secure the backing of some institution to pay his legal expenses. Even the cost of defending oneself on a criminal charge is often very high and frequently beyond the means of those charged. The most perfect system of laws in the world is not much use if the public cannot avail themselves of it; and the fairest criminal laws and procedure are likewise not much use if the accused cannot afford a lawyer. So what can be done to make the legal system more accessible to the public?

Unfortunately, the answer to this is that many ways have been tried over the years, and none has proved very successful. One way is to introduce new courts of a simpler and more streamlined character, designed for small litigants and minor cases. But courts like this have a way of developing over the years into more important courts handling more serious work, and so, as this happens, they tend to become more expensive to use, and not much less complex in their procedure than the ordinary courts. For instance, the present-day County courts began life in 1846 designed for simple debt-collection and minor litigation, but today more and more serious litigation takes place in the County courts, whose proceedings are only a little less formal and expensive than those of the High Court. A new kind of small-claims procedure now also exists where minor cases can be heard in the County court before a district judge sitting as an arbitrator, and this is sometimes used by consumers and other individuals without legal representation, relying on manuals or handbooks to assist them. But even these courts are somewhat daunting for the average person, and anyhow their powers are at present confined to the hearing of very minor cases, that is, those involving claims of under £1,000.

Other reforms are possible, though some of them involve an almost despairing acknowledgement that litigation and ordinary law are not for ordinary people. Recently, for instance, there has been a huge burgeoning in the number of ombudsmen who can investigate and deal with complaints at their own expense, and can often award compensation to claimants. Indeed, they are sometimes more useful than ordinary litigation because they can rely on standards of fair practice as well as on the law itself, so claimants may find it easier to obtain substantial justice from an ombudsman than from the law, where claimants can still be defeated by technicalities. Today ombudsmen exist for several distinct types of commercial activity, such as the work of banking, insurance, and building societies. The legal professions also have an ombudsman of their own. In addition there are ombudsmen for many public services, such as the National Health Service, and local government services, as well as the national ombudsman who can investigate allegations of maladministration in the civil service or government departments, though only at the behest of an MP. All this is very useful, but it does not necessarily eliminate the demand for ordinary litigation. Ombudsmen work in offices, privately, issuing their findings in discreet reports which may receive little publicity. Many would-be litigants are not satisfied by this. They may have a burning and wholly legitimate desire for their day in court, for an open confrontation with the other party, for a public hearing and vindication. So reforms of this character go only a limited way to meet the needs of potential litigants of moderate means.

Other kinds of legal reforms may be possible within the legal system itself. Perhaps courts could rely on court-appointed experts to save the parties the huge expense of each having their own expert witnesses, sometimes several such witnesses or experts, in one simple piece of litigation. Perhaps courts could change their procedure to allow more work to be done in writing, to take more written evidence, to reduce the length of oral legal argument on appeals, and so on. But it must be said that reforms of this kind—though the search for them must always go on—are only palliatives and are unlikely to make a great deal of difference to the costs of litigation and of legal services. The fact must be faced that lawyers will always be expensive so long as the law is complex. It takes many years of hard study to train a lawyer, and it may take many hours and even days of hard work to research a relatively minor point of law. In our system of precedent, when judgments in some cases run to twenty or thirty pages, or even more, a lawyer may have to read hundreds of pages in the law reports with a great deal of care to form a professional opinion on a relatively simple point. (He also has to maintain a very expensive library of law books.) This kind of thing will never be cheap. And recently our entire legal system has become even more complex as a result of the European dimension, which often means that two almost entirely separate legal systems have to be studied before the law on a point can be ascertained.

Then again, legal procedures, in their search for high-quality justice, are not cheap either. Much modern litigation, and even many criminal cases, generate enormous quantities of paper, and these papers have to be read by qualified lawyers, or anyhow by paralegals like trainee solicitors. To take one example of how the search for greater justice can produce huge extra costs, the Court of Appeal recently decided that the prosecution in a criminal case must disclose to the defendant all documents which they have obtained for the case in hand, and all witness statements taken, except for those taken from witnesses whom they intend to call to give evidence in court. Now in a complex criminal case hundreds of statements may be taken, thousands of documents may be seized and examined, all of which may ultimately turn out to be irrelevant, or may perhaps be put aside because the prosecution chooses to concentrate on other issues. All this material must be disclosed to the defence, which means that defence lawyers must wade through it all just on the chance that something favourable to their client's case may be found. Of course the cost of doing this is high even in a minor case; in a major fraud case, it is a nightmare.

In order to help poorer citizens gain access to law there have been for many years two systems of legal aid, one for civil cases and one for criminal cases. Unfortunately, these systems have been, in the economic jargon used today, 'demand-led', which means that no Treasury-imposed ceiling has so far been used. Anybody who qualifies according to the criteria used by the two systems has so far been entitled to legal aid. In recent years the results of this have been soaring costs. In a relatively short period the costs of the legal aid system have climbed from a modest few millions around 1970 to about £1.4 billion in 1993. Until the changes recently announced (which are discussed in the next paragraph) the rate of increase was such that the cost would have risen to over £2 billion by the mid-1990s. This huge, and very rapid increase has, not surprisingly, led to Treasury pressure on the Lord Chancellor, who in turn has been desperately looking for ways to keep the bill down. Equally unsurprising has been the result that the relationship between the legal profession and the Lord Chancellor has been steadily deteriorating for some years.

All this pressure has led the Lord Chancellor to introduce major changes in the eligibility for civil legal aid. This has always been a means-tested programme, but recently the tests have been tightened up very severely, so that now few people qualify to have their total legal costs covered in civil litigation except those on state benefits. Others will now have to contribute quite substantially to the costs of litigation if they are granted legal aid, and a person on a modest middle-class income may easily be found to be outside the eligibility bands of legal aid altogether. The Lord Chancellor acknowledges that there has been a shift in the philosophy underlying the whole system. It is no longer assumed that people are entitled to be able to litigate, where they appear to have a reasonably arguable case, in the same way that people are entitled to free medical treatment when they are ill. The new philosophy requires would-be litigants to bear a good part of their own costs, if at all possible, and this means that they are now expected to ask themselves whether the cost of litigation is worth the benefits it may bring. This is getting close to treating litigation as a commodity in the market, like other commodities. Naturally, some people find this highly objectionable. People go to law to get justice, they claim, and justice is not an ordinary commodity in the market. But unfortunately, justice can often only be obtained by use of the services of skilled lawyers, and lawyers, like all other members of the community, do provide their services in the market-place and naturally expect to be paid for their work. So there is an almost insoluble dilemma here. In times of great pressure on the government, when the Health Service, schools, roads, and all public services are constantly having to justify every pound of expenditure, it is not surprising that the government is no longer willing to fund legal aid on an open-ended basis.

One result of all these difficulties is that the Lord Chancellor (and indeed, the law itself) is now cautiously opening the door to new ways of financing litigation, especially the contingent fee system. It is now permissible for lawyers, subject to various restrictions, to agree to take a case on the basis that they will only charge a fee if the client is successful. This kind of fee arrangement is particularly useful in personal-injury litigation where substantial damages may be won by the client, and it is often quite easy to predict that the client will almost certainly win some damages. Indeed, in many cases, defendants (or their insurers) admit that they are liable, and the only argument is about the amount of the damages. In these cases this new fee arrangement may work reasonably well. In the United States the contingent fee system is very widely used to enable poor people to bring legal actions which they could never otherwise afford, but the American system has been the subject of various abuses which it is hoped to avoid in England. In particular, American lawyers are able to contract that their fee should be a proportion—often 30 per cent, and sometimes as high as 40 per cent—of the damages recovered. This means that an enormous fee can sometimes be recovered which is not at all commensurate with the amount of work involved. The American system has also led to still worse abuses, such as the notorious ambulance-chasing system, under which lawyers or their touts may go round hospitals seeking accident victims, and trying to persuade them to sign a contingent fee contract with a lawyer. There is no reason why these abuses should get a foothold in England; and within limits the introduction of contingent fees may prove a beneficial reform. It certainly opens the door to the possibility of litigation by the poor or persons of modest means.

It may well be that the problem of cost, and the accessibility of the legal system to those of modest means, require some very fundamental rethinking about the nature of legal procedures and civil litigation. A review of this nature was being conducted in 1994 by Lord Woolf, a lord of appeal, but it is hard to believe that a one-man inquiry by a person who has other duties to perform is going to do more than identify a few lines for further inquiry and research.

The system of criminal legal aid is also in some crisis because of the cost. Although this too is means-tested, the trouble is that most of those accused of serious crime simply have no means. Indeed, there have been some well-publicized cases recently in which persons with relatively wealthy life-styles have been able to obtain criminal legal aid when accused of frauds and other serious offences, because their assets have been frozen while civil litigation is pending against them. Criminal legal aid is granted at the discretion of magistrates, subject to the means test, and subject also to some consideration of the nature of the charges. But in virtually all serious crime, especially where the defendant is at risk of being sent to jail, but also where his reputation rather than his freedom may be at stake, it is now normally automatic for legal aid to be granted if the defendant cannot afford representation. It is virtually impossible for the government to reduce or cut down this right, because in modern times it is widely regarded as a fundamental right of a person accused of serious crime to have a lawyer to defend him. In the United States it would be an unconstitutional denial of due process not to fund an accused person's legal representation; and it seems pretty clear that the European Court of Human Rights at Strasbourg would take the view that the denial of legal representation would equally be a violation of the Human Rights Convention.*

The result is that the Lord Chancellor has been desperately seeking other ways of cutting the criminal legal aid bill, though with constant opposition from the legal profession, often supported also by the judges. One recent change has been the introduction of standard fees for minor criminal work in the hope of encouraging lawyers to be more efficient and speedy in their disposal of such cases. Obviously, a system in which the fee is based on the hours of work

* See further Chapter 5 below, pp. 161 ff., on this Convention.

done encourages lawyers to be more thorough in their work, and possibly over-thorough and wasteful, where the bill is to be paid by legal aid. On the other hand, the legal profession is loud in its complaints that much legal aid is even now scarcely enough to cover their costs, and that the system of standard fees will simply encourage slovenly work. The Lord Chancellor is also experimenting with the idea of 'franchising' firms of solicitors to do special classes of legal aid work. Presumably the hope is that franchised firms will specialize in different types of legal aid work, and then be willing to do cases of this type for a lower fee, in return for an assured flow of work.

Two peculiarities of the English judicial system

Before closing this brief survey of the English court as a decision-making body, it is worth drawing attention to two peculiarities of the English judicial system. Both are largely paralleled throughout the common law world,* but the second is particularly pronounced in England. The first of these is that the trial process in common law countries is almost invariably based on an 'accusatorial' rather than an 'inquisitorial' procedure. What this means is that basically the English trial is designed to resolve a dispute between two contesting parties, rather than to conduct an investigation, or even to ascertain the truth. The judge is to a great extent an umpire who presides over a contest between two parties. He listens to what they have to say and *only* to what they have to say; he may, of course, go away and consult his law books. But he does not generally consult anything to which he has not been referred by the parties or their lawyers, and he certainly does not himself call any witnesses or demand the production of any documents, even though he may feel unable to ascertain the truth without such a course. If he is unsure where the

* The 'common law world' is an imprecise term, generally used to refer to those countries which have inherited the essential elements of the English common law. Besides England itself, it includes Australia, New Zealand, Canada, and the United States (with the exception in Canada of Quebec, and in the United States of Louisiana). Former parts of the British Empire, such as India, Pakistan, and Nigeria retain common law characteristics. Some legal systems (Scotland, South Africa, Sri Lanka) are a mixture of common law and other systems.

truth lies at the end, he will say so, and the party with the burden of proof then loses.

Further, the judge is not expected to conduct the proceedings in too interventionist a spirit. He may ask questions of witnesses to clear up obscurities or ambiguities, but he must not take charge of the case and conduct the examination of the witnesses himself. It is widely thought by common lawyers that a judge who oversteps the mark in these respects loses the appearance of impartiality, and gives the impression of making up his mind before he has heard the whole case.

This accusatorial process underlies criminal cases as well as civil ones. A criminal case is a contest between prosecution and defence. The Crown (in trials on indictment) and the police or other complainant (in magistrates' courts) is one party to the case, and the accused is the other party. A criminal trial is not an investigation conducted by a judge or jury or magistrates. It is based on a charge made by the prosecution which it is for the prosecution to prove. So, for instance, the accused will not be asked any questions in court, unless he voluntarily chooses to go into the witness box and give evidence. Nor, indeed, need the defence say anything at all; the accused (or his lawyer) may, in effect, say to the prosecution: prove your case if you can.

This concept of the trial as a contest between two contending parties is deeply ingrained in the common lawyer's make-up. He is often unhappy in proceedings of a different character, where an investigation is the purpose of the exercise. In fact, the only court whose proceedings are of this nature in England is the coroner's court, which is not generally regarded by lawyers as a very important institution because it makes no decisions, but merely records findings. There are, however, other semi-judicial investigations of an *ad hoc* character which are held from time to time, for instance, inquiries into major disasters, or into political scandals and the like. Here also lawyers have often felt uncomfortable with the proceedings, largely because they often seem to be pointing an accusing finger at one or more persons under suspicion, and yet these persons do not have the usual protections and safeguards of an accused in a trial on indictment. No specific charges are formulated, the inquiry is of a roving character, and new allegations may suddenly appear in the course of lengthy and expensive proceedings.

There is no doubt that the accusatorial system has great strengths, above all, that it preserves the appearance of judicial impartiality. But there is a price to be paid for this. It sometimes happens that the only evidence that a person has committed a serious crime consists of a statement he has made in a form which is not admissible in evidence at all. For instance, a person may confess to having committed a crime, but his confession may be inadmissible because it has been induced by improper police interrogation. In the English system of trial, the case against the accused will then collapse if there is no other evidence; indeed, if it is clear to prosecuting counsel that the confession will be inadmissible he will probably advise against proceeding at all. Another disturbing kind of case arises when it is certain that one of two or more persons has committed a serious crime, but it is not known which of them is responsible. For instance, a baby may be seriously injured by being battered in its own home. It may be clear that one or other parent is responsible, but if both take refuge in silence there is no way of mounting a prosecution at all. In an inquisitorial system of trial the parties would themselves be questioned by or before a judge, and the truth might then emerge. However, the right of the accused not to answer questions is a basic feature of English criminal procedure closely associated with the accusatorial nature of the trial process. Indeed, to some it is even more—a basic human or constitutional right, as in the United States. This may seem rather curious today: why should a person be unwilling to answer questions properly put to him by duly authorized courts or officials? And if he is unwilling, isn't it likely that this is because he has something to hide? Why (as Bentham asked many years ago) should we protect criminals by inventing a rule which is the very one they would themselves choose as the first principle of criminal procedure?

Historically, it seems clear that the right to keep silent (or the privilege against self-incrimination, as it came to be known) was a reaction against torture and other unacceptable modes of questioning prisoners. And even today, it seems probable that the main force behind the opposition to any change in the law comes from doubts about police methods of interrogation. Undoubtedly this is true in America, where the main purpose of the continued vitality of the privilege against self-incrimination is to protect the citizen from 'third-degree' and other intolerable modes of questioning. Of course, it may be said that this is no reason for preventing a judge or court from asking questions of the accused; but the issue is not as simple as that. The accusatorial nature of our criminal procedure requires that a person should not be brought before a court unless the prosecution feels that it has sufficient evidence to lay before the court showing at least a prima-facie case of guilt. If the prosecution, or the judge, was entitled to question the prisoner even before a prima-facie case had been shown by the evidence of other witnesses, there would be a danger that the most innocent person could be hauled into court and charged with an offence, and then cross-questioned in an attempt to show his complicity. The only way in which this danger could be avoided would probably be to bring the judge (or magistrate) actually into the police investigation, as is done in France, so that the judge is (at least in theory) in charge of the investigative process. This would undoubtedly represent such a break with traditional English ideas that it would almost certainly be unacceptable. There are, it seems, clear advantages in letting the police make their own investigations and insisting that the results be laid before an impartial judge or magistrate who then adjudicates (with a jury if appropriate) on the rival cases of the two parties.

But even within the present structure of the adversarial system of procedure, the 'right to silence' can be protected to a greater or lesser degree. While it remains the case that nobody brought before a criminal court can be questioned by the judge or magistrate or prosecutor if he chooses not to go into the witness box to give evidence, the Criminal Justice Act 1994 introduces important new provisions which have been widely criticized as abolishing the 'right to silence', although they do no such thing. What these new provisions do is actually something very minor: they simply permit the court or jury to draw inferences against the accused from the fact that he has said nothing at various stages of the case—for instance, at the time of his arrest, or when interrogated by the police, or on his trial. In other words, a judge can now tell a jury that (for instance) the fact that the accused said nothing when arrested to explain his presence at the scene of a crime may be put into the scales and treated by them as an additional piece of evidence against the accused. But this only *permits* an adverse inference to be drawn; it does not compel the jury to draw such an inference. If they feel that there may have been very good reasons why the accused said nothing when arrested, even though he may have been innocent, then his silence will not add anything to the prosecution case. Hitherto the judge has not been allowed even to suggest to the jury that they may draw an inference against the accused because he kept silent when arrested or when questioned by the police. The judge has been compelled, if he mentioned the matter at all, to tell the jury that the accused was not bound to say anything when arrested, and they must not infer anything against him because he chose to exercise that right. But the judge has always been allowed to suggest to the jury that they may draw adverse inferences against the accused from his refusal to give evidence in court, so the changes made by the Criminal Justice Act 1994 only extend to the pre-trial period the same rules that have long applied to the trial itself.

So in some ways this is a very minor reform. But it has nevertheless generated very wide controversy. It was not recommended by the Royal Commission on Criminal Justice, and it has been very strongly opposed by the legal professions and many civil-liberty groups. And indeed, as we have already seen, it has been treated as abolition of the right to silence, which is absurd. The reasons for all this controversy are to some degree related to the long string of miscarriages of justice which have been discussed above. The legal professions have grown very distrustful of the police and perhaps even of the judges themselves in many ordinary criminal prosecutions. They are very worried that judges may not appreciate that people of low intelligence, or education, people who are regularly harassed by the police, who find all authority intimidatory, may simply be too frightened to say anything when found (say) in some compromising situation, even though they may have been innocent of wrongdoing. While a self-confident and articulate middle-class person may be able to offer an explanation for his presence or behaviour to a police officer, others may take refuge in silence. If judges fail to understand this, they may direct juries in terms which suggest that a strong adverse inference may be legitimately drawn against the accused in such a case. While this danger undoubtedly exists, there seems no reason why defence counsel cannot make this point adequately, nor why juries should not be able to understand it for themselves. In any event, after the long series of miscarriages of justice, so frequently due to police malpractice and dishonesty, it seems reasonable to assume that judges will be careful in directing juries what inferences may appropriately be drawn in difficult cases.

Another important new development concerning the 'right to silence' arises from the *Saunders* case which was recently decided by the European Court of Human Rights. Although (as stated above) it remains a firm principle of criminal procedure that the accused cannot be questioned if he chooses not to give evidence, there are some other unusual statutory powers that require a person to answer questions in some pre-trial inquiry, under threat of penalties if he refuses. For instance, companies are sometimes investigated under statutory powers for the detection of fraud, and an inquiry of this kind was conducted into the affairs of the Guinness corporation when Ernest Saunders was chairman of the company. He was compelled to answer questions, and his answers were then used against him in his subsequent trial for offences in connection with the same matters. This procedure was condemned by the European Court of Human Rights, which insisted that it was contrary to the very basis of a fair trial to use compulsion against the accused to obtain answers to questions before the trial, and then use those answers against him. This presumably means that amending legislation will have to be introduced to give effect to this ruling, which may also have implications for the powers of the Serious Fraud Office to compel suspects to answer questions in pre-trial inquiries, even though their power to use those answers is limited to cases where the accused's answers differ from his evidence given in the court.

The ruling in the *Saunders* case probably has no bearing on the amendments made by the Criminal Justice Act 1994, because there is nothing in that Act which compels a person to answer questions under threat of penalties. Since the European Court ruling would apply to other European countries which generally use an investigative mode of criminal procedure in which the accused is questioned by the judge as a matter of routine, it is hardly possible that that Court could adopt an extreme view on the right to silence which would prevent such questions even being asked. Yet it has been reported that the changes made by the 1994 Act may be challenged before the European Court of Human Rights.

The accusatorial trial can also raise difficulties in civil cases. The full truth in some cases may never emerge because neither party wants to call a vital witness. The contest-like nature of the proceedings may conceal some important public interest which neither party wishes to discuss. And where a novel point of law is involved, it is more than a little curious if the judge is restricted to choosing between rival formulations of the law offered to him by the parties; this is, indeed, so unsatisfactory that judges sometimes rebel against it, and reject both parties' contentions. But this too has serious difficulties in our adversarial system, because it means that the solution adopted by the judge may not have been searchingly tested by the arguments placed before him.

The second peculiarity of the English legal system is, surprisingly, one that has escaped much public comment or criticism. It concerns the great extent to which the legal system relies upon single judges to make decisions. All county court and nearly all high court litigation comes before a single judge in the first instance; and in criminal trials on indictment, the judge has sole responsibility for the sentence. The power wielded by a single judge in these cases is awesome. It can make or break a life. Yet even the possibilities of appeal are very limited. Most appeal courts are loath to upset a decision on a point of fact, or an exercise of discretion, unless it is grossly and manifestly wrong. A sentence of, say, five years' imprisonment is unlikely to be upset by an appeal court, each member of which would only have passed a sentence of four years if he had been trying the case. An award of £50,000 in damages is unlikely to be upset by a court of appeal, each member of which would have personally awarded £60,000. An assessment that an injured plaintiff was 30 per cent responsible for his own injuries might well be upheld by an appeal court, each member of which would have assessed the plaintiff's responsibility at 20 per cent.

And that difference of 10 per cent may cost the plaintiff, in a bad case, £20,000 in damages. The main reason for this sort of behaviour on the part of appeal courts is probably the desire to discourage frivolous appeals. If appeal courts were willing to substitute their own discretion for that of a trial judge, even where they only differed from him by some trivial amount, litigants might (it is feared) come to the view that an appeal is always worthwhile: an appellant would have nothing to lose and would always have a chance to gain something, however small. At present, counsel familiar with the reluctance of appeal courts to interfere, except in cases of gross deviation from a norm, will often advise that an appeal on sentence or amount of damages is pointless for these reasons.

But the result of this is that the powers vested in trial judges are enormous. The fact that so little comment has been directed to this state of affairs may be testimony to the high quality of the judges, but some may wonder whether such great powers should ever be vested in single individuals, or perhaps, whether appeals should not be treated in a different sort of way. And these doubts are likely to intensify as more and more discretions are substituted for decisions by fixed rule.

2 Law outside the courts

Legal institutions

Courts may be central to the way in which lawyers think about law. But most people have very little actual contact with courts. The great majority of the population probably never see the inside of the High Court or a County court in their lives. Many people, no doubt, have minor brushes with the criminal law in magistrates' courts, and many others receive county court summonses for simple debts—which are usually paid before attendance at the court is required. But the courts are not institutions of central and daily relevance for the ordinary person. On the other hand, there are numerous other institutions which may be much more important to ordinary people. There are, for a start, major constitutional institutions, like Parliament, government, and Cabinet. True, the ordinary citizen may have little more direct contact with these than he does with courts, but he does at least have a chance to vote for his local Member of Parliament every few years, and he is certainly likely to read and hear a great deal more about these institutions than about the courts. Moreover, what these institutions do is likely to impinge on his life in a more obvious way than what courts may do, except of course in cases in which he is personally involved. Then there are other institutions, like local authorities, and local branches of central government departments, such as the local offices of the DSS, the local tax inspector, and so on. So, too, there are the law-enforcement agencies, and in particular the police. Standing somewhat apart from institutions of this character are private bodies like companies, trade unions, and professional bodies, though in practice many bodies have functions which uneasily straddle the line between private and public, such as the post office and the universities.

Now there is an important sense in which all institutions of this character are actually creations of the law, not just in the sense that it was the law which originally established the institution (which indeed is not true of all institutions, for instance, Parliament or the monarchy) but in the sense that an institution is not a physical object or even a group of people. Parliament as a constitutional and legal institution is *not* the pseudo-Gothic structure topped by Big Ben which we all tend to call to mind when we think of Parliament. Nor is it even the individual MPs and lords who sit in the two Houses of Parliament who comprise Parliament as an institution. If an atom bomb fell on Westminster and obliterated the Houses of Parliament and all who sat there, the institution of Parliament would not be destroyed. The reason for this is that Parliament as an institution does not consist of buildings or individual people but of *rules of law*. It is, indeed, a very complex skein of law, and perhaps to refer to all this law as 'rules' may be misleading; but the essential point is that institutions of this character are in a sense just part of the law. It is the law which says what Parliament *is*; it is the law which says that what Parliament does—provided it follows certain prescribed procedures and forms—creates an Act of Parliament which can change the law; it is the law which says that these 635 individuals are members of the House of Commons with the right to sit and vote there; and it is the law which regulates the electoral process by which we can identify these 635 persons as being those entitled to call themselves members of the House of Commons; it is even the law which says that courts will not interfere with the internal arrangements of the two Houses and which therefore leaves the Houses free to follow their own procedures as they choose.

As I have already indicated, this is not to say that all institutions of this character were historically created by law. As we saw in the last chapter, this was not the origin of the early courts of common law, nor was it the origin of the monarchy, or even of the Parliament of England.* These institutions were not created by law; 'they just grew', like Topsy. They have, of course, been amended. Acts of

---

* A Scots lawyer might object that the present Parliament is indeed (in part) the creation of the Acts of Union between England and Scotland in 1707. But that raises issues I prefer to leave aside as irrelevant here; see *below*, p. 92.

Parliament have altered the succession to the throne several times, most recently on the abdication of Edward VIII in 1936; they have frequently amended the composition of the House of Commons, and even the Lords (for instance, by introducing life peerages and peeresses), and they have also altered the balance of power between Commons and Lords in the Parliament Acts of 1911 and 1949. But all this is not strictly relevant to the point being made here. This is that, no matter how institutions may have originated historically, in a developed and complex legal system like ours all institutions come to be treated as part of the very law itself. They must be fitted into a framework of law which defines their composition, procedure, and powers. The chief reason for this is the simple fact that it is the only way in which we can control and regulate the exercise of power. In the absence of some legal framework which defined how, and when, and by whom the policeman or the soldier could in the last analysis be ordered to bring his physical force to bear, there would be no way in which the citizen could distinguish between lawful authority and just plain force.

What I have said of Parliament is also true of all the other institutions mentioned above—local authorities, companies, trade unions, and the like. In the case of companies, much juristic discussion has centred on the nature of corporate personality, but as a matter of plain law there is no argument that a company has a legal identity as a sort of person created by law. And here again, it is necessary to bear in mind the distinction between the physical world and the legal world. Legally speaking, a company does not consist of buildings, plant, workers, and managers. Most lawyers would say that a company is an artificial legal person with a legal identity which enables it to own property, make contracts, and so on. But this is a somewhat confusing, if traditional, point of view. A natural person is a physical being, but his legal identity is not a physical fact, any more than that of a company. The law and the physical world do not exist on the same plane as each other. Companies, like human beings, have both a physical existence and a legal existence. The only relevant distinction is that all human beings are recognized to have a legal identity (except perhaps in slave-owning societies), while not all companies have a legal identity.

Law and the physical world

The above discussion leads to some more general questions of interest and importance. In modern developed societies, law and legal institutions are so pervasive, and have in general such stability, that we come to think of many legal (or 'institutional') facts as though they were physical facts. I have in my pocket a round piece of metal, which looks like gold but isn't, with an engraving of the Queen on one side. I call it a pound coin, and so does everyone else. It *is* a pound coin. But (although, of course, the coin is a physical object) its character as money, as a *pound*, is not a physical fact; it is a legal or institutional fact. In order to explain how this piece of metal is legally treated as a pound I would have to trace a good many laws and regulations concerning the authority of the Bank of England and the Treasury back to their ultimate legal sources. But it would be so rarely that anyone, even a lawyer, would need to do this, that for all practical purposes we think of pounds (whether coins or notes) as physical objects.

A great deal of law operates in this sort of way, to such an extent, indeed, that it permeates much ordinary language and even thought. Many of us think we have 'money in the bank'. But that isn't a physical fact at all. Strictly speaking, as has been well said, the only person who has money in a bank is the bank itself. What the customer has is a legal right to obtain money from his bank in various ways, and subject to various limitations. Many ordinary words in everyday use (for instance, 'wife' or 'husband') can only be fully understood by reference to a complex and interwoven network of law and regulation. Of course, for ordinary purposes nobody has all this in mind when using such words. But the background is taken for granted, and it is a background which rests on law. Words like this naturally *relate* to the physical world, and one can conceive of simple societies in which such words could be used solely to express a physical fact or relationship. In some societies the word 'wife' or its equivalent, for instance, might just mean 'the woman I live with'. But in a developed society it does not mean that: your wife remains your wife even if you don't live with her, and the woman you live with doesn't, by that fact alone, become your wife.

Words indicating possession or ownership or other relationships are another common illustration of ordinary linguistic usage which rests ultimately on assumptions about the background of law. 'My house', 'your car', 'his country' are all phrases which *can* be used to refer to a purely physical relationship (the house I live in, the car you drive, the country he was born in), but in practice words like this tend to be used in a more complex and subtle way which presupposes much background law. 'My house' is often mine because I own it, or rent it, and to own or rent a house is to be involved in legal relationships.

Two comments are worth making about the relationship between the legal and the physical world. The first concerns the *pervasiveness* of law in developed societies. Law is everywhere; all actions, all relationships, even many facts and events which appear to be purely physical phenomena, can be (and sometimes must be) described in legal terms and slotted into legal classifications. One result of this pervasiveness is that we often tend to think of the law as though it had itself a physical existence, as though it were 'a brooding omnipresence in the sky'. That quotation comes from a judgment of a famous American judge (Oliver Wendell Holmes) who was at some pains to reject this concept of the law: his point was that there is no such entity as '*the* common law' which is the same everywhere at all times, and in particular he was rejecting the notion that the common law had to be identical in all the American states. But although most lawyers would today agree that the law is not a brooding omnipresence in the sky, there is still a tremendous temptation to reify it and think of it as though it were an entity of some kind. To take a simple example, lawyers would be very loath to admit that there might actually be *no law* on a point. They would readily admit that on such and such a point the law is doubtful, and that until the courts have decided what it is, nobody can say for sure, or advise his clients what they are likely to decide. But they would reject the idea that this somehow means that the law has a gap, a hole. There *must be* some law to cover everything that happens. This is a reflection of the way lawyers tend to think of law as something that 'exists', a tendency powerfully reinforced by the ease with which we identify physical objects like printed Acts of Parliament, or law reports, with the law itself. For most ordinary purposes it is quite harmless to think of the law in this sort of way—indeed, perhaps it does some good, as will be suggested below. But it can also lead to confusion for the person who seeks a deeper understanding of the nature of law.

The second point to be made about the relationship between the legal and the physical world is that the gap between the two must be bridged if the law is to be efficacious, indeed, if it is to be a proper system of law at all. The most perfect code of laws would be a mere abstract set of ideas if it had no actual relationship to the world of reality, if it was never observed or followed. So there must be ways and means of bridging the gap, of striving for a correspondence between the legal and the physical world. How is this to be done? It cannot be done directly, because laws have no power over the physical world. Laws cannot, by themselves, build houses, prevent accidents, stop inflation. So it must be done indirectly, by operating through human beings. By persuading or compelling people to behave in this or that way, laws can indirectly have a profound effect on the physical world. To the extent that human beings can control their own environment, laws can operate to produce results in the environment of widely varying characteristics.

Persuasion and compulsion in the observance of law

To achieve these results laws must, then, persuade or compel people to behave in the desired fashion. It is often thought that compulsion is the more important of these two. In the last resort it is of course true that most laws are backed by force, although there is much juristic controversy about the possibility of genuine laws which cannot be enforced, or which contain no sanction for breach; for example, some rules of international law. And unquestionably, in any modern state there is a practical need for the use of force in the last resort to enforce much of the law. There is no point in labouring the obvious. But there is a need to emphasize that the use of force in this way is very much a matter of last resort, that a great deal of the law does not rest upon the daily use of force for its operation and that it would in practice be extremely difficult, if not impossible, to govern a country if regular and habitual compliance with the law could only be secured at the point of the bayonet. Even the most monstrous tyrannies would find it difficult to operate effectively unless they could rely on the remote threat of force rather than its immediate threat, still less the actual infliction of force, to secure compliance with the law. In practice most tyrannies find it necessary to control the sources of information available to their citizens— the press and the modern media—in order the more effectively to mobilize the powers of *persuasion*. For it is, in the end, not so much naked force but the power of persuasion which secures most compliance with the law, although it is obviously true that, in tyrannies, the persuasion may be more effective for the threats of force which lie close at hand.

But in free societies—indeed, this is one of the marks of free societies—most of the law is observed most of the time by most of the citizens without the constant threat of immediate force. This is not to say that the psychological reasons which induce certain patterns of behaviour are uniform or simple. No doubt different people observe the laws for different reasons, and the powers of persuasion operate in many different ways. They are most effective of all when they are taken for granted, and not consciously examined. Those who observe the law from habit and custom without thinking about it may not be consciously responding to the persuasive powers of the law, but they may well be responding to training from earlier life.

The persuasive power of law has also derived much of its strength from its mystique and majesty. The element of mystique was much greater in earlier days, particularly when law remained strongly associated with religion. In less developed societies it is commonly found that law and religion are not separate elements in the rules that provide how people are to behave. In such societies law is commonly conceived as something mysterious and discoverable only to an élite, originally a priest class, who gradually get transmuted into a professional lawyer class. The mass of the people then have to accept the law as some awesome and profound mystery whose requirements are translated for them by these professional experts. Furthermore, under these conditions law is not thought of as something which is capable of instant and perpetual change by human beings. Its close association with religion gives it a stability and permanence, and its vaguely divine source conceals the extent to which the law in practice is used by some human beings to maintain power over others. Similarly, the formal trappings and ritual traditionally found in English courts and legal institutions may historically have contributed much to the powers of persuasion of the law. The element of majesty, represented for Englishmen until relatively recent times by the regular visitations of the assize judges, resplendent in their scarlet robes and huge wigs, may have added its part to the grasp which the law used to have over men's minds.

In modern times much of the mystique and majesty of the law have disappeared. The association of law and religion has, for most people, been decisively broken; the source of the law, as it is made, unmade, and remade by successive Parliaments, is seen only too clearly to lie with mortal men and women; and the formal trappings and ritual of the courts may seem to many an absurd and outdated deference to forms and traditions. To many, these changes in attitude are welcome signs of liberation from superstition. To them, law can now be more clearly seen for what it is, a human institution for the regulation of conflict in society, and for the better facilitation of the due fulfilment by men and women of their individual aspirations. What remains doubtful about this vision, however, is the extent to which the disappearance of superstition will be replaced by rational calculations of enlightened self-interest. For the removal of the mystique and majesty from the law may lead (indeed, surely has already led) to a great weakening of the persuasive powers of the law.

No doubt the habit of law observance is still strong in societies such as ours. This observance of law through habit, custom, and early training is of profound importance to the stability and efficiency of modern societies. Where these habits and customs are less strong, the law will depend more on actual force for its implementation, and under those circumstances both political and social stability may break down. Political stability breaks down because it is very difficult to use force to compel observance of political and constitutional power—at least it is very difficult to do so for any length of time. Hence, the recurrence of *coups d'état* in many modern African and Asian countries where the custom and habit of respecting a particular constitutional arrangement has not become established. But social stability can also break down where people constantly weigh up the advantages and disadvantages of observing a law, before they choose to obey it. For it is only too obvious that most laws in a modern state must operate to the advantage of some and to the disadvantage of others. Ideally, the aim should be to produce laws which, *on balance*, will be to everyone's advantage. But even if a society approximates to this ideal, many laws will disadvantage some, and if those disadvantaged by them decide to defy them, or to resist them, or even to refuse their co-operation unless and until compelled by force, a society can quickly descend into chaos. The habit of obedience to laws is very much more difficult to establish than it is to break down, as is vividly illustrated by the rapid changes in the former Soviet Union since the collapse of communism. It is also more difficult to maintain the habit of obedience to the law in times of great change, because then people must constantly be adapting their behaviour to the new requirements of the law, and that is hard to reconcile with the idea of habitual or traditional observance of the law.

So it is clear that the law must, if it is to function well, generally operate with the consent (or at least without the active dissent) of the mass of the people, and that its ultimate enforcement by the power and coercion of organized force, though also necessary in the last resort, must generally remain a matter of last resort.

In England this point has been well illustrated by the fate of the poll tax which was introduced in 1989 and eventually abolished and replaced by the new council tax in 1993. The poll tax, as it was popularly called (though its official name was community charge) was introduced to replace domestic rates which had themselves become unpopular, and which certainly operated very unfairly in many respects. But the rating system was easily enforced because the liability was always that of the occupier of the property. The occupier is very easy to identify, and the legislation anyhow allowed the rating authorities to distrain (i.e. to seize goods in the house and sell them) in the event of default. So the rating system had struggled along, in need of reform, but still readily enforceable. The new community charge eliminated some unfairnesses and adopted as its basic premiss the idea that every voter should contribute something towards the cost of local government. Even the poorest members of the community were required to pay some part of the normal charge; those on state benefits, for instance, had to pay 20 per cent of the charge, but benefits were raised by 20 per cent of a notional or average charge to enable them to do so. Unfortunately, many councils levied a charge far higher than this notional charge, so those on benefits were generally much worse off than before. On the other hand, those who lived in huge, valuable houses, far above the average level of prosperity, were much better off because the charge, unlike the rates, did not differentiate against those who lived in better-off houses, or who had higher incomes.

The community charge was hugely unpopular with a large segment of the country from the start, and protests and demonstrations against it were commonplace. But governments often ride over this kind of unpopularity, and insist that the law should be enforced. Unpopular laws, say successive governments, can be amended or repealed in Parliament, if necessary after a change of government at the next election. In the meantime people should observe the law. That is what the democratic process requires. In general this is doubtless a good answer, but it was not good enough in this instance for two reasons. First, the extent of opposition to the charge was much greater than normal political opposition to government legislation. Here a large section of the community was not merely opposed to the law, but was prepared actively to disobey it. And the second reason why the normal respect for the law failed to save this legislation was that it was exceedingly difficult to enforce. The charge was a personal liability imposed on every individual adult member of the community, with rare exceptions. It could not be enforced against houses, or goods seized from those houses. It could only be enforced by summons in the local magistrates' courts. But when millions of people defy a law of this kind, enforcement by these means becomes almost impossible. A large segment of the population—unmarried young adults, for instance—are fairly mobile. They moved readily from one temporary residence to another, and claimed they were not resident wherever they were served with a claim for the charge. Thousands of summonses were issued; huge numbers of those summonsed turned up at the courts to argue that the summonses were invalid for one technical reason or another; others turned up to plead that they could not afford to pay anyhow. The courts could not cope; the system became clogged; council revenues fell off alarmingly, and many councils detested the whole procedure anyhow because they were strongly opposed to the charge for political reasons. The rest, as they say, is history. Mrs Thatcher had been credited with pushing through the legislation against all opposition within her own Cabinet and party; and after her resignation, the first act of Mr Major, as the new Prime Minister, was to set up a committee to find some way of replacing the community charge. The committee reported speedily and new legislation was introduced at the earliest possible moment. The community charge was consigned to the scrap-heap.

This little episode is an object lesson for governments and parliaments. It shows how, in a democratic society, there are real limits to the kind of laws which can be passed and enforced even by a legally unrestrained parliament. Nobody ever doubted that the legislation introducing the community charge was legally valid. But the extent and intensity of the opposition, combined with the legal difficulties of enforcement, made the law in practice unenforceable. Nor is this the only illustration in recent years of the impossibility of enforcing legislation against a large and actively dissenting segment of the people, even if they are a minority of the population. The Heath government's Industrial Relations Act 1971 was similarly derailed in a few short years by the opposition of the entire trade-union population. It is salutary for governments to realize that, even where they control Parliament with a large party majority, and even though Parliament may have the legal powers to pass the sort of laws they want, it simply is not possible to enforce certain kinds of laws against the will of a large section of the community.

Unfortunately, in the course of highly political controversies like this, a number of critically important issues have tended to get less attention than they deserve. One is that, although it may not be possible to enforce laws against large numbers of actively defiant citizens, the tradition of customary observance of the law is so necessary to the stability of society that it is hard to condone those who advocate such mass defiance. Of course, it may be said, and perhaps with justice, that part of the responsibility here must lie with those who pass laws which they ought to realize will in fact provoke mass defiance. And it is of course true that, in a free society, honourable and decent citizens may sometimes find particular laws so bad that their conscience dictates disobedience. The tradition of civil dissent and civil disobedience is an important one, and society needs to understand and respect those whose conscience drives them to such extremes of behaviour. Sometimes this kind of behaviour is what first alerts the rest of the public to serious injustice in the law. And when tyranny threatens, even under the cloak of law, civil disobedience and peaceful protest may be the only weapons that citizens have. At the same time, these arguments are much weaker in a democratic society which does genuinely give the public the opportunity to throw out a government at elections every few years. In such a society laws must normally—and indeed, whenever possible—be given the benefit of the doubt. It must be accepted in the ordinary way that some laws will disadvantage some members of society; elections are held to decide how these things are to be arranged, and so long as fundamental rights are duly respected, it cannot be left to the dissident to decide what laws he will obey. That way lies anarchy, because most people will find some objectionable laws in any society; and if everyone is entitled (even morally entitled) to judge what laws he will disobey because he thinks them unjust, a society will quickly collapse into chaos.

A second point which has perhaps received less attention than it should in this political controversy is that it is part of the responsibility of the government to provide the necessary framework of laws which will *persuade* the reflective citizen that it is indeed in his overall interest to comply with laws which disadvantage him, provided he can be assured that others will do the same. This proposition may also seem controversial, because it is put in the context of a highly political issue. But the proposition itself lies at the root of all government, and of many things that governments do. It derives from the simple fact that there are a great many circumstances in which it is in everyone's interest that a certain course of conduct should be followed, but this result cannot be spontaneously arrived at by individuals following their own interests. As Thomas Hobbes pointed out in his celebrated work *Leviathan* (1651), it is in my interest and in your interest that we should each respect the other's right to his own property; but in the absence of a government to enforce property laws, I cannot safely assume that you will not try to evict me from my property, and for that reason I may try to evict you from yours. By instituting a government which enforces (through its courts and its law) both our rights, each of us is better off. So this principle underlies the very institution of government itself. But it also underlies many particular laws. For instance, it is in my and in your interest that neither of us should keep a gun; the more guns there are in private ownership, the more danger there is of violence and death to innocent citizens. But, unless there are laws which regulate the keeping of guns, both you and I may choose to buy guns in our own self-interest. Only if I know that the law will be enforced against you will I be willing to forgo my own right to buy a gun. This is why, in the United States, where there are virtually no serious gun-control laws, many people buy and carry guns who would very much prefer that the private ownership of guns should be legally regulated.

In the last resort, all society rests on the willingness of the citizens to observe the laws which disadvantage them. When they are satisfied that, by and large, others do the same, or are if necessary compelled to do so, most citizens observe most of the law by custom and habit. But if the citizen sees that others do not observe the laws which disadvantage them, his own habit of obedience to the law may rapidly crumble away.

A third point which has rarely been made in this context is that the moral and persuasive power of law can, if it is adequately supported by the nation's leaders, provide a powerful example which may ultimately change people's attitudes. This has often been insisted upon in different contexts; for instance, it has often been said (usually by politicians of the right) that you cannot change emotional and public feelings about race by legislation. Hence, it has often been urged that the law is of very limited efficacy in dealing with matters such as racial discrimination. On the other hand, it has been said (usually by politicians of the left) that the law can set an example, can demonstrate what Parliament authoritatively believes to be a matter of moral right, and that in this way the law can actually lead and mould public opinion. On this particular issue, recent history in the United States suggests that—anyhow, given appropriate circumstances—the left may be more correct than the right. In 1954 the Supreme Court of the United States declared that the practice of racial segregation in state schools was a violation of the constitution. The initial reaction of many Southerners was violent and defiant. It was widely predicted that the Supreme Court's decision would never be enforceable because it was not possible to eradicate social prejudices by law. In fact these predictions proved wrong. In the twenty-five years following the Supreme Court decision a social revolution occurred in the United States, especially in the southern states. Racial segregation by law, by official fiat, disappeared; and social prejudices also changed with a rapidity which few would have thought possible. Today one sees blacks in the same schools, jobs, buses, restaurants, and even legislatures as whites. This is not to suggest that all social resentment has disappeared, nor that blacks have ceased to be disadvantaged in many ways. But it is a remarkable illustration of a social revolution in public attitudes that was almost entirely the result of a change in the law.

There are other areas where the influence of the law on public attitudes is today of some importance. There is, for instance, growing anxiety in some quarters that the extreme permissiveness of modern society in relation to sexual behaviour, co-habitation without marriage and parenthood, has eliminated all stigma from child-bearing outside marriage. While the elimination of stigma from the children themselves may be welcomed, what is increasingly worrying some people is whether the law is now giving the 'wrong signals' to the public. It is, for instance, widely thought that many people choose to have children even though they are in no position to maintain them financially, and that the law should at least discourage this. But it remains very controversial whether the law has much influence on human behaviour in matters of this kind, though even a marginal influence may be of great importance over society as a whole. In this area it is the Conservatives who tend to believe that the law does influence public morality and behaviour, while those on the left tend to deny it.

3 The law, the constitution, and the European Community

The law and the constitution

The importance of persuasion as opposed to force as the backing to the law is of particular relevance to the central constitutional position for at least three different reasons. First, and most obviously, the persuasive power of the law is likely to be immensely greater in a country where the constitutional system itself commands the assent of the great mass of the people. Secondly, much of the law in a modern society concerns the relationship between the citizen and the state. In practice, laws of this kind cannot actually be *enforced* against the State if the State resists. If the government refused to pay an award of damages made by a court against the Crown in its nominal capacity, there would be no way in which the citizen could invoke force to compel the government to pay. In fact British governments do not refuse to observe such awards; indeed, they very rarely refuse openly to observe any law, once it has been clearly defined and ascertained by judicial process. But they observe the law, not because they are compelled to do so by force or the threat of force, but because they basically accept the system. The cynical might be moved to add that they do so the more readily because, at least in modern times, it is relatively easy for the government to persuade Parliament to change the law in case of real need. But this cynicism may be unjustified. In many other countries (for instance, Australia, Canada, the United States) governments show a similar respect for the law even though they do not always have the power to carry through changes in laws they dislike.

The third reason why persuasion is so important in the British constitutional system is because so much of it still rests upon convention and not law at all. It was convention, not law, which compelled Mr Callaghan to call an immediate general election in 1979 when defeated (even by one vote) on a vote of censure in the House of Commons. It is convention, not law, which requires the government to respect the rights of the Opposition to adequate debating time in Parliament. And it is even convention, rather than law, which prevents Parliament from repealing the law which requires an election to be held every five years, if not sooner. Clearly, if laws depend so heavily on public acquiescence, the case of conventions is an *a fortiori* one. Nothing compels their observance other than custom and tradition and the force of public opinion.

Until very recently, the basic constitutional position in Britain was well known. The country had no written constitution and the sovereignty of Parliament was thought to be legally untrammelled. This meant that in the ordinary way there was simply no limit to the laws which could be passed by Parliament. Parliament could prolong its own life, alter the succession to the throne, or redefine the relationship of the two Houses. In fact it had done all these things. It could also deprive citizens of their rights, nationalize all private property (without compensation, if it so wished), abolish the monarchy, and take over or censor the press. Some, though not all, of these things it also did, but only in time of war. To say that Parliament could legally do any of these things only meant that there was no agreed written constitution which limited Parliament's powers in these respects, and that the judges of British courts disclaimed the power to declare Acts of Parliament legally void for any reason whatever. This was not to say that if Parliament in fact tried to do any of these things in peacetime it would have succeeded. There is a point beyond which citizens and officials—perhaps even judges— might simply refuse to obey Parliament. Perhaps judges would resign if faced with laws they regarded as grossly unconstitutional, for instance, a law which indefinitely prolonged the life of Parliament.

There are also other possible limits on this sort of parliamentary action. An Act of Parliament requires the consent of the Queen, and though, in ordinary times, it is a firmly established convention that the Queen must assent to all bills passed by Parliament, nobody could predict how the monarch would respond to a bill which was itself a gross breach of fundamental constitutional conventions. These are, fortunately, realms of fantasy and we can leave them to turn to more serious issues.

Until very recently English constitutional lawyers have almost unanimously accepted the view that Parliament retains today the legal sovereignty discussed above, thought by many to have been politically settled by the Revolution of 1688. This position was set out with great clarity and elegance in A. V. Dicey's classic work, *The Law of the Constitution* (first published in 1885), and most lawyers in England were brought up to regard this work as a sort of constitutional bible.

Only one serious doubt was ever raised about this conventional view. The doubt emanated from Scotland. The Parliament we have today is the Parliament of the United Kingdom of Great Britain and Northern Ireland, and it was formed by, first, the Act of Union with Scotland in 1707, secondly, the Act of Union with Ireland in 1801, and finally the Government of Ireland Act of 1920 which excluded Southern Ireland (now Eire) from the United Kingdom. Now some Scots lawyers argue that there is no reason to assume that the present Parliament has taken over all the attributes of the old Parliament of England, when it is quite clear that a new Parliament was being created in 1707. The Parliament of England, they say, actually came to an end with the Acts of Union in 1707, which were passed by both the English and the then separate Scottish Parliament, and which provided for the merger of the two in a new Parliament, the Parliament of Great Britain. Further, the two Acts of Union provided quite explicitly some limits on the powers of the new Parliament so far as Scotland was concerned; for example, the Acts prohibit the conferment on English courts of appellate jurisdiction over Scottish courts. It is hard to suppose that the new Parliament of Great Britain was being invested with the legal capacity to abrogate those limits whenever it felt inclined. Hence, it is argued, the present Parliament does not have unlimited sovereignty so far as Scotland is concerned. There is a good deal of force in this argument, the only weak point being that it remains uncertain whether the limits on the powers of the old Scottish Parliament were ever regarded as justiciable by Scottish courts; but that is not necessarily decisive of the position regarding the present-day powers of the Parliament of the United Kingdom.

But with this possible exception relating to Scotland, the sovereignty of Parliament had not—until a few years ago—been seriously challenged since 1688. In this sense sovereignty was a strictly legal concept. It simply meant that the courts had no power to declare invalid anything enacted by Parliament. No matter what Parliament put into an Act, no matter how unjust it might seem, no matter that it might involve a serious breach of democratic political conventions, no matter that it might involve a breach of the UK's international obligations, the courts simply had to observe and enforce the law as laid down. If Parliament did anything wrong the remedy lay in the political sphere—that is to say, through protest in Parliament itself, and through the electoral process.

The European Community

Now all this has changed in very dramatic fashion, and it has become clear that the sovereignty of Parliament is today subordinate to that of the European Community.* When the UK first joined the European Community and passed the European Communities Act 1972 this result was not clearly anticipated, and it is a sad commentary on the level of the legal advice on which the government acted at the time that this was so. Many people, including most politicians and lawyers, thought in 1972 that joining the European Community was not very different from joining many other international organizations (like the United Nations, for example). An ordinary international treaty does not impinge on the sovereignty of Parliament in the legal sense, because the only effect of failure to comply with such a treaty is to put the country in breach of *international law*. That is no doubt a matter of some seriousness, and indeed the UK government probably

---

* There is today widespread discrepancy in use of the terms 'European Community' and 'European Union'. This discrepancy comes from the Treaties themselves. The Community is still the correct legal term for those matters which are subject to the control of the European Court and in respect of which the law itself governs the relationship between members. The further matters dealt with by the Maastricht Treaty, such as the attempt to have a common foreign policy, and eventually monetary union, are matters in respect of which European Union is the correct term.

treats a breach of international law more seriously than most other governments in the world, but at the same time, it is in a sense less serious than a breach of our own national law. The reason for this is that courts in the UK must observe and apply the law of England (or Scotland, or Northern Ireland as the case may be); every court in the country must do this, so if criminal charges or civil proceedings are brought in England, the court must as a matter of course apply English law. Equally, any person can bring proceedings in those courts, so if the government acts illegally it can usually be challenged quickly and easily in our own national courts. But a breach of *international law* does not have these immediate effects. The only court which can establish that there has been such a breach is the International Court of Justice, which is a mighty but ponderous institution. Frequently nobody has the right to institute proceedings before the International Court anyhow except other governments, and it usually takes years to get a decision from that court. And even when such a decision has been rendered it has no effect on our own national law. English courts would still be obliged to enforce English law even though it might by then be clearly established that English law was contrary to international law in some respect. Of course, a government which takes its international obligations seriously can usually be relied on to take steps to deal with a situation once it has been shown that there clearly was a breach of international law. It may offer compensation, for instance, to those who have been injured by the breach, and it will probably initiate a change in its own national law to put the matter right for the future, though the speed with which these steps are taken may well depend on the context.

When the UK first joined the European Community it was widely believed that the European Treaties were much like other international treaties. It was of course appreciated that things would be different in some respects. For instance, it was obvious, and well understood, that joining the Community required the UK to make many legal changes to give effect to the Treaties. And it was also appreciated that there would be an ongoing obligation to give effect to new European Community laws, as and when they were made. Moreover, the Community, unlike most international organizations, actually had its own Court of Justice which was empowered to decide cases on the interpretation and effect of the Treaties, as well as of other new laws such as Directives. And so the 1972 Act gave effect to all these obligations. It recognized the Treaties as part of our own national law, and declared that all future acts and judicial decisions would become law so long as they were legally valid as part of the Community laws. It also enabled the government to make statutory instruments to give effect to changes in our own law which were required by Community law, and even enabled these instruments to override or repeal Acts of Parliament. It also required our courts to submit questions to the European Court when issues of Community law arose, and declared that they would be obliged to follow decisions of the European Court. To that extent it was always understood and appreciated that the European Community was a little different from other international organizations. But one thing was certainly not clearly understood or appreciated, and that was the effect of joining the Community on the sovereignty of Parliament, that is to say, on the relationship between Parliament and our own courts.

The first surprise came with a decision of the new European Court that some Directives made by the Community Council of Ministers— provided they were sufficiently clear and precise—could have *direct effect* in the member states and thus become part of our own national law without any further action to implement them in the UK. It had originally been thought that Directives were—as their name implied— solely addressed to the governments of the member states, requiring them to change their laws to give effect to them; and that, until they were implemented, therefore, they would not become part of the internal law of the member states. But cases then arose in which member states had failed to implement some Directives, and in legal proceedings in their own courts relied upon that very failure as a defence. In order to prevent governments from taking advantage of their own laxity in this way, the European Court declared that some Directives could have *direct effect* and thus become law in the member states—at least as against their own governments—without further implementation. This was a surprise, but it did not strike at the heart of parliamentary sovereignty. It simply meant that Directives of this kind had to be treated rather like subordinate English legislation made under the authority of an Act of Parliament as, indeed, in one sense, they were. They did, however, go beyond ordinary subordinate legislation in one important respect, because such Directives were often inconsistent with existing Acts of Parliament. It would be very unusual for ordinary subordinate legislation, made by ministers under statutory powers, to amend or repeal an Act of Parliament—indeed, in modern times this would be almost unheard of, except for statutory instruments made under the European Communities Act. And these were at least made by UK ministers, responsible to Parliament. Yet Community Directives were made by the Community Council of Ministers, and it now had to be admitted that they could also have this effect.

But all this was a trifle compared to what was still to follow. The profound effects of membership of the Community on the sovereignty of Parliament were not fully demonstrated until the dramatic *Factortame* case,* when it first became apparent that English courts now had the power to declare Acts of Parliament to be void or invalid because they contravened European Community law. In this case the Community had allocated fishery quotas to its members, but a number of Spanish fishermen attempted to evade the effect of the quotas by registering companies in England, and then transferring their trawlers into the names of these companies, which were thus English companies. Their trawlers fished in British waters, but continued to land their catch in Spain. Not surprisingly, the British government thought that this was an evasion of the whole system of quotas and they introduced into Parliament a bill which was in due course enacted as the Merchant Shipping Act 1988. Under this Act the companies, though registered in England, were to be treated as Spanish companies because their owners were Spanish. This Act of Parliament was then challenged as invalid on the ground that it contravened one of the basic corner-stones of European Community law, namely, that member states were not allowed to *discriminate* against nationals of other states. In this particular case the non-discrimination principle was invoked in a highly technical way, and

* This was one of a set of cases between the same parties, of which the most crucial was the second, the full name of the case being *R.* v. *Secretary of State, ex parte Factortame* [1991] 1 AC 603.

because the fishery quotas had actually been agreed by the Community, it was obviously somewhat unfair that the Spanish fishermen were able to invoke it. But that is not really relevant to the crucial importance of the case. What happened when the case first reached the House of Lords was that it was held that as a matter of English law it was impossible to challenge the validity of the Merchant Shipping Act, and it was not even possible to suspend the operation of the Act while the case was referred to the European Court. But the matter *was* referred to the European Court, which decided that since European Community rights were at stake (the right not to be discriminated against) the English courts *had* to have the power to suspend the operation of the Act pending a full hearing of the issue at the European Court. The House of Lords then decided that it should suspend the operation of the Act, and following the full hearing by the European Court which declared the Act to be contrary to Community law, it was eventually declared invalid by the High Court. The Act was then amended to remove the offending provisions.

In one sense this decision was little more than a practical necessity. If national courts could not declare their own national law to be invalid when it conflicted with European Community law, the practical working of the European Community legal system would be immensely cumbersome. It would mean that any conflict of this kind would have to be decided in defiance of Community law, the government would then be obliged to introduce amending legislation, and in the meantime, anyone whose rights had been adversely affected would be entitled to compensation, but there would be no machinery by which that compensation could be secured in an English court. So it would take years to enforce rights accorded by Community law, and if governments dragged their heels, the whole system would collapse into chaos. In this connection, it must be appreciated that conflicts between our national law and Community law are potentially very common, far more common than conflicts with international law or ordinary treaties. Even though the UK government has one of the best records among members of the Community in giving effect to Community Directives and other decisions, it has become increasingly apparent that many conflicts arise because our ministers and their advisers have not fully appreciated the way in which the European Court was likely to interpret Community law. So, in a practical sense it is really imperative that national courts should recognize the precedence of Community law over national laws, and the courts of all other member states in the Community in fact do recognize this. It must also be said that this is an absolute prerequisite of a federal state, and although the Community is not yet a federal state, it may eventually evolve into one. Without the *Factortame* decision it is doubtful if that could be done.

So the *Factortame* decision was a practical necessity. But at the same time it was, in a legal sense, a revolutionary decision. It was the first time for more than 300 years that an English Court had declared an Act of Parliament to be unenforceable in law. What this means, therefore, is that English law is now subject to European Community law. If there is a conflict between them, the English law may, and sometimes *must*, be declared invalid by English courts. In a sense, therefore, we have now acquired a written constitution—consisting of the various European Treaties—and laws contrary to that constitution will in future be invalid. So the sovereignty of Parliament seems to have been dethroned from its pivotal point at the centre of English constitutional law with very little appreciation of that fact by Parliament, politicians, or the public.

How has this happened? Many lawyers thought that the sovereignty of Parliament was the centre-piece of our unwritten constitution, and was something which simply could not be surrendered or abandoned. Every Parliament was traditionally thought to be legally sovereign and so capable of altering any previous law simply by passing a new Act. Why therefore was the Merchant Shipping Act of 1988 not treated simply as altering all previous law and, if necessary, the European Communities Act itself? If this had been done, the UK government would have been in breach of the Treaties and would have been under an obligation to amend or repeal the Merchant Shipping Act, but at least the traditional doctrine of Parliamentary sovereignty would have been preserved. In fact, the judges in the House of Lords did not deny that this *could have been done*. Parliament could have phrased the Merchant Shipping Act to make it quite clear that it was to be applied whether or not it was in conformity with European law. In that case, said the judges in the House of Lords, they would have obeyed the Act, and so the sovereignty of Parliament would have been respected. But of course the government and Parliament did not *want* to pass an Act which violated European law. They thought that the Act they passed was good in law, but it turned out that they were mistaken. So the judges in the House of Lords thought that they should look at the Merchant Shipping Act as though Parliament had said at the beginning of the Act:

The following Act is passed on the assumption that it is not in violation of European Community law; if it is contrary to Community law, do not enforce it.

In this way the traditional respect for Parliamentary sovereignty was to some degree reconciled with the practical need to recognize the supremacy of European Community law.

In one sense this reconciliation may seem pretty empty. It now seems quite clear that we shall see many Acts of Parliament challenged in future as contrary to European law, and some of these challenges will be upheld. Moreover, it will not, of course, be open to Parliament to overrule these decisions by passing another Act, unless Parliament chooses openly to defy the Community Treaties— which could only provoke a political crisis of the first order. So, to a limited extent, we shall have what many politicians (and perhaps the public and the press) intensely dislike, 'government by judges'. On the other hand, there is also reality in the way the House of Lords approached this problem, because it is very unlikely that Parliament will ever pass an Act which is clearly and plainly invalid as contrary to European law. Where it happens at all, it will nearly always happen by accident or mistake, and it may well accord with Parliament's intent that if the Act is found to conflict with Community law, it should not be enforced.

It must not be thought that all this means that English law can be challenged as invalid because (for instance) it is contrary to French or German law. It is only invalid if it is contrary to European Community law, which is the central law of the Community. In this respect the Community increasingly resembles a federal system of law, like that of the USA or Canada or Australia, where there is a federal government and a federal legislature, on the one hand, and state governments and state legislatures on the other. There are two sets of laws, each perfectly valid within its own sphere, but state laws which conflict with (valid) federal laws are invalid. In a strict legal sense, the situation in the European Community is thus similar to that of a federal state.

A Federal Europe?

But although the Community legal system is thus in some ways like that of a federal state, in other ways it still remains a long way removed from a federal state. It still has no common currency, nor the power to levy taxes over its citizens. It has no federal executive authority like those of genuine federal states. It has no President or Prime Minister, it has no Cabinet or elected ministers at the head of its civil service. It has no means of actually enforcing its laws because it has no police force or army, though a police force (Europol) is now in process of being created. It does have the Commission, a very powerful executive body, based in Brussels, which is responsible for executing and overseeing Community laws; but the Commission is fundamentally a bureaucracy rather than an executive. It is the *civil service* of a federal Europe, but has no executive ministers in control of it. Similarly, the Community has no genuine federal legislature. The European Parliament, which is now directly elected by the citizens of the member states, has very limited powers, generally only of a supervisory or consultative nature.

The real legislature of the Community is the Council of Ministers, which confusingly is not the executive of the Community, as its name might suggest. The Council simply consists of the ministers of the separate member states, meeting together on particular issues. Thus, if the matter under discussion is agriculture, the Council consists of the various Ministers of Agriculture in the member states; if it is finance, it consists of the various Finance Ministers; and so on. The Council has the power to make Directives which are binding on the member states, though generally these are made only on a proposal from the Commission, and today the Council is sometimes obliged to consult the Parliament before it can legislate.* In general the Council has to act unanimously, though it can sometimes act by majority, and as the Community increases in size, it is evident that more decisions will have to be majority ones because of the practical impossibility of securing unanimity among fifteen states. But a majority decision at the Council does not merely depend on a majority of the states; the members have different voting numbers according to their size, and a majority decision has to be by a 'qualified majority' to be effective. If the Community institutions are looked at from the perspective of a federal legal system, it seems clear that the Council is rather like the upper House or Senate of a federal Europe, except that the states have one member each, who has several votes, instead of having several members, each with one vote. But in real federations, the lower House—elected by the people at large—has most of the political power, while in the Community it is the upper House which has the real power, and the Parliament which is in effect the lower House. This is why it is often said that there is a 'democratic deficit' in the Community institutions. As at present organized, its institutions are not very democratic.

The upshot of all this is that the Community is not yet a federal state, though it may evolve into one, by agreement of its members; the necessary legal groundwork for this evolution has been laid, but it is not of course an inevitability. To create a true federal state the existing Treaties would require many changes, and these changes could only be made by agreement between all the members. No single member could be outvoted by the others on such issues, though one member could find itself in such difficulties if it attempted to block a change on which all other members were bent, that it might find itself virtually compelled to go along with its partners, however reluctant it might be to do so. The development of the Community certainly appears to have a built-in momentum, though the very narrow majorities obtained in referendums in some member states for some of the recent changes, as well as in new members who joined the Community in 1995, may halt this process. In 1996 an

---

* Some further details about the Community's legislative machinery is given in Chapter 6 below, p. 177.

intergovernmental conference is scheduled, at which the next stage in the building of the Community is due to be reviewed. This will certainly require a decision about the inclusion of new member states from Eastern Europe, as well as the possible European currency, but more important, it may well involve some fundamental moves towards a federal Europe, even if only on the part of a few of the member states in the first instance. This conference threatens to be difficult and perhaps stormy.

There is a tendency in some quarters to suggest that it would be unthinkable to move to a federal Europe because of the democratic deficit in the Community institutions and the weakness of the European Parliament. Of course this is true as the Community now exists, so evidently fundamental reform of its institutional arrangements would be necessary before it could evolve into a true federal union. These reforms would have to include the creation of a proper legislature in which the Council would be replaced by an upper House, perhaps of partly elected and partly appointed members, and the legislative power would then be vested in the two Houses jointly. Equally, executive ministers, drawn from and accountable to one or other of the Houses, would have to be put in charge of the Commission, which would have to be downgraded from its present high status to convert it into a genuine civil service, accountable to democratically elected superiors. And, presumably, a federal Cabinet, with a federal Prime Minister would have to be contemplated, although the present mood in the UK Parliament makes it very improbable that such a proposal could be carried in the near future. All this could produce a reasonably democratic federal Europe; but it is probably a pipe-dream to think that a United States of Europe could ever exist as closely integrated as the United States of America. Apart from anything else, it is very difficult to believe that the European Parliament composed of representatives of fifteen (or more) countries speaking eleven (or more) different languages could ever function as an effective law-making body. It would certainly be very different from our own Parliament, where the detailed wording of bills can be the subject of minute scrutiny, amendment, and debate. And control over the detailed wording of legislation is regarded by English lawyers as an important aspect of the democratic process and the Rule of Law.

A European Parliament could only legislate on matters of broad principle, leaving the detailed wording to others, versed in the minutiae of all the Community languages and legal systems. So a federal Europe would have still further and major implications for the very nature of the laws which govern us.

The ultimate supremacy of European Community law over domestic British law does not of course mean that most day-to-day law in English courts will gradually be superseded by European law. The Community is still primarily an economic institution and most of its laws and regulations concern public economic issues, rather than matters of private law. Thus, the criminal law, family law, much of the ordinary law of contract and tort, and certainly the law of procedure and evidence will remain largely unaffected by Community law. Even if Europe eventually does become a fully federal state, there is no reason why English law should be changed on matters of this kind. But it is of course true that a genuine federal Europe would need to have many more genuine federal laws than presently exist. A federal union means monetary union, so laws relating to the currency would have to become federal laws, and that might include much banking law as well. In addition, commercial subjects like company law, bankruptcy, patents, trade-marks, and copyright would need to be increasingly harmonized (a process already under way, indeed), if not made completely federal. So also immigration laws would have to become federal laws if the Community becomes a genuine federation, and that might lead to a need for a common European nationality or citizenship. Social security and welfare law is perhaps a borderline area. As is well known, the Community is in general now moving into these areas, though the UK has at present 'opted-out' of these moves. If the Labour party wins the next general election, this opt-out will almost certainly be abandoned.

In many other respects, our own laws and legal traditions could still remain under our own control. But it is historically true that minority legal systems in federal countries (e.g. Louisiana in the United States, and Quebec in Canada) have tended over the years to become greatly influenced by the majority systems, and in the very long run this might also happen in Europe. It is also true that the present bureaucracy in the Commission appears to be bent on imposing requirements for the harmonization of law on the whole Community in many areas where such harmonization does not appear to be in the least necessary. For example, the Council adopted a few years ago a Commission proposal to impose on the whole Community a uniform law of 'products' liability', that is, a law defining the circumstances in which manufacturers should be held liable for injuries caused by defective or dangerous products. The only justification for requiring such a harmonization of laws appeared to be that it would eliminate distortions of competition, which is one of the basic aims of the Community. Formerly (so it was said), a company doing business in one country might be subject to different legal liability rules from companies doing business in other countries, and this could encourage companies to set up business where the liabilities were lowest—thus distorting the free-market competitive system which it was the aim of the Community to foster. But the argument loses much of its strength when it is appreciated that in the United States—certainly the most powerful and efficient free market the world has ever seen —the law on matters of this kind remains entirely a responsibility of the states, and there are considerable divergences between them.

The Rule of Law

Lawyers and politicians in Western societies, and perhaps especially in countries whose legal systems are based on the common law, frequently make the claim that their countries are subject to 'the Rule of Law'. But this concept, like many other ideological concepts (including, for instance, the concept of democracy), is very hard to pin down or define. To say that a country is subject to the Rule of Law means, at one level, simply that a country is governed by laws— fixed, legal rules—and not by the arbitrary diktat of individual men (or women); and the phrase 'a government of laws and not of men' is itself used with much the same ideological meaning as the 'Rule of Law'. But the difficulty with many such concepts is that on analysis they tend to appear either vacuous or based on politically biased ideologies.

The concept may be vacuous because in one sense all government is, and must be, a government both of laws and of men (and women).

Men and women must actually conduct governments; they must have the power to make, change, interpret, and enforce the law, and, indeed, most modern government shows that officials must generally be given a good deal of discretionary power if a state is to be conducted with a tolerable degree of efficiency. So in this sense, all governments must be the government of men and women. But no government can do wholly without law. Even the most tyrannical despot, who may operate on the basis that his whim is law, soon discovers that his whims will be most effectively enforced if they are translated into 'real' law. To make them laws gives them some degree of permanence and generality. Moreover, it enables the tyrant to recruit as an ally in the enforcement of his whims the considerable power of persuasion that law traditionally carries. In so far as law is still seen as having mystique and majesty behind it, it usually helps a government to recruit the law. One of the first things a modern government does when it seizes power in a *coup d'état* is to take control of the government printing presses and start issuing 'decrees' which look like duly enacted laws.

So in this respect it may seem that the concept of the Rule of Law appears pretty empty: at any rate it is reconcilable with a high degree of tyranny. As has often been said, Nazi Germany was, in one sense, governed by the Rule of Law—in the sense that Hitler was appointed Chancellor of the German Reich by due legal authority, and was formally voted the supreme power in the state by the Reichstag, which had arguably the power to do that. More plausibly, perhaps, it may be contended that South Africa remained subject to the Rule of Law even during the darkest days of repression. There, at least, the façade of government according to law continued to exist. Courts appeared to be (and to a large degree were in fact) independent of the government, they appeared to operate in much the same manner as courts in countries with more genuine democratic political systems, laws were still made by legislatures elected by (some of) the people, and so on. But the repugnant nature of the policies of South African governments, and the fact that most of the population in that country was effectively disenfranchised, made many people reluctant to concede that the Rule of Law still operated under such conditions. A major reason for this was probably that the police and military security forces appeared to be above the law, in the sense that whatever the law may have said in theory, it was not in practice possible (at least for the black and coloured people) to assert ordinary legal rights against these bodies.

At the other extreme, the Rule of Law has sometimes been associated with a large number of purely political ideals. For instance, a much-quoted statement of the International Congress of Jurists at a conference in 1959 declared: 'The function of the legislature in a free society under the Rule of Law is to create and maintain the conditions which will uphold the dignity of man as an individual. This dignity requires not only the recognition of his civil and political rights but also the establishment of the social, economic, educational and cultural conditions which are essential to the full development of his personality.' The obvious trouble with definitions of this kind is that they equate the concept of the Rule of Law with the *types* of law (and social and political systems) which some people wish to see established.

Despite the difficulties, however, many lawyers remain reluctant to abandon the concept of the Rule of Law as something without meaning or value. Many people—and not only lawyers—do feel that there is something of special importance about the law in a society subject to the Rule of Law. There have been many attempts to identify what that element is. One attempt, which has been taught to many generations of law students, was made at the end of the last century by A. V. Dicey in his book *The Law of the Constitution*. Dicey argued that the Rule of Law consisted of three elements. First, that the government itself was conducted by law and not by the use of wide discretionary or arbitrary power; secondly, that everybody was equally subject to the law; and thirdly, that basic constitutional rights in England were the result of ordinary legal case law, and were not enshrined in high-flown constitutional documents. Unfortunately Dicey's account of the Rule of Law, which was not really adequate in his own day, is now quite unacceptable. It is no longer true that government has no wide arbitrary or discretionary power; equality before the law may be a necessary part of the Rule of Law, but it does not go very far by itself; and the notion that basic constitutional rights have to be derived from ordinary case law in order that a country be considered subject to the Rule of Law would mean that the United States was not subject to the Rule of Law. There seems something perverse in arguing that constitutionally guaranteed rights are actually inconsistent with the Rule of Law, though of course it remains true that the value of such rights depends on the degree to which they are respected and enforced in practice.

More recently, academic lawyers have suggested that the Rule of Law is a concept with an identifiable content, much of which has to do with the procedures governing the making and enforcing of the law. For instance, it has been argued that although wide discretionary powers are not inconsistent with the idea of the Rule of Law, it is necessary that such discretions should be exercised and guided by open and relatively stable general principles of law. Similarly, it has been said that the Rule of Law requires that laws should generally be prospective (and not retrospective), that they should be open, published, and reasonably intelligible to those whose conduct is to be guided by them. So also the independence of the judiciary and the accessibility of the courts may be said to be requirements of the Rule of Law. Perhaps also it may be argued that certain fundamental requirements attend the making of new law by the legislature if the Rule of Law is to be observed. New laws should, in general, be made after due publicity and after the opportunity for debate and consultation; adequate discussion should be allowed during the legislative process itself, and adequate warning should be given of legal change to those most affected. It is implicit in all this that the basic requirements of a democratic system should be in place, and should be observed, if a country claims to be subject to the Rule of Law.

In this connection it is of some interest that the High Court of Australia recently held invalid legislation designed to control and restrict television broadcasting in a pre-election period (see *Australian Capital Television Pty. Ltd.* v. *Commonwealth* (1992) 177 CLR 106). The Australian Constitution contains no Bill of Rights to protect the citizen, but the High Court was able to hold that the Constitution contained within it an *implied* freedom of communication, based on notions of representative democracy and responsible government. So it seems fair to suggest that the ideal of the Rule of Law, which embraces within it the concept of democratic government, has inherent requirements about the laws needed to sustain the workings of democratic government.

If it is complained that all these turn out, after all, to be just another list of political ideals, rather than any specifically legal set of concepts, one answer may be given: requirements of this kind arise from the basic nature of enacted law as an instrument for guiding the behaviour of the people. If we begin by assuming that this is, after all, one of the chief functions of all law, it might be widely agreed that it follows that laws should be widely published, reasonably intelligible, made after adequate warning, and so on. For if these requirements are not observed, the effectiveness of the laws in securing their objectives will be impaired. Up to a point, this answer may be accepted, but it should be noticed that the answer makes certain presuppositions about the purposes and nature of law. These presuppositions tend to be those we associate with traditional liberal values—in particular, the basic presupposition that individuals are autonomous human beings, who plan their lives, and therefore need adequate notice and warning of the law in order to enable them to do this the more effectively. To those who do not accept these liberal values, who assume, for instance, that the right of the individual to plan his own life is not the basic right which the state exists to protect, but that the welfare of the whole body of citizens is the supreme good, then some of these presuppositions about the chief purposes of the law may be unacceptable.

It is right to add that the whole value of the concept of the Rule of Law has, for these reasons, been a somewhat controversial one among those on the left of the political spectrum. To some, the Rule of Law has traditionally reflected a politically biased ideology, because it stood for a legal system in which the chief aim of law was to maintain a stable and predictable legal framework within which individuals could plan their own lives. Within such a framework, power and property tend to gravitate to the shrewd and unscrupulous, as well as to those who already start out with more than their 'fair share' of power and property. So for the Marxist, and perhaps other supporters of the radical left, the whole concept of the Rule of Law has often been rejected as part and parcel of traditional liberal (or 'bourgeois') ideology. But with the collapse of communist regimes, and the gradual shift to the centre of most socialist political parties in recent years, these controversies are probably over for the time being. Virtually everyone in British and even European politics today accepts the ideals enshrined in the concept of the Rule of Law. To most of us, it is precisely the presuppositions about the purpose and function of law which give meaning to the concept of the Rule of Law, and which mark the distinction between a tolerable and an intolerable form of society. The assumption that the individual is an autonomous human being in charge of his own life, within a framework of law provided by the society of which he is a member, is, to most of us, the mark of a civilized society. It is just this which sets apart a modern Western democracy from a totalitarian state.

But although most Europeans accept these ideals in a broad way, there may well be cultural differences in our attitudes to some aspects of the Rule of Law. As a result of British membership of the European Community, these differences threaten to become of great importance in future. One facet of the ideal of the Rule of Law is that governments should themselves respect the law and see that it is enforced, even, where necessary, against their own officials. If the law is unsatisfactory, the traditional and very long-standing British approach has been that the law should be amended or repealed by the normal democratic processes, but that in the meantime it should be respected, and where necessary, enforced. Of course, there is always some degree of discretion as to the zeal with which the law is enforced; and it has not seemed in the past inconsistent with the Rule of Law if governments or other public authorities should ease up a little on enforcement of very out-of-date laws, especially where there is every likelihood that the law will soon be altered by Parliament. But that is a totally different thing from tolerating widespread flouting of the law, even where change is likely in the near future. For instance, even after the government had announced that the community charge legislation would be repealed, the government did not agree that the legislation should not be enforced while it remained in operation.

It is true, of course, that one reason that governments in Britain have nearly always displayed such respect for laws even where they disagree with them is that our governments have for many years found it very easy to amend laws they do not like. Because governments are always drawn from the majority party in Parliament, and because of the strength of party discipline, it is nearly always possible for the government to amend or repeal laws it does not like. So it has been easy and relatively painless for governments to declare that all the law must be respected and enforced, no matter how bad or unpopular it may be. But countries in the common law tradition often have governments and legislatures with restricted powers, especially federal countries like the United States, Australia, and Canada. In these countries, too, governments generally respect and enforce the laws, even those they do not agree with, and cannot change. In countries with strong traditions of respect for the Rule of Law one is, therefore, entitled to hope and expect that governments will observe and enforce the law even though they dislike it. Now, however, this tradition is under threat, and one reason for that is Britain's membership of the European Community.

One of the most obvious results of our membership of the Community is that we as a nation are no longer free to do what we want with many of our laws. Many national laws are now subject to Community law; and sometimes national law in conflict with Community law will be invalid. Sometimes it may not actually be invalid, but it would be a breach of our Community obligations to adopt (or retain) laws contrary to Community Directives or other processes. So there will increasingly be occasions when the British government is compelled to secure the passing of laws which it does not like, or conversely, will be unable to pass laws it would like to pass. And naturally this means that there will be more law which has to be enforced but which the government actively dislikes and would change if it could; equally, there will be laws which the government would like to enforce but cannot, because to do so would be to violate Community law. These problems are well illustrated by the furore which recently arose with regard to Sunday shop opening.

Under an old and very out-of-date piece of legislation, the Shops Act 1950 (which actually perpetuated many laws much older than 1950), shops were severely restricted in what they could sell on Sundays. It was well known that the laws were irrational and extremely arbitrary in operation, and enforcement (which was the responsibility of local councils) was very sporadic and half-hearted. But a first attempt to repeal all the restrictions and leave shops to open whenever they pleased was defeated in the House of Commons in 1986. So the unsatisfactory situation continued. A few years ago a number of large stores who wanted to open on Sundays hit upon the idea (no doubt with the help of their lawyers) of arguing that Sunday shop restrictions were invalid as restrictions on trade contrary to the European Treaties. Although the point never had much likelihood of success in the long run, two successive cases had to be taken to the European Court before it became quite clear that the member states of the Community were entitled to impose whatever Sunday restrictions they wanted. And while these cases were awaiting decision, large stores around the country routinely decided to open on Sundays. All attempts to enforce the Shops Act were blocked because the courts insisted that pending the European Court decision the old law could not be enforced while its validity was in doubt. For several years, therefore, the law remained in a sort of limbo. There were many complaints about this state of affairs. Demands were made in Parliament for the law to be enforced. The Attorney-General was, perhaps not surprisingly, unable or unwilling to explain clearly that he could not enforce the law because neither he nor anybody else could know what the law was until the European Court had spoken.

Eventually all this mess was brought to an end. The European Court handed down its second decision making it clear that member states were free to do (more or less) what they wanted about Sunday opening, and new legislation was finally passed and is now in force. But for several years there was largely a vacuum in the law, and this kind of thing will undoubtedly happen more often in future, if the experience of complex federal legal systems is anything to go by. Those who live in federal countries no doubt get used to this sort of thing, but the British have long been accustomed to a formal legal system in which the public expects *the law to be enforced*; indeed, to many, this is itself a necessary ingredient of the Rule of Law.

But there is today an additional problem which did not really arise in the case of the Sunday opening laws. The European Community is churning out a vast amount of new law all the time, and a good deal of this law is simply not being implemented by many member states. Sometimes they drag their heels about actually passing it into law, and though some Community laws and Directives become part of national legal systems without further ado, many others require to be passed by national legislatures before coming into operation. In other cases member states pass laws to implement the Community legislation, but then in practice fail to enforce or observe those laws. All this is no myth; it is well documented, and it is giving rise to great concern in the European Commission and indeed elsewhere. Now one can see that if respect for this facet of the Rule of Law is less strong in other member states than in Britain, the British people and their government may well find their own respect for the Rule of Law becoming slowly undermined. We already begin to hear public complaints that Community laws are implemented and enforced far more rigorously in Britain than in many other members of the Community, and there is no doubt that this kind of thing, if it persists over time, will lead to pressure on our own government to turn a blind eye, from time to time, to breaches of Community laws, or even to breaches of our own laws and regulations which have been passed to give effect to Community requirements. There are important long-term implications in all this for our laws, and our national culture, and the relationships between citizen and state, all of which are tied up with our respect for the Rule of Law. There is a worrying possibility that we may in course of time lose something very valuable as a result of our membership of the European Community, namely, our long-term respect for the Rule of Law. To say this is not to adopt a 'holier than thou' attitude to our neighbours in Europe. It is merely to recognize that we do have different traditions with regard to law, as well as to much else.

Law in theory and law in practice

One thing which makes people sceptical about the Rule of Law (and other inflated claims by lawyers of the virtues of law) is that there often seems to be a substantial difference between the way things work in practice and the way the law says they ought to work. Lawyers themselves, indeed, know this better than anybody, and it can contribute to legal cynicism as well as lay scepticism. Why does it happen? And what are the implications?

One reason for the divergence between theory and practice is that (as we have seen) much of the efficacy of law rests on persuasion and not force, and if those responsible for enforcing the law can be neither compelled nor persuaded to observe the law, then the law is in practice likely to be disregarded. As we have already noted, one of the main reasons that South Africa was widely thought not to respect the Rule of Law under the former regime was that the law was not in practice enforced against the police and the security forces. Any government which systematically permits the state's own laws to be violated, and protects those guilty of the violations, clearly has little respect for the Rule of Law.

Even in modern Britain it is today widely believed by lawyers that the law relating to police interrogation of suspects is systematically violated by many policemen. Since the police are themselves the chief instrument for the actual enforcement of the law, it is only too obvious that enforcement of the law against them is exceedingly difficult, even where the government in all good faith desires to see the law observed. So all depends on the persuasive power of the law, and if the police are not persuaded that strict observance of rules of interrogation is desirable they will not observe the rules. In this situation, indirect methods of enforcement may have to be adopted, even though these are not very satisfactory. The only indirect means of enforcing the law about police interrogations is for the courts to throw out prosecutions where they feel the law has been violated, but this has the obvious disadvantage that it may involve acquitting the guilty because of police misbehaviour. American courts do this a great deal—often to the great fury of the public—and English judges are beginning to follow suit, though less frequently and with great reluctance. But there is still probably a wide gulf between what ought to happen and what does happen in many police stations.

But there are many other, less sinister, reasons why the law in practice may diverge from the law in theory. One simple reason concerns the difficulties of proof. Facts that cannot be corroborated by documentary evidence are often difficult to establish in court. Of course, such facts can be proved by witnesses, but it is unhappily the case that a false story told plausibly by a confident witness will often be more readily believed than a true story told haltingly by an inarticulate witness. So, for instance, the evidence of police witnesses is often likely to be believed even when it is exaggerated or mistaken or deliberately false, while the evidence of an uneducated or illiterate misfit may come out in so jumbled and confusing a fashion that it is simply rejected. On the other hand, these difficulties of proof are often exaggerated by laymen. One often hears it said that a fact cannot be proved, 'because it is only my word against his'. This demonstrates a serious misunderstanding of the working of the legal system. One person's word may be sufficient proof of a fact, even though it is contested.

There are other reasons why law in practice and law in theory may be quite different. It often happens that laws are in practice modified or adjusted, or sometimes completely superseded, by those who operate them. This may be done in quite formal and semi-authoritative ways, or completely informally. For example, there are a number of 'extra-statutory concessions' made by the Inland Revenue (presumably with the authority of the Chancellor of the Exchequer) under which tax which would legally be payable is waived. These concessions always operate, of course, in favour of the taxpayer, but those who fall just outside the line drawn by the Revenue may well feel aggrieved that the precise position where the line is drawn depends on the discretion of the administration rather than on statutory authority. There has been some judicial criticism of the whole practice of granting these concessions, and it is somewhat curious that they have never been the subject of parliamentary authorization.

Another informal example of the way in which laws can be superseded in practice concerns the establishment and operation of the Motor Insurers' Bureau. This body, which is operated by the insurance industry, has a contract with the Department of the Environment under which it undertakes to pay compensation, subject to various conditions, to persons injured in road accidents who are unable to obtain compensation from another person responsible for the injuries. Since the Bureau is financed by those who pay third-party premiums for motor insurance, and since the payment of such premiums is legally compulsory for those who drive vehicles, there is one sense in which the Bureau, with the government's encouragement, is using the law to provide compensation for those who are not legally entitled to it. There is, of course, nothing sinister about this—indeed, many people would think the objective highly laudable—but it illustrates the way in which the law does not always regulate what actually happens, nor even what is, in one sense, supposed to happen.

Another example of the way in which practice can come to supplement the law concerns the discretion of public authorities, chiefly the police, to decide when they will prosecute for breaches of the law. Since a large number of minor and technical offences come to the notice of the authorities where a prosecution would often be high-handed and perhaps pointless, it is widely accepted that the prosecuting authorities must have a discretion in deciding which cases to pursue. In other cases a warning may be administered, or no action at all may be taken having regard to all the circumstances. As with other examples of practice supplementing the law, there is in principle nothing sinister about the existence of prosecution discretions. Indeed, they are inevitable. But in recent times such discretions have come to be studied and commented on by academic lawyers and others, as their potential implications have been more fully appreciated. For such discretions are capable of abuse. The police may (for example) decide not to bother at all with certain classes of offences in order to concentrate on others: is that a permissible exercise of discretion? Or again, it may be found that the practice of warning rather than prosecuting children suspected of offences is operated in a discriminatory way: perhaps coloured children are more likely to be prosecuted, white children to be warned. It is no use protesting to the court before which a coloured child is brought, because the fact may be that he is indeed guilty of the offence charged: his grievance is not that he has been charged, but that others similarly situated have not been charged. But such a grievance is irrelevant to the actual case before the court. When this kind of thing occurs there often arises pressure to bring the extra-legal practices within the control of the law and the courts. And that is precisely what has been happening with regard to police discretions about prosecutions. The Home Office, for instance, has been issuing circulars offering guidance as to these discretions, and there are increasing demands that these discretions should in some way, and to some degree, be subject to some judicial control. Cases have even been brought before the courts challenging the discretions in particular cases, though so far the courts have been very cautious on these matters.

4 The purposes of law

Does law have any purposes?

In the first three chapters we have been looking at law as a somewhat static phenomenon. We have looked at the legal system and the legal profession in order to get some understanding of the central role which courts occupy in the lawyer's world; and we have looked too at the nature of law outside the courts, but only as something which 'exists' in some strange way outside the physical world. And we have looked at law as the foundation of our constitutional arrangements, and our membership of the European Community. In this chapter we look at law from a somewhat different point of view; we look at the way in which law can be used as an instrument to achieve certain purposes or goals. We begin with the question posed at the beginning of this chapter: does law have any purposes?

Lawyers and laymen alike often talk as though the law has purposes—both law in general and particular laws. For example, one of the main purposes of the law in general is to maintain order, and to provide an outlet for the peaceful resolution of disputes; one of the main purposes—perhaps the only real purpose—of the rule excluding hearsay evidence is to prevent courts from acting on unreliable information. General statements of this kind are, no doubt, harmless, and it is very hard to avoid all reference to the purposes of law in any serious discussion about the nature of law and its role in society. But further inquiry reveals that there are difficulties about the idea that the law has purposes, and that it may be dangerous to draw conclusions from the supposed purposes of the law.

In the first place, the law is an abstraction, a set of rules, principles, and ideas. The notion of law having a purpose implies a teleological view of law, with a purposive mind behind it, but the law itself has no mind. Those who make the laws may certainly have purposes which they wish the law to achieve, and sometimes it is clear enough what those purposes are. When this is the case it is relatively easy to transfer the purposes of the law-makers to the law itself, and assume that the purpose (or policy) of the law is to achieve this or that objective. The purpose of the Competition Act 1980 (to take one example) is to stimulate competition and to enable inquiry to be made into certain anti-competitive practices. It is easy to see what are the purposes of the Act in general by reading it; and it is also possible (for the lawyer or layman, and nowadays even for a court) to read *Hansard* and see what was said there about the purposes of the Act.

But in many circumstances it is very difficult to say what are the purposes of the law. A particular section or paragraph of an Act of Parliament may be extremely obscure, and its purposes may be as enigmatic as its effect. Further, the common law, or even statute law, once encrusted with interpretative case-law, is not the work of a single mind, or even of a small number of minds. Much of the common law is the work of generation after generation of judges, layer upon layer of juristic interpretation and commentary and classi-fication. To discern general purposes in the laws thus made is often quite impossible. An interesting example of the difficulty this sort of thing poses concerns the question whether, and to what extent, penal or exemplary damages should be permitted in tort actions, that is, actions for civil wrongs such as libel or wrongful arrest. This ques-tion has sometimes stirred up a good deal of controversy in the courts, and in *Cassell* v. *Broome* [1972] AC 1027 some of the judges in the House of Lords attempted a partial answer to the question by asserting that it was the purpose of the civil law to provide compen-sation for injuries and not to punish wrongdoing. But other judges pointed out that this was assertion rather than argument. It was quite consistent with the existing law to suggest that the punishment (and hence deterrence) of wrongdoing could be a legitimate, if secondary, purpose of the civil law even if compensation remained the primary purpose. The decision in *Cassell* v. *Broome* was to the effect that penal or exemplary damages should not normally be permitted in libel actions, so it would seem that the House of Lords endorsed the limited purposes of the law in this class of actions; but there is a sense in which this case involved a semantic exercise only, for the House also approved the practice of awarding 'aggravated damages' in libel actions, that is, damages for the general hurt and injury to the plaintiff's feelings as well as his reputation, and the judges recognized explicitly that such damages may have the effect of punishing the defendant. (They also decided that in exceptional cases—of which *Cassell* v. *Broome* was one—even exemplary or penal damages may be awarded in libel actions subject to a number of caveats.)

Leaving aside, then, the purposes behind particular laws, or sets of laws, is it possible to postulate any general purposes to law as such, law in itself, as it were? In one sense this may be said to be impossible. Law, it may be urged, is fundamentally an instrument, a tool, for the achievement of social purposes. The purposes are not those of the law as such, but of the people who make and enforce the law. Laws can be made to serve diametrically opposite aims, as is perfectly obvious from a casual look around the world. Laws can be used to censor the press or uphold its right of free speech; laws can be used to suppress trade unions or to give them legal privileges and immunities beyond those of ordinary citizens or other bodies; laws can be used to prohibit discrimination or even to recognize slavery; laws can be used to protect rights of property and so punish theft or trespass, or they can be used to provide for the confiscation of property without compensation. There is no need to multiply instances further.

It is easy to conclude from examples of this character that the law is not an independent, autonomous institution with purposes of its own; but that, on the contrary, law is merely a tool, an instrument, by which policies and goals otherwise decided upon can be aimed at by those who make and enforce the law. Many lawyers and legal theorists over a wide spectrum of political opinion hold this position, with varying degrees of emphasis. At one end, for instance, is the traditional Marxist view which postulates that the only reality is the economic or materialist circumstances of a society. Economic conditions lead to a class structure, and the dominant class controls and manipulates the law to maintain its control and to achieve its purposes. The purposes of law, in the Marxist view, are therefore the purposes of the dominant class: if economic conditions lead to a capitalist system of production, for instance, the law will stress the sanctity of private property and freedom of contract which are necessary instruments of a capitalist regime. Those who own the means of production, the bourgeoisie, will be those who own the private property protected by property laws, and those who employ labourers under the system of freedom of contract. When, after the inevitable revolution, the proletariat eventually come to power, it is less clear what the role of law is to be; early Marxists often spoke as though law would no longer be needed in the ultimate communist Utopia, because there would be no classes left, and hence there arose the idea that the law (and the State) would ultimately wither away. Modern Marxists are understandably less sure that the need for law will ever disappear, though it is not always clear what they perceive as the role of law in the wholly communist society.

Many would accept some features of the Marxist analysis without in any way accepting the inevitability of the revolution, or the idea that all social power groups can be seen and understood in class terms, or the notion that laws respond only to economic conditions. Up to a point, it seems clear that the law *is* an instrument of those who wield power. Indeed, it is part of the ideology of liberal democracies that this should be so. Governments and legislatures are elected by the people, and one of their functions in any democratic society is to prepare and enact laws designed to reflect the wishes of the majority who have elected them. One does not need to be a Marxist to recognize that when a Conservative government is in power, legislation tends to benefit those who vote conservative (for example, by lowering taxes on high incomes), while when a Labour government is in power, legislation tends to favour those who vote labour (for example, by expanding the rights of tenants in council houses, or enlarging trade-union immunities).

At the same time, there are many features of the Marxist analysis of law which simply appear inconsistent with the facts. It is not the case that all power groups can be defined in class terms, nor is it the case that all law is a simple one-way instrument designed to enable the dominant class to maintain its power. In a democratic society there are many power groups (or lobby groups) representing the interests of this or that business, profession, region, minority, or religion, and it is unreal to see such groups entirely in terms of class. There are also groups who band together for some purely ideological purpose, such as the environmentalists or animal rights' groups, who certainly cannot be seen in class terms. Nor can racial minorities be said to be a class, and legislation designed to prevent discrimination against such minorities can hardly be seen as an instrument of class power. Moreover, the Marxist analysis overlooks the fact that a great deal of law, indeed most of the law, is concerned with disputes which arise among members of the same class. Property owners may sue each other about (for instance) the use made of land by some at the expense of others. Laws are needed to settle disputes of this kind as much as to settle disputes between members of different classes; what is more, it is, in general, *the same law* which governs the relations of those involved in disputes both of an intra-class and an inter-class character, and this makes it impossible to see all law as the biased law of one class.

It also seems unreal to believe that, even if law is generally an instrument designed to serve other purposes, those purposes must always be economic purposes. The fact is that many laws are designed to serve ethical purposes. Those who make laws—judges and legislatures—usually make laws which they believe to be morally right, not just laws which are in the economic interests of themselves and their supporters. Of course there is a tendency for most people to believe that what is in their interests is morally right, but there are many examples of laws being passed primarily for moral reasons in which the legislators were either indifferent to their own interests or willing to accept the adverse consequences of the law to their own interests. Modern anti-discrimination laws, for instance, or laws decriminalizing homosexual acts between consenting adults have been passed because they are believed to be right, not in order to further the economic interests of the ruling classes.

Similarly, it is mistaken to think that law can never be used to change social attitudes, to lead by example. Marxists tend to think that the law always *responds* to external, primarily economic, forces, so that economic conditions determine what the content of the law will be. Of course there is some truth in this: an economic system based on the free market requires laws of a different character from an economic system in which the free market is suppressed, and an economic system based on agriculture requires different laws from an economic system based on industry. But, as I have suggested earlier (p. 89, above), laws can change, as well as respond to, social and economic conditions. The astonishing social changes in the status of black people in the United States since the Supreme Court decision banning segregation in schools are one vivid example of social change flowing from the law rather than the law responding to social or economic change. Another example is brought to mind by a comparison of modern English and French farming conditions: English farms tend to be larger than those in France, where land-ownership is much more fragmented. The reasons for this lie largely in the result of several centuries of different inheritance laws. In England, primogeniture and freedom of testation tended to preserve landed estates; in France, the rights of succession of children to a share of the parental lands tended to break up landed estates. So present-day economic and social conditions in these respects are the consequences of differing laws; possibly these laws were themselves the outcome of previous economic conditions when they first came into existence, but even if that were the case, it is plain several centuries later that the law is a cause and not just a consequence of economic conditions.

Nevertheless, many contemporary theorists would accept the thesis that the law at any given moment can be used in an instrumental way, that it is possible to change and adapt the law in order to attain a given objective. Does this mean then that the law can be used for *any* purposes at all? Does it mean that lawyers have no particular aims, policies, and values different from those of society, or of the ruling classes? Does it mean that we should not talk of the purposes or aims of the law, but talk instead of the purposes or aims of society or of the government? Before we hasten to this conclusion we need to enter a number of caveats. Four possible claims may be made to the effect that law, as such, does have certain autonomous purposes, which may be different from those of society at large, or the governing classes.

First, it may be argued that there is something about the very nature of law which requires that law in general must aim at certain purposes. For instance, it may be asserted that one of the essential and necessary purposes of law is the maintenance of order and the suppression of violence. But this is rather an uninteresting claim because it is obvious that in this respect the aims of the law and of society (*any* society) must largely coincide.

A second, and more interesting, claim might be that law is inherently and necessarily tied to the aim of justice. In practice we all know that the law can sometimes be unjust, but it may be urged that justice must always be the goal to which the law aspires. In this respect, it may seem that law and lawyers may sometimes have purposes or aims which differ from those of society or the State. No doubt society and the government will also in general claim that they serve the ends of justice, but there are circumstances (for example, when tightening the means test for legal aid) in which the government or Parliament in effect says: 'This may be unjust, or rough justice, but it is an urgent necessity, forced upon us by the demands of public financial control.' On the other hand (it may be said), the law ought never (or even, can never) be perverted in the same way. The law cannot bow to the claims of expediency: justice must be done, though the heavens may fall.

This is a noble ideal, but there are, all the same, serious difficulties about treating the aim or goal of justice as something peculiarly tied to the law. For one thing, we have the only too obvious problem that ideas of justice are highly variable, so (unless one accepts the idea of a divine justice) there is no unique set of aims which one can identify as those to which law must aspire. Once again, then, law seems to become merely an instrument for attaining goals previously selected upon grounds which do not necessarily have anything peculiarly legal about them. But, secondly, the conflict between justice and expediency is not one which is confined to governments. Courts and lawyers may also have to face this conflict, and although it would be rare for them openly to admit that they are sacrificing justice to expediency, in practice this may sometimes be necessary. To take a simple example, time-limits for the various steps which have to be taken in the course of litigation have a somewhat prosaic function. Obviously, compliance with such limits is in general a necessary part of an efficient system for the administration of justice, although doubtless exceptions may be permitted. But if a party who has failed to comply with a time-limit (perhaps on several occasions) is finally shut out from the seat of justice, the result could easily be seen as one in which justice is sacrificed to expediency. Or again, courts from time to time start passing heavier sentences for offences which they regard as particularly prevalent in order to heighten the deterrent power of the law. It is unlikely that a court would openly admit that it is doing anything unjust in passing such a sentence; but it is nevertheless faced with a conflict of goals—passing a 'fair' sentence for the particular criminal as against deterring possible future criminals—and that conflict could well be called a conflict between the demands of justice and expediency.

Thus, the aim of justice is no more absolute for courts and the law than it is for any other institution, or for society as a whole. Although some moral philosophers appear to think this is the case, it is in practice impossible to say that the demands of justice always outweigh every other consideration. Indeed, there may be something misleading even in the suggestion that we can identify the demands of justice as something clearly distinct from the demands of expediency. Perhaps there are simply conflicting goals, both or several of which are prima facie desirable, and we have to choose between them. In this respect the law is no different from other social institutions, lawyers no different from governments and politicians.

A third, more modest, claim might be made about the purpose of law. Although it may be conceded that there are no absolute goals inherent in the idea of law to which law must always aspire, it may be argued that in a particular society, at a particular time, it is possible to identify some goals as ones which the law has traditionally sought to further. In England today, for instance, it may be argued that the purposes of the law include the protection of private individual rights to a degree greater than would be warranted by social values generally. So here we may find that there is a conflict between the aims and policies of the law and lawyers, and those of politicians and parliaments. If that is so, we seem to have a clear instance of a case where the law is not merely an instrument of the ruling classes; but an alternative explanation is that, *for some limited purposes*, the lawyers and judges in fact constitute (or at least share power with) the ruling classes. That is an explanation which may be closer to the truth than appears at first sight. If governments and parliaments tolerate a judiciary which consistently aims to further certain goals and values which are different from those pursued by governments and parliaments, then it may well be that this is because it is in practice beyond their power to change these characteristics of the law. And the only plausible explanation of why this is beyond their power is presumably that public opinion would not stand for it. If that is a correct assessment of the position, then it would be quite accurate to see the courts and the judges as sharing power with the politicians. More needs to be said on this question of the traditional goals and values of English law, but it seems preferable to postpone further discussion until we come to consider law avowedly as an instrument. For it is surely clear that even if the law has traditionally pursued goals which differ somewhat from those presently being followed by society and governments, it is not because these are goals inherent in the nature and purposes of law.

There is a fourth, still more modest, claim which may be made about inherent goals or values of the law. This concerns those institutions which, as we understand the function of law in Western societies, are specially central to law, that is, the courts. In Chapter 1 we saw how lawyers have developed the concept of due process of law as a set of ideals governing the making of decisions by courts, and to a more limited extent by administrative and other agencies. It is plausible to suggest that, in so far as law and lawyers follow a goal of their own, over and above and distinct from goals followed by other social institutions, that goal is the pursuit of the ideal of due process. There is no doubt that it is in this sphere above all others that lawyers can claim to possess a collective experience and expertise which is not shared by other bodies wielding power in society. Moreover, since due process is largely, if not entirely, a procedural matter, there is a sense in which the law's pursuit of this goal need not obstruct society's pursuit of other, more substantive, goals. So when the law requires decisions to conform to the model of due process, lawyers are not telling governments and parliaments what they must do, but only how they must do it. In this sense the character of law as an instrument for the pursuit of goals not selected by the law itself remains largely unqualified.

Law as an instrument of policy

If, then, law is very largely an instrument of policy, a means by which goals or values can be pursued, it remains to inquire somewhat more closely into the nature of some of these goals or values. But it should by now be clear that there are many circumstances in which the precise nature of these goals or values is not really a matter of great importance—or at least not of peculiar importance—to the law and lawyers. At the level of high policy formulation, for instance, when (say) the Cabinet is discussing how to attack the rate of inflation, a number of possible courses of action will doubtless be discussed, some of which will involve the instrumentality of the law, while others will not. In deciding which instruments to use, the Cabinet will largely be concerned with their probable effectiveness, and with the disadvantages which each brings in its train. Much the same sort of choice of instrumentalities may take place at lower-level policy decisions. For instance, a highway authority discussing how to reduce accidents at a bad road junction may canvass the choice of redesigning the road layout (an engineering instrumentality) or imposing a speed limit (a legal instrumentality). Again, the relative effectiveness and cost of each alternative will require consideration if decisions are to be rationally made. In cases of this nature, whether of high- or of low-level policy, the nature of the law as a mere instrument is clearly seen, and the policy being served is not something that would be of peculiar concern to lawyers. The only reason why the lawyer has perhaps a special interest, and a right to be heard, when the law as an instrument of a particular policy is being discussed is to enable him to remind non-lawyers that some laws are not easy to enforce, and that damage can be done to the persuasive powers of the law in general by passing laws which are likely to be difficult to enforce.

In passing on to consider policies and values which the law is extensively used to further, we are, however, dealing with goals and values which are not easily pursued by non-legal methods. Even here, other instrumentalities may be available to some degree, but the major instrument is—in the broadest sense—law. It is worth beginning by distinguishing two sets of goals and values. The first set are those which have been traditionally associated with the law in England as a matter of historical fact, for example, the protection of freedom, of private rights of property and contract, the protection of individual interests and rights in reputation, in the family, and in bodily safety. The second set of goals and values are those which are associated more with modern legislation, and in particular with the pursuit of more collective goals and values. For instance, laws relating to the establishment of the National Health Service, the maintained school system, and the social security system are all examples of the use of law in the pursuit of broad social goals. There are very deep differences in the way the law is used in the pursuit of these two sets of goals.

The first difference is of course the chronological fact that the first set of goals, and therefore the laws giving effect to them, pre-date the second. Despite some qualifications which recent research suggests may need to be made to the traditional picture of eighteenth-century judges and their work, it remains broadly true that through the eighteenth and nineteenth centuries the primary function of law was conceived as the protection of these individual rights of freedom, the protection of property, and so on. Only towards the middle of the nineteenth century did the law come to be widely used for the pursuit of collective social goals. The second difference between these two sets of goals is that the first was generally protected by the common law, while the second mostly owes its origins to legislation. I pointed out in Chapter 1 that the very earliest part of the common law (dating back to the twelfth century and perhaps beyond) naturally dealt with the most basic requirements of law—criminal laws against murder, robbery, and rape, for instance. Now the law of the eighteenth and nineteenth centuries was a long way removed from these very early days, but the common law remained throughout these centuries primarily concerned with the rights of individuals as conceived by the judges of their time. To some degree it still remains true today that lawyers and judges tend to think of the common law as the repository of the most basic legal principles and values. Legislation is still often thought of as a secondary source of law in this sense; it is of course primary in the sense that it can override the common law.

A third major difference, related to the previous one, is that much modern collectivist law is not made enforceable by giving individuals legally enforceable rights. Naturally, the common law method of pursuing goals was developed through the process of common law litigation, and almost necessarily, therefore, the courts rested on the idea that the proper way to pursue a particular goal was to give individuals the right to take action in defence of rights which would forward that goal. If the goal was to reduce railway accidents, the proper remedy was obviously to allow injured railway passengers to sue in the courts for their injuries; if the goal was to stop newspapers publishing scurrilous information, the remedy was to permit those aggrieved to sue for damages in the courts. Now much modern collectivist legislation does not create individual rights in this way. The National Health Service, the maintained school system, and many comparable parts of the modern welfare state do not in general give individuals the right to sue in court if the services supplied sometimes fall short of what is required. It was at one time assumed by those responsible for the establishment of such institutions that no legal enforcement would be needed because the institutions were public ones, under the control of public authorities, and it was taken for granted that they would always seek to comply with their legal duties. Today, there is perhaps less complacency about the operation of public institutions, but it is still widely thought that if they fail to comply with their legal duties, the proper remedy is a political one. Elected bodies may be turned out by the electorate, and non-elected bodies can be disciplined by the appropriate minister or other public body to which they are accountable, but it is not open to the individual citizen to argue in court that (for example) the local schools are not up to scratch. There are signs that the Conservative party is beginning to grasp the fact that there is a real need for some way in which individuals can pursue complaints against such public services. In recent years, the establishment of ombudsmen for various public services (such as the Local Government ombudsmen and the Health Service ombudsmen), as well as the Citizens' Charter, show some slight moves in this direction. We can probably expect more in the future.

It would anyhow be wrong to think that modern welfare legislation never gives individuals legally enforceable rights. The social security system, for instance, does create a tremendous battery of rights which the individual can pursue, though not in the ordinary courts. He must apply, in the first instance, on the appropriate form, for the appropriate 'benefit' from the DSS office, but if he is refused his rights there, he can appeal to the independent appeal tribunals established for this purpose. Nevertheless, it is undoubtedly true that the method of collective enforcement is far more often used for the purpose of ensuring compliance with modern collective law. In this respect there is a striking difference between the pattern of law in England and that in the United States, where individual action in the courts is still the preferred method of enforcing the law, even much modern welfare law. A good example of the difference in approach is to be found in much consumer-protection legislation concerning unsafe or dangerous goods. At common law, a person has the right to sue a manufacturer if dangerous or defective goods are (negligently) put on the market and cause injury to him, and under the Consumer Protection Act 1987 this right extends also to many situations where the goods were defective even though no negligence can be proved against the manufacturer. But in modern times this right is reinforced by an array of statutory controls over different types of goods. These controls, under regulations made usually by ministers exercising powers conferred by statute, do not generally (except sometimes incidentally) give rights of action to injured consumers. What they do is make it an offence to manufacture or sell goods contravening the specified standards. Such contraventions then become punishable through the criminal law, and responsibility for bringing prosecutions passes to public authorities. In the United States, by contrast, the control of dangerous goods remains still largely a matter for ordinary litigation and ordinary courts, with the initiative resting entirely in private hands. Both systems have their advantages and disadvantages. What is being stressed here is that they represent two very different ways in which the instrumentality of the law can be used to achieve identical goals.

The differences are, moreover, ideological as well as practical. The modern English approach depends not merely on a belief that collective enforcement through the machinery of the criminal law is more effective and cheaper than enforcement by civil litigation; it arises in part from the paternalistic traditions of modern welfare law, which seem to assume that most people are incapable of protecting their own interests. By contrast, the American tradition still rests on the firm conviction that the individual is the right person to entrust with the task of law enforcement, because he has both the right and the responsibility to take the initiative in bringing suits before the courts. Equally, the English tradition starts from the premiss that the minister, representing the government, which in turn is supported by the elected House of Commons, is the right person to specify the standards of safety to which manufactured goods must conform. The American tradition, on the other hand, starts from the premiss that the jury (even in civil cases), representing a random cross-section of the public, is the right body to make decisions of this character. This is not to deny that other factors may contribute to the American tradition, for instance, the greater power of business concerns to block legislation of a regulatory nature, and the strength also of lawyers who have an interest in preserving the litigation process. But the differences in ideology are also important. In matters of this kind the American tradition is much closer to the English tradition regarding the *first* set of laws referred to previously.

Economic goals

The distinction between these two types of goals pursued through the instrumentality of law closely parallels the distinction between different economic ideals and perhaps different economic goals. Private enterprise economics, from the days of Adam Smith onward, has tended to take it for granted that the individual pursuit of individual satisfaction within a minimal framework of laws will produce the maximum economic advantage for everyone. The views of many of the early economic adherents of *laissez-faire* theories have today been so often exaggerated, caricatured, and ridiculed, usually by those who have never read them, that simplified accounts of their views must be taken subject to many qualifications. But it is broadly true that many of these economists thought that it was a demonstrable truth that the main function of the state was to maintain laws of property and contract within which individuals could pursue their own interests. Property laws were thought to be manifestly necessary, for who would bother to sow crops if others could push him aside at harvest time? Freedom of contract, and enforcement of contracts, were likewise thought essential, for it is through the medium of contract that all exchange and trade takes place. The labourer exchanges his labour for a wage; he then exchanges his wage for food and clothing. The farmer likewise exchanges his money in return for the labourer's work, so that he can produce a crop which he can then also exchange for money; with the money he can pay his rent and other expenses. Each party to a free contract necessarily gains, for if he did not gain he would not make it; hence, laws which restrict people from making any contracts they choose *must* be harmful since they deprive two would-be contracting parties of the right to make an exchange which benefits both.

There is no doubt that much of the common law from the late eighteenth century onwards was profoundly affected by these economic theories, and many of the traditional rights protected by the common law were closely associated with them. So it would not be inaccurate to suggest that much of the common law of the past two centuries was in a broad and general way designed to further economic goals—the goal of economic 'efficiency'. We enter here very controversial territory which there is not space to traverse in any detail. But it must at least be stressed that efficiency to an economist is often a goal with a rather special meaning which does not necessarily accord with its popular meaning. Broadly speaking, the *laissez-faire* economists assumed, like the utilitarians, that an individual is the only judge of what satisfies him. Hence, an efficient solution is, roughly speaking, a solution which maximizes human satisfaction. Put thus it is perhaps somewhat clearer why many people in the last century found this an attractive goal for the law to pursue. Lawyers today sometimes find it unconvincing to suppose that nineteenth-century judges unconsciously forwarded economic goals by their decisions on common law questions; but once the economists' meaning of the term 'efficiency' is grasped, the supposition becomes more plausible.

Now much modern collectivist legislation and welfare law is clearly based on differing economic theories, and therefore can be seen to pursue different economic goals. We can identify here two separate strands of development. First, there are laws which are still designed largely to give effect to private enterprise economic goals, but which have been modified to take account of neo-classical (or modern) economic theory. Secondly, there are laws which really are based on a rejection of private enterprise economics altogether. In a 'mixed economy' it is not surprising if we have mixed laws. In the first category are, for example, laws relating to restrictive practices and monopolies, which are basically designed to strengthen the operation of the free market. Similarly, there is now a much wider recognition that contracts between two parties, even if they benefit both parties, may be contrary to the public interest because they inflict harm on third parties—the problem known to economists as that of 'externalities'. So, for instance, public health legislation may prohibit a landlord from packing tenants into an overcrowded house—not so much in the interests of the tenants as of the public at large. It is, too, much less readily assumed today that people always know what is in their own interests, although economists have great difficulty in knowing what to put in place of this assumption. But at any rate, much modern law does recognize that people make hasty or ill-considered decisions which are contrary to their long-term interests. In all these and many other similar respects, a good deal of modern law can be said to be still based on, or geared to, the advancement of goals closely linked to those of private enterprise economics.

In other respects, much modern law is directed towards goals which clearly require rejection of the basis of private enterprise economics. Planning laws, for instance, which deprive the landowner of the right to decide how to develop his land, and replace that right with a system of public control, are based on the assumption that public elected agencies will arrive at better decisions than individuals pursuing their own interests in a free market. Similarly, the very large number of laws which prevent a person exercising an occupation without some sort of licence or permit from a statutory authority, rest on the belief that the consumer is not the best judge of his own interests in these respects, and needs the assistance of some agency to distinguish the competent from the incompetent. More obviously still, the European Community's common agricultural policy, which subsidizes much agricultural production, is a negation of the free market in the products to which it applies.

A bias in favour of traditional values?

It is implicit in what has already been said that there is no cause for surprise in this multiplicity of goals and values which the law serves. In so far as the law is an instrument which can serve virtually any purpose which the lawmaker wishes to pursue, it is quite natural that in a mixed economy and a pluralistic society with a succession of different governments of different complexions, we have, at any given moment, many laws serving conflicting goals and values. But there is one facet of this question which calls for further comment. As previously indicated, many of the more modern collectivist and welfare goals pursued by the law are not widely enforced through the ordinary courts. This means that the legal profession and the judges do not have a great deal to do with laws of this character, and continue to work primarily with laws of the more traditional sort, even though much modified and amended to take account of modern ideals. This in turn probably means that the values underlying the traditional goals pursued by the common law still tend to be dominant among lawyers and judges, and may well have a strong influence even in those relatively unusual cases which do involve strongly collectivist ideas and which occasionally come before the courts for decision. In short, it may well be that there is a sort of bias in the law dealt with by courts in favour of the traditional values.

The causes of this bias, however, run more deeply than may be suggested by the above distinction between traditional and more collectivist goals. Another cause of this bias may well have something to do with the characteristics of the legal profession and the judges themselves. The Bar, as presently organized in England, is a highly individualistic profession. Barristers are not permitted to work as employees or in partnership. Each barrister stands on his own two feet. If he succeeds, he owes his success largely to his own natural endowments, plus, no doubt, the traditional element of luck which may be needed to get started. Barristers are the sort of people who are likely to be good judges of their own interest, and to be good managers of their own interest. Moreover, barristers have little direct contact with clients from the poorer and less articulate classes. Naturally, those who use legal services are those who can pay legal fees, and these people tend to be more middle-class and more articulate—indeed, many of them are likely to be professional people like the barristers themselves. The very fact that a client seeks to litigate is often itself testimony to his belief in the rights of the individual to take the initiative and to use the courts as a means of vindicating his rights. There are growing changes today which require some of these remarks to be qualified—for instance, the increase in legal aid, especially in criminal cases, does bring a larger number of poorer people into the network of the common law system—but the general picture of the civil law still remains of a profession of individualists, working for individualists, to vindicate individual rights. All this may help to explain, though perhaps not to justify, the bias in the legal profession and the courts towards traditional goals and values. But there is one further point to be made which does perhaps constitute at least a partial defence for this state of affairs.

Much modern collectivism exacts a price from individuals. Welfare legislation, like the social security system, is perhaps exceptional in not normally hurting individuals; but it is rarely possible to pursue collective goals without causing harm, and sometimes serious harm, to individuals. Planning laws, for instance, may be essential in the public interest, but they carry a price. The individual property-owner loses his freedom to develop his land, and this loss of freedom extends from the large landowner who cannot turn his farmland into a housing estate, to the small house-owner who is deprived of his freedom to change the use of his property in a way which might cause no harm to anyone else. Naturally, the decision to enact planning laws means that government and Parliament have (one assumes, or hopes) considered these costs and decided that they are a necessary price to be paid for a system of rational land use. To that extent, it would be wrong of lawyers and courts to challenge or undermine the basic values underlying the planning system. But in fact they rarely, if ever, do that. Where the traditional individual values tend to surface is when things have in some sense gone wrong with the machine. Mistakes are made by the planning authority, for instance, incorrect information is given, or unauthorized conditions are imposed on a planning permission, inordinate delays hold up a project to the great cost of an individual property owner, and so on. Cases of this kind are often not specifically anticipated when the legislation is enacted, and even though Parliament may in a general way be aware that they may occur, it is much easier to suppress sympathy for those affected when they are only potential victims of a possible future wrong who at present have no identity or individuality. But when the machine does go wrong, and individuals *are* affected, it is the lawyers who see them and learn of the particular hardship which they have encountered. Under these circumstances it is natural for lawyers and judges to feel sympathy for the individuals affected and to look at the legislation carefully to see whether they cannot uphold the rights of the individual without destroying the general collectivist goals.

Perhaps the example from planning law is not well chosen, because the land 'speculator' has a poor image and few would shed many tears over the landowner refused planning permission even where there has been much greater hardship or loss than normal. But it is not hard to find many other examples of the same sort of thing. Much trade-union activity formerly gave rise to acute conflicts of this nature; and although these are not making the headlines today, they could easily become more important again in the future. The trade-union movement has historically rested very heavily on its solidarity because it is only solidarity that gives it strength; and one cannot doubt that in general terms members of trade unions have gained from this solidarity in the past. But when particular individuals find themselves in disagreement with their union, say, over a strike, and wish to continue working when a strike has been called, the conflict between the individual's rights and the collective rights of the union members as a whole is very acute. Lawyers almost instinctively side with the individual in such circumstances. Indeed, the very nature of the conflict is likely to be perceived in a different way by those on either side of this sort of controversy. To the trade-unionist, the issue is often posed as one concerning 'the right to strike'; to the individualist, and the lawyer who tends to side with him, the issue is not the right to strike but the right to compel others to strike when they do not wish to strike.

To the individualistically minded common lawyer, one of the less attractive aspects of collectivism is that the collectivist often gives the appearance of not wanting to look too closely at the cost to individual rights of his grand plans and aspirations. The legislative process is, on the whole, one that tends to encourage broad appeals to abstract goals; the litigation process, by contrast, is one which tends to emphasize the hardship and cost to the individual of the pursuit of these goals. So a bias in favour of traditional individualistic values and goals may well be inherent in the litigation process, and may even be a desirable counterweight to the generality and abstractness of legislation. But it is no doubt a fair point to make, that lawyers and the litigation process offer small consolation to those who pay the costs of those parts of the system which are based more on private rights and individualist goals—for these too, of course, have costs.

General rules and particular decisions

Whatever goals are pursued through the instrumentality of law, one nearly always finds that the law can be used in two different ways. The law can consist of general rules, or it can take the form of making particular decisions in particular cases. Typically, of course, one thinks of legislation as providing the general rules, and litigation as providing the *ad hoc* decision in the particular case. But the full picture is rather more complex than that. For a start, the common law itself is now a body of general rules, drawn from individual instances. Then again, judges do not generally decide cases on a completely *ad hoc* basis. They first formulate the general rule or principle which they think should govern all like cases, and then they apply that rule or principle to the case in hand. And on the other hand, not all parliamentary legislation is so very general. Parliament sometimes delegates to ministers or courts the job of settling issues in particular cases without giving them general rules by which they are to be guided.

This distinction between general rules and particular decisions is of the greatest importance. From the days of the Greek philosophers it has been a well-understood phenomenon of general laws that they do not always do justice when applied to the facts of particular cases, and that therefore some modification or adjustment, some application of mercy or equity, may be needed in the particular case. In the development of English law, this fact has historically been recognized in various ways. The royal prerogative of mercy, for instance, has been available from time immemorial as a way of mitigating the harshness of criminal convictions where the result, though in accordance with the law, has seemed unjust. Some of the cases in which the prerogative of mercy was regularly used in the medieval common law arose out of the fact that much of the early common law was very crude, not to say barbaric. For instance, homicide, even when accidental, or by way of self-defence, was originally accounted capital murder, and the only way the unfortunate killer could escape the death penalty was by obtaining the royal pardon. Later the common law became less crude, and itself began to distinguish between accidental killing, killing by way of self-defence, and killing with 'malice aforethought', which was murder.

In civil cases a somewhat similar use of the royal power was handed over to the Lord Chancellor around the fifteenth century, and he resorted to basic ideas of equity as a way of modifying the ordinary common law where it seemed to produce unacceptable or unjust results. Gradually, the Lord Chancellor began to sit regularly like a judge, his sittings came to be called the Court of Chancery, and 'equity' itself became a regular body of rules, supplementing the common law. It was eventually incorporated into the general body of the law in the late nineteenth century. But lawyers still talk of rules of equity as distinct from rules of common law, though in this sense equity has the technical meaning of rules developed by the Lord Chancellors in the Court of Chancery. Today rules of equity are just as much general rules as rules of common law, though they still bear traces of their origin, in that (for instance) equitable remedies remain to this day discretionary. Thus, you can demand, as a matter of right, damages for breach of contract (a common law remedy), but if you want the court to order the defendant actually to perform his contract (an 'equitable' remedy), you can only ask the court to exercise its discretion in your favour. In practice, the difference is smaller than this may suggest because equitable discretions are exercised in general according to established principles, if not fixed rules.

The historical process by which cases at one time dealt with by the prerogative of mercy, or by *ad hoc* equitable decisions, are today dealt with by actual modifications to the law itself is a revealing one. The law has, over the centuries, tended to become more and more complex as attempts have been made to provide for more and more subdivisions, or exceptional cases, by way of rule rather than by way of mercy or equity. This shows the power of the ideal that laws *should* be based on general rules, and not on particular decisions, even though—despite all the increasing complexity—we still constantly find that general rules produce unjust results in particular cases. Whence derives this great ideal of *generality* in law?

In earlier times it probably arose, at least in part, from beliefs about the very nature of law itself. Those who thought of law as some eternal body of rules of right or justice, especially when law was associated with religion, naturally assumed that there must always be some general principle which could be found to govern any particular dispute. Moreover, this vision of law placed the judges, like everybody else, in a position in which they were subject to the law. If the judge who decides a case is subject to the law, then he cannot just settle the dispute in front of him in an *ad hoc* way; for that would make the judge a sort of *cadi*, administering 'palm-tree justice'. The very notion of judges being subject to the law assumes that there is always a legal rule or principle to govern every dispute, which it is the job of the judge to discover.

In more modern times lawyers have had difficulty with the idea that law somehow exists in the sky, and pre-dates its 'discovery' by the judge who has to apply it. But this has not seriously dented the ideal that laws should consist of general rules and principles. Belief in the generality of law in more modern times probably stems from certain liberal principles about the role of law and the individual. General rules of law are thought to enable the citizen to plan his life in such a way as to conform to the law in the way he thinks best. There are many respects in which the individual simply cannot rationally plan his life or even his daily conduct unless he knows what are the rules of the game—whether it is the businessman who wishes to know what important regulations may affect a long-term contract he wants to make now, or the taxpayer who wishes to adjust his affairs so as to minimize his tax liabilities, or the ordinary consumer who wishes to insure his house or his car with some reasonable confidence that he is getting the cover he expects, or the employer who wishes to know whether he can safely dismiss a worker for incompetence. So there arises the demand for certainty and generality in the law. 'Let us know where we stand' is the demand of the liberal individualists, 'so we can get on with our lives.' If judges decide cases according to their individual sense of justice the law will vary from judge to judge (according to the length of his foot, in the old legal saying), and nobody will ever know where he stands.

But there is a second factor of great importance in the ideal of generality of law, namely, the strength that it gives to its persuasive power. It is easier to learn, and understand, a general principle or fixed rule if the message comes through simple and unqualified. 'Do not kill' is a simpler message than 'do not kill with malice aforethought', or even 'do not murder'. 'Do not take other people's property' is a simpler message than 'do not steal, that is, take other people's property with the intent of permanently depriving them'. There are grounds for thinking that in the eighteenth century, at least, one of the ways by which the landed aristocracy maintained its power with the minimum of force was by harnessing the immense persuasive power of *simple* and unqualified laws. The more general are the laws and rules laid down for the guidance of the mass of the people, the simpler they are, and the more readily intelligible. In eighteenth-century England, for instance, much of the apparent crudity and barbarity of the criminal code arose from the fact that the laws against theft, violence, and so forth did not incorporate mitigating factors to the extent to which they do today. On the face of it, the law often appeared ferocious and bloodthirsty: don't do this, or that, on pain of death. In practice, a large proportion of capital sentences were commuted, so that mitigating factors could be, and were, taken into account in the end; but it may well be that the mass of the people were unaware of the extent to which mercy in fact modified the apparent severity of the law. In this way the people were being fooled into believing that the law was more severe than it really was.

Laws relating to debt appear to have been subject to similar factors. On the face of it, debtors were threatened with dire and instant penalties for default; but in fact mitigation was possible through the intervention of the Court of Chancery in some cases, and through other forms of mercy (periodically emptying the debtors' prisons) in other cases. So here too it may be that a deliberate balance was being maintained between preserving the generality of legal rules and principles—so that they would remain simple messages to the public—and permitting modification on merciful or equitable grounds in particular circumstances.

Even in the nineteenth century this balance may have continued in some respects. There is at least evidence that working-class children were often brought up on a stark code much cruder than in fact the law actually was, as witness the following passage from Flora Thompson's delightful book, *Lark Rise to Candleford*: 'Any statement which departed in the least degree from plain fact was a lie; anyone who ate a plum from an overhanging bough belonging to a neighbour's tree was a thief. It was a stark code in which black was black and white was white; there were no intermediate shades.' (Penguin edn. (1973), 183). It is arguable that this illustrates one of the reasons why, in earlier times, modifications to the way the law actually worked were *not* incorporated in the law, but left to be dealt with by mercy or equity as residuary, non-rule-based discretions. For one of the curiosities of English legal history is the way in which equity, even after it had become a regular body of rules of its own, was not incorporated with the law (until 1875) but in theory coexisted with the law. It seems possible that leaving standing the nominal force of rules of law (even though in practice it was known that they were modified by the separate rules of equity) helped to strengthen the persuasive powers of the law.

Clearly, one reason why this argument no longer appeals is because it rests upon an élitist assumption that the mass of the people can be fooled into observing laws by persuading them that they are harsher and cruder than they really are. With the spread of education and the mass media, it is unlikely that the people can be so easily fooled; and with the spread of democracy, it would be widely thought that the people should not be fooled even if they could be. But some doubts may remain on both scores. It is, for instance, extremely unlikely that most people understand the extent to which the law today would protect them against the consequences of (say) non-payment of hire-purchase or mortgage instalments, or even gas bills or other debts. And niggling doubts must remain as to whether it is not on the whole desirable that some element of mystery concerning the law must remain so that its powers of persuasion are not weakened beyond repair.

However, there is no doubt that in modern times the pendulum has swung against this ideal of certainty and generality in law. We now find an increasing tendency in very many spheres of law for wide discretions to be vested in decision-makers. The courts themselves have enormous discretionary powers, of which some examples have previously been given (see p. 51, above), such as the power to award maintenance out of the estate of a deceased person, the power to carve up matrimonial property on divorce, the power to strike out unfair clauses in many types of contract, and so on. Other wide discretions are also vested in administrative agencies and decision-makers of all kinds, such as the powers of the local planning committee of the council to approve or veto an application, and the power of the area health authorities to decide what priority to give various forms of treatment or surgery under the Naional Health Service when there are inadequate resources for everyone to receive immediate treatment for all conditions.

Why has the pendulum swung in this way? There are several reasons. First, of course, is the waning power of the liberal ideal itself. The right of the individual to plan his own life, and even his daily conduct, is no doubt still highly prized, but it is not treated so absolutely as in earlier times, particularly when it comes up against other values and goals. Secondly, and relatedly, those who have power and authority (in particular, governments and administrators, but including also judges) often prefer to have discretionary power rather than to be bound by fixed rule. Everyone who has had to make decisions knows that decisions bound by fixed rules often produce unexpected results. Further, they produce a greater demand for accountability. If the decision-maker has to follow rules, then his decisions will be scrutinized by those affected, who will complain if he appears to be making inconsistent decisions. It is much easier to shelter behind a discretionary power than to justify apparently (and perhaps genuinely) inconsistent decisions. The often-repeated pronouncement of decision-makers: 'This decision is not to be cited as a precedent', is the despairing cry of those who know that their decisions ought to be consistent but cannot guarantee that they will be. Thirdly, and this too is closely tied up with the last two reasons, the growth of paternalism in modern societies has often led to situations in which decision-makers wish to reserve a greater freedom of action than they may have under a fixed-rule regime. Because some people may enter into foolish or unfair contracts, the law will not always tell them in advance what sorts of contracts they may enter into: it will wait until the contract is made and then decide whether it is unfair.

Fourthly, there has been, at any rate in some quarters, a growing scepticism about the genuineness of the certainty that general rules provide anyhow. There is good ground for thinking that even where the laws appear to be based on fixed rule rather than discretion, the judges, in their anxiety to do justice in particular cases, will bend or modify the law, or interpret the law or the facts so as to enable them to achieve the result that seems right. Indeed, it is sometimes suggested that it is actually easier to predict discretionary decisions than rule-bound decisions, which is only to say that it is often simpler and clearer to identify (and agree upon) the justice of a case than the law. Further, many laws may appear to be relatively certain and take the form of fixed rules, only because their rules are largely empty of content. The entire law of civil liability for negligence, which is today of immense practical importance, and fills the courts with claims for damages for personal injury and other forms of loss, rests almost wholly on the rule: thou must take reasonable care not to injure thy neighbour. But what is 'reasonable care' is something which is never decided or laid down in advance: the courts give guidance, certainly, but actual decisions are only made after the event. So, for instance, a professional firm, say, of accountants, can never find out in advance whether the inquiries and investigations they think adequate for an audit will be enough to satisfy some future judge that they have taken 'reasonable care'.

But it has perhaps also become more clear that not all laws concern situations in which the citizen needs advance knowledge of how he is going to be treated. Some laws, for instance, are specifically designed to deal with accidents and untoward events. Much of the law of negligence is designed to cope with the aftermath of an accident, to clear up a mess after it has occurred. One can, of course, take steps to guard against accidents and to deal with the contingency of an accident should it occur, for instance, by taking out insurance. But in the nature of things the full aftermath of an accident is not a foreseeable eventuality, and so perhaps laws designed to deal with such events have less need to be spelt out in advance. A parallel set of laws often deals with windfalls—the most typical case in recent years being the profit which may be made on sale of a matrimonial home by a couple who are separating or becoming divorced. Here too it is very difficult to anticipate the nature of such a windfall, and the circumstances in which it is likely to arise, so few people would lose much by laws which were designed to operate *ad hoc* after the event.

So for these and perhaps other reasons, the tendency of much modern law is to become less fixed, less rule-oriented, and more discretionary. The rule with a residual discretion to set it aside in exceptional circumstances is becoming very common in modern law, except perhaps in the criminal law and the law of taxation. It remains to be seen whether the cost of this trend will become excessive, in terms of the weakening of the persuasive powers of the law, and the difficulties it places in the way of those who wish to plan their lives, conduct, and business.

5 The legitimacy of law

Does legitimacy matter?

By what right do the acts of parliament become Acts of Parliament and hence, law? By what right does a judge order that a man be sent to gaol for ten years? By what right does the policeman thereupon confine the man and hand him over to the prison authorities, and by what right do they imprison this man? By what right, indeed, does the State demand allegiance from its citizens and threaten them with dire penalties for treason? Questions of this kind are often called questions about the legitimacy of the State, or the legal order, or the law. To some people, the search for legitimacy is of the utmost importance. It is only the legitimacy of a law or a legally authorized act which distinguishes the order of a policeman from the howls of a mob, the order of a judge from the demands of a gunman. If the only reason that I ought to obey the policeman is because I know that he has the physical power to arrest me and, if I resist, that he has other policemen who will come to his help, then the only distinction between the policeman and the gunman is that there are more policemen.

The ordinary legal practitioner is unlikely to have much interest in questions about the legitimacy of the law. To him, it is perfectly clear that there are established bodies of authority and power who make, enforce, and administer the law. So far as he is concerned, 'the law is the law is the law'. But to theorists there have always been some very basic questions about the legitimacy of the whole legal order that need examination, although curiously enough it is political theorists rather than legal theorists who have traditionally been most interested in these issues.

In modern times the concept of legitimacy and of government by consent has largely come to be replaced by the much simpler idea that governments must be elected by the people. This is a concept of international political morality rather than of law, but it is gaining strength and, indeed, practical significance in the international community. Elected governments are still not infrequently overthrown by military or other coups, but in the absence of any serious international political or judicial system, it is unfortunately difficult to suggest that all elected governments are more legitimate than all coups. Some elections are so corrupt and some governments so tyrannical that a coup to dislodge them, with the prospect of genuine elections later, is often to be welcomed rather than deplored. But even dictatorships are coming to discover that the disapproval of the international community is no light matter. Foreign aid, for instance, may be withheld from governments without genuine claims to legitimacy. The threat of this has produced results, in Kenya for instance, where the government has been forced to recognize the rights of opposition parties to participate in the political process. In other countries, international observers have often scrutinized elections and so helped to confer legitimacy on the results. The collapse of the communist regimes of the Soviet Union and Eastern Europe has also led to a great increase in the number of elections held in that part of the world, and with it, a great gain in the legitimacy of the governments concerned.

But legitimacy in this broad sense, as part of the international legal or moral order, is not my concern. In this book I am more interested in internal legitimacy, as it were; in the legitimacy of particular laws, for instance, even where it is indisputable that they emanate from an elected Parliament. What sort of questions are these? They are not questions about strict law, as such. The question of *legal* legitimacy is just an ordinary question of law, like any other: if a policeman orders someone 'to move along there', we can look up the law concerning policemen's powers to see how far they extend. As we shall see, there is a long tradition in English legal theory which holds that this is all that concerns the law. But when questions about legitimacy are posed, it is other issues which are usually being raised. These are often seen as being moral issues: by what (moral) right does the judge order a man to be gaoled, by what (moral) right does the State demand allegiance, and so forth? Others again might see them as raising sociological or psychological issues. For example, it might be thought to be a question for sociological inquiry how it is that most people come to perceive lawful and established authority and power as something different from mere might or force. So too, it might well be important to an understanding of deviance and law-breaking to ask how and why rebels and deviants reject the general acceptance of established authority. Do they, for instance, reject established authority while accepting its legitimacy, or do they deny its legitimacy altogether? Similarly, there may be psychological issues of interest concerning the habits of obedience to lawful authority which most people acquire. Here, I shall do no more than offer a few tentative suggestions about the practical importance of questions of legitimacy, and then say a brief word about the traditional political and legal theories concerning these questions.

It may be suggested that legitimacy matters to lawyers primarily because of what has been previously referred to as the persuasive power of the law. Unless the mass of the public feels that there is some moral obligation to observe established law, then the law may come to be unenforceable. In recent times the poll tax may well be thought to illustrate the problems surrounding the attempt to give legitimacy to highly controversial political policies by clothing them in the form of law. There seems no doubt that the Conservative government which passed the Local Government Finance Act 1988 thought that, however controversial its policies might be, once they had been duly enacted by Parliament, and converted into law, the normal law-abiding habits of the British people would assert themselves, and the Act would be observed and accepted. It seems equally clear that the opponents of the tax who decided to flout the Act totally rejected this attempt to give legitimacy to policies which they thought (rightly or wrongly) were an unfair and unacceptable violation of the traditional basis on which local taxes are levied. The result is well known: the hasty repeal of the legislation, and the replacement of the poll tax by the council tax in 1993.

Although this was not the first occasion in modern times that the Conservative party had made such a mistake (the Heath Government

Industrial Relations Act 1971 was a precursor), it may be hoped that it has now learnt the lesson that governments cannot confer legitimacy on their policies just by legislation: if large numbers of the people just do not accept the moral right of the government to legislate as they have done, they will not accept the resulting laws as having the legitimacy which entitles laws to be obeyed without question in most circumstances. For a while it seemed uncertain whether the Labour party had learned the same lesson, although, in industrial affairs, it was that party which constantly hammered home the idea that governments must operate by consent of the people. In 1980, for instance, the Labour party conference passed a resolution to make it illegal for people to send their children to private schools. It seems very doubtful whether the many thousands of parents who do this would have accepted the legitimacy of a law of that nature. Fortunately the Labour party has more recently abandoned such extreme policies.

It is, perhaps, not inconceivable that more fundamental problems of legitimacy may confront this country in the decades ahead. For nearly 300 years the supremacy of Parliament, and latterly of the House of Commons, was the unquestioned basis of our constitution, and hence, ultimately, of our law. It was precisely this long tradition of stability in political and constitutional matters which generally made legitimacy a matter of little practical importance in this country. For this long tradition tended to make arguments about legitimacy seem theoretical and fanciful. What was the point of arguing about the legitimacy of this or that piece of law, when we knew that (nearly) everybody (nearly) always accepted the right of Parliament to pass whatever laws it pleased? However, much has happened in recent times (apart altogether from the changes following our membership of the European Community) to suggest that things may be changing. In particular, there has recently been much more interest in and discussion of three basic and important constitutional issues which are closely involved with issues of legitimacy. These are, first, the electoral process itself, with our 'first past the post' winner-takes-all system; secondly, renewed controversy about the future of the House of Lords; and thirdly, increasing interest in the possibility of a Bill of Rights which might actually impose limits on the power of Parliament. I will return to these three issues later in this chapter.

The positivist tradition

As indicated above, English lawyers have not generally taken much interest in questions of legitimacy. One reason for this is undoubtedly the strength of the 'positivist' tradition in English law, which for nearly two centuries has encouraged lawyers to concentrate on purely formal issues of legitimacy. Formal questions of legitimacy are pure questions of law about the formal source of the authority of a particular law, or rule, or order. Judge Bloggs in the Lawshire County Court, for instance, orders Mr X to produce some documents in an action brought against him by Miss Y. Is that a lawful order? Strictly, to answer that question one would need to inquire into a number of things: first, who is this man purporting to make the order? The answer is that he is a judge of this court because he was appointed to that office by Lord Z. Of course Lord Z only had the power to make that appointment because he was the Lord Chancellor (having been duly appointed by the Queen—in accordance with any legal formalities and other requirements as to his qualifications); and the appointment of Judge Bloggs was made under some statutory provision. Then one would have to inquire into the nature of the order made by the judge: where does he derive the power to make that order? The answer probably is that it comes from the County court rules; but we can then ask further, what are these rules, how do they have the right to be called laws? And the answer to that is that they have been duly made by members of the Rules Committee (duly appointed in accordance with other statutory or legal requirements) pursuant to an Act of Parliament which actually confers this power. But perhaps the rule in question does not on its face cover the sort of order the judge has made: then we might need to know that there is a precedent in which the Court of Appeal (duly sitting as required by law, and comprising judges duly appointed as required by law) has interpreted the rule in question in a particular fashion. And we shall also need to know that, under the rules of the doctrine of precedent, that decision of the Court of Appeal has made law which binds the present Judge Bloggs.

Eventually, the lawfulness of any order, rule, or law can be traced back in this sort of way to some ultimate source or sources. For all practical purposes there are only two such sources in our legal system, namely precedents and Acts of Parliament,* and the whole immense set of laws and rules and specific legal orders which comprises the legal system can be seen as a sort of pyramidical structure in which the legal authority or legitimacy of anything in the lower parts of the pyramid can be traced through several layers until we arrive at some ultimate or basic 'norm'. This pyramid is often seen as having at its apex the basic 'norm' that whatever is duly enacted by the Queen in Parliament is law, and all other laws, rules, and orders must ultimately be traceable back to this norm. This norm is a basic postulate of the legal system which comes to be accepted by actual observance by society, but all other rules and laws derive their validity from higher norms or laws. This is not the place for any extended critique of this particular theory of law, which is associated with the work of Hans Kelsen (1881–1973), an Austrian judge and jurist, who later lived in America and became renowned as an exponent of the 'pure theory of law'. It is enough to say that theories of this kind of analytical jurisprudence are concerned almost entirely with the formal sources of legitimacy of law. To Kelsen and his supporters, the question of legitimacy is, in its nature, a formal question which has nothing to do with the actual content of the law in question.

This kind of analytical jurisprudence had its origins in the work of Jeremy Bentham (1748–1832) and John Austin (1790–1859). Bentham was a great law reformer and critic of legal and social institutions, and one of the things which he was reacting against was the tendency of lawyers, as he saw it, to assume that law had some legitimacy over and above that given to it by its own creation or observance. Eighteenth-century lawyers often justified particular laws and legal institutions by talking the language of 'natural law' and

---

* Of course the reality is now much complicated by the European Community dimension; originally all Community laws derived their validity in the UK from the European Communities Act 1972, but it is no longer realistic to treat Community law as though it were all derivative in this way, because (as we have seen) UK law is now *subject* to Community law. But I ignore this complication for the purposes of the theoretical analysis in the text.

'natural rights'. For example, rights of property were seen as 'natural' and the function of property law (and hence the law of trespass, theft, and so on) was therefore to preserve the natural rights of the property owner. Much of this in turn derived from the works of John Locke, whose (second) *Treatise on Civil Government* came to be regarded as an apologia for the Revolution of 1688 and was treated as a sort of political bible by the Whig landowners through most of the eighteenth century. To Locke the only function of government was to preserve and protect the natural rights which men had 'in the state of nature'; it had to be assumed that men in the state of nature had voluntarily consented to the establishment of the State by a 'social contract'; it was this which gave legitimacy to laws and the State, and once the ruler neglected to do his job properly (as of course James II had done) it was right and justifiable for the people to overthrow him by revolution.

But to Bentham, all this talk of natural law and natural rights was just nonsense—'nonsense upon stilts' he called it. The 'state of nature' and the 'social contract' were pure fictions. Property rights did not antedate the existence of society and law; on the contrary, it was only in a society and through law that the very idea of ownership of property had any meaning. So it was impossible to insist that societies existed in order to protect pre-existing property rights. Laws were a human creation, made by humans, for humans; there was nothing sacred or mysterious about them, and bad laws could be and ought to be changed. In propagating this message Bentham was, in the long run, completely successful. None of Bentham's ideas has more powerfully taken root than the notion that laws are mere human creations which can be made and unmade at man's mere pleasure. Indeed, it is permissible to wonder (as previously suggested) whether we are today not too prone to think that modern societies can get along happily without the elements of mystery and majesty and sacredness about law. But to recognize Bentham's triumph in these respects is not to say that the Lockean tradition is completely dead; there is still powerful support for the idea that the State and the laws derive their legitimacy from the consent of the people; and the notion that the function of society and law is to protect pre-existing moral rights is still vigorously defended by some modern theorists.

One of the curious by-products of Bentham's work was the positivist tradition which has had such a profound influence on the development of English law and legal thinking since his time. 'Positivism' is a label which has been used somewhat imprecisely for a variety of theories and ideologies, but, for present purposes, the principal beliefs associated with the positivist tradition can be said to be these: first, laws are commands of human beings addressed to other human beings; secondly, there is no necessary connection between law and morals; thirdly, the analysis of law and legal concepts is a true 'scientific' inquiry which is concerned with the formal requirements of valid law, and not with its content; and fourthly, judges, when deciding new points of law, must confine themselves to 'legal' arguments and not rely upon moral or policy arguments.

It may well be that no particular jurist or thinker ever actually entertained all these beliefs (though Bentham and Austin certainly entertained the first three); and it may also be true that these various ideas were not, and indeed are not, *necessarily* connected with each other. But it is also easy to see how closely they fit together. The idea that all laws are commands is today regarded as a gross over-simplification (for instance, some laws confer permission or power, some create institutions, and some laws merely repeal other laws), and in this it is clear that Bentham and Austin were mistaken. But although the detailed analysis of all laws as commands is unacceptable, it may still be true—and this was certainly the central point of Bentham's ideas—that all law is the creation of human beings who are responsible for the way it is made and the way it works. The second point—that there is no *necessary* connection between law and morals—has been much discussed by jurists and philosophers in modern times, and it remains highly controversial. Most would readily concede that there just are certain features of law which make it inconceivable that in practice a legal system could work if it did not in large measure reflect the morals of its society; but some theorists still believe that the formal characteristics of law do not logically entail any relationship with morals. However, there is one way in which many jurists believe that law and morals *must* be related. Every time the law is unclear and judges have to decide what the law 'is' they must, in the nature of the case, decide what it 'is' by reference to what it 'ought to be'—though that usually means, *not* 'what it ought to be in an ideal world', but what it ought to be, given all sorts of constraints and existing rules which must be accepted for the moment. To this extent at least, law and morality do appear to be inextricably, and of necessity, linked together. But it is unlikely that Bentham would have denied that, though to him, of course, morality was itself (like law) a human institution designed to further 'the greatest happiness of the greatest number'. What Bentham did object to was the assumption that all existing laws had some sort of moral basis to them; especially when it was also assumed that this moral basis was in some way sacred or mysterious so that it would be dangerous to tamper with it. If Bentham wanted to separate law more sharply from morality, it was largely in order that he could more easily train his guns on bad laws and so establish the need for radical reform. Paradoxically, the stress on the distinction between law and morality has often, since Bentham's day, become a somewhat conservative stance; the positivist can proclaim his lack of concern for morality as a ground for defending the legal *status quo*.

The third characteristic of positivism, that legal theory is (or perhaps ought to be) primarily to do with the analysis of legal concepts, undoubtedly stems, as a matter of historical fact, from the analytical and theoretical work of Austin, who built largely on Bentham's foundations. Indeed, until quite recently, the study of jurisprudence or legal theory in English law schools was almost entirely devoted to a study of the Austinian theory of law. Whatever useful insights this kind of jurisprudence may have produced, it is difficult to believe that its long dominance has not impoverished both legal theory and English law. For stress on the exclusive importance of formal analysis has led (until very recent times) to an unwillingness on the part of English lawyers to pay serious attention to issues of morality or policy and their interrelationship with law. It is, for instance, still quite common (though becoming less so) for English judges to refuse to discuss moral issues in their legal judgments, and to assert baldly that moral ideals play no role in the formulation of the law by the courts; though it is equally common for judges to appeal to ideas of fairness and justice where this seems appropriate.

The fourth aspect of the positivist tradition—that judges should indeed confine themselves in formulating principles of law to purely 'legal' arguments and deliberately avoid drawing on moral or policy arguments—is not one which can be fathered on Bentham or perhaps Austin either. But it is closely related to the other three, and despite its declining importance in recent times, it is still often the 'official' theory of the law that this can and must be the chosen method of developing new legal rules or principles.

Positivism and the constitution

It does not seem far-fetched to suggest that the positivist tradition has also been closely associated with another characteristic of English legal and constitutional thought over the years. Put crudely, this is the belief that political issues can be *settled definitively* by majority vote, and that no serious moral, legal, or constitutional issues arise once the majority has spoken in due course of law. Legally, this tradition is of course intimately tied up with the sovereignty of Parliament, and the fact that (as seen above) questions of legitimacy have not generally troubled English lawyers. Once the majority has properly made its decisions, the law is duly enacted, and that must be the end of the argument. Even constitutionally, this has generally been the accepted tradition in England, though increasingly subject in recent years to the qualification that, if the majority changes its mind at the next election, what has once been done can readily be undone. And among lawyers and constitutional theorists, and perhaps even practical politicians, what has been true of the legal and constitutional position has been, in general, also the accepted moral viewpoint: majorities, in other words, have traditionally been seen in England as settling moral argument as well as legal and political argument.

Historically speaking, this tradition can be seen as the result of a series of rather strange accidents, all the more strange because of the different course of events in the United States. As was mentioned earlier, Bentham's positivism was in part a reaction against the natural-law theories which had in England been closely associated with the ideas of John Locke. Much that Bentham advocated was violently opposed to the Locke tradition. Where Locke had argued

that men had natural rights which in some sense pre-dated the existence of civil society, government, and laws, Bentham argued that
natural rights were nonsense and that all rights *derived* from society,
government, and laws. And where Locke had argued that, because
of the existence of natural rights, society, government, and laws had
and should have only limited powers over men, Bentham argued that
the only limits which needed to be observed by society in its powers
over its people derived from the principle of utility.

Throughout the eighteenth century it was Locke's ideals which
generally had the upper hand with the ruling classes—the landed
aristocracy. But precisely because they *were* the ruling classes they
never felt the need to take steps formally to limit the sovereignty of
Parliament to bring the constitutional position more into line with
the theories which they espoused. But when the American colonies
rebelled in 1776 and eventually established their own system of
government, the ideals which were adopted by the founding fathers
of the American constitution were the ideals of Locke. Hence, the
American constitution rejected outright the concept of a supreme
or sovereign legislature with unlimited legal power over the people.
The American system of government rested from the outset on the
belief that political power belongs to the people, not to governments
or legislatures, to whom only limited authority is delegated. And
very shortly after the establishment of the United States, the Bill
of Rights—consisting of ten amendments to the federal constitution
—was duly passed. The Bill of Rights consisted essentially of a
statement of certain basic or fundamental rights which were believed
to belong to the people, and to be *inviolate* at the hands of government. So neither the federal government, nor the Congress, nor
the state governments or legislatures had or have the legal power to
take away these constitutionally guaranteed rights. Among the most
important of these rights are the right of free speech, the protection
of life, liberty, and property (which can only be taken away 'by due
process of law'), and rights of peaceful assembly and association.
Later amendments have added other fundamental rights, such as the
guarantee of the equal protection of the laws.

At the time when the American Bill of Rights was passed it is
unlikely that there was much in it to which the English ruling classes

would have taken serious exception. But, as suggested above, being conscious of their own position they never felt the need to limit the constitutional powers of Parliament and government in the way that the American rebels did. So the ultimate supremacy of Parliament remained the leading characteristic of the English constitution through the centuries, and as political power manifestly no longer rests exclusively in the hands of one ruling class, the question is being increasingly discussed whether limitations do not need to be imposed on the power of Parliament, the House of Commons, or both. As previously mentioned, this discussion is today centring on three particular issues: the electoral system, the House of Lords, and a possible Bill of Rights.

Alteration of the electoral system does not necessarily raise questions about the unlimited powers of Parliament, but it is, all the same, closely associated with the other issues. For it is well known that the present electoral system produces extreme disparities between the total popular vote and representation in the House of Commons. This affects, in particular, minority parties like the Liberal Democrats. In recent elections the Liberal Democrats or their predecessors, the Liberals (or the Liberal/SDP Alliance) have polled as many as 20 per cent of the total votes cast in a general election while only obtaining a little over 2 per cent of the seats in the House of Commons. But it also affects the majority parties, in that a party can actually secure a majority of seats in the Commons with a minority even of the total votes cast; and more commonly, it can happen that a party loses votes in the country but increases its representation in the Commons, or vice versa. These facts are well known, and it is surely something to do with the long tradition of positivist constitutional and legal thought which has so far prevented them from raising doubts about the legitimacy of the political and constitutional process. For they do and must raise such doubts, since the reason why the major political parties are unwilling to discuss serious reform of the electoral process is precisely because they are the beneficiaries of the present system. Traditionally, the electoral process is seen as a political question to be resolved in the last resort by Parliament itself; but dissatisfaction may increasingly be felt about this traditional answer when the very question at issue is whether

Parliament as at present elected adequately represents the people. Questions of legitimacy are especially likely to be raised if (for instance) a future Parliament were to vote for still further strengthening of the European Community without consulting the electorate in a referendum.

In the United States, analogous (though different) questions have been raised by shifts in population which have led to some population centres being grossly over- or under-represented in their state legislatures. In a famous case in 1962 (*Baker* v. *Carr* 369 US 186 (1962)) the Supreme Court of the United States declared that such a state of affairs violated the rights of the electors to the equal protection of the laws which is guaranteed by the fourteenth amendment of the federal constitution. In England, of course, no recourse to the courts is possible, though the Liberal party did present a petition to the European Court of Human Rights in 1980 claiming that the British electoral system was a violation of the European Convention on Human Rights. A finding against the British Government would of course have been gravely embarrassing, but in the event the petition was found inadmissible, and was never judged on its merits.

The second issue referred to above concerns the position of the House of Lords. This too is related to the other questions, although it would be quite possible to change the composition and nature of the upper House without altering the fundamental constitutional supremacy of Parliament as a whole. But the questions are closely connected, because one check upon the legal powers of Parliament is that there are two Houses; and although the Lords has, in general, power only to delay legislation passed by the House of Commons, one important legal power it still retains relates to the duration of the life of Parliament. A bill to prolong the life of Parliament still requires the consent of the House of Lords, and if that House were totally abolished there would be no legal check of any kind (the European dimension apart) on the constitutional supremacy of a temporary majority in the House of Commons. Reform of the House of Lords has not been a very live issue since the Labour party dropped its threat to abolish the House of Lords without replacing it, though Labour may well take the subject up again if it wins the next election. It seems, however, that that party now favours reform rather than abolition of the House of Lords, so legitimacy is unlikely to be in issue.

A Bill of Rights?

The third possible change referred to above is the enactment and entrenchment of a Bill of Rights in this country. A Bill of Rights is generally taken to mean some set of constitutional guarantees which are given a special status by law. This status must normally mean that rights so guaranteed cannot be reduced or taken away by ordinary executive or even legislative actions. So even an Act of Parliament which impinged on a Bill of Rights would be void.

As we saw earlier, until the *Factortame* case recognized the supremacy of European Community Law over that of the UK, it was not possible, as a matter of law, to recognize any fundamental rights as having any special legal significance. Of course, we have long been a democratic nation, and many rights are, in a political sense, fundamental to democracies: the right to vote, for instance, and the right of free speech and a free press. And in some countries these rights have some sort of guaranteed status, which means that it may not be possible to overturn them or violate them by ordinary legislation. In the United States, for instance, the Bill of Rights—consisting of a series of amendments to the federal constitution—limits the legal power of Congress, and the state legislatures in a variety of ways. Legislation which contravenes the Bill of Rights can be declared void by the courts, and in this way the rights of the people may be better protected than where the legislature is legally uncontrolled.

The arguments in favour of a Bill of Rights are, in brief, that there are certain basic human rights which ought not to be at the mercy of a government or legislature; that governments and legislatures derive their powers from the people, and that the people cannot be assumed to have granted away unlimited and despotic powers just because they have elected a parliament (by a process set by parliament itself); that a majority of the people is no doubt entitled to elect a majority government and parliament to represent their views, but this does not give, and ought not to give, that government and parliament unlimited power to oppress the minority or minorities; and that in particular the basic structure of the democratic pocess— which alone gives legitimacy to the powers of governments and parliaments—ought to be entrenched so as to be unalterable by parliament. Additionally, it is often argued that, in times of stress, a government or legislature can be whipped up by a sort of mass hysteria into legislating oppressively against minorities, and that a Bill of Rights, passed when passions are cooler, may actually reflect the popular will more genuinely than such legislation.

For a long time these arguments have seemed theoretical in the British context. The sovereignty of Parliament was for so long the central feature of our constitution that English lawyers and politicians were rather inclined to disparage the idea that a constitution should contain a Bill of Rights. Indeed, it was often suggested that our record on the protection of fundamental human rights—even without constitutional guarantees—was actually better that that of most other countries. But the trend around the democratic world is undoubtedly in favour of the principle of a Bill of Rights. Canada and New Zealand have both moved in this direction in recent times. In Australia, where the constitution contains nothing in the nature of a Bill of Rights, the High Court (as we have seen) has managed to find an implied right to free communication of opinions. And even in this country, discussion of the legal role and status of fundamental rights has begun to assume major practical importance as a result of two important developments. The first of these is the *Factortame* decision which, as we have already seen, establishes the supremacy in our own courts of European Community law. Now the European Treaties do not have a general or broad-based Bill of Rights on the American model, partly because the Community did not start as an attempt to create a political entity in which the central focus might have been on the rights of citizens and the powers of state institutions. Instead, the Community began as a common market with its main focus on the ideas of free movement of labour, capital, and goods across the member states. At the same time Community law does protect certain rights which are central to the whole idea of a common market. For instance, the right of free movement for people across the national boundaries, and the right to work in any member state are rights guaranteed by the Treaties. The Treaties also contain a provision guaranteeing equality of treatment in employment for both sexes, and this has proved a major source of anti-discrimination litigation before the courts. National laws which contravene the Treaties are now invalid, so these new rights are in the legal sense fundamental rights which cannot be interfered with or cut down by ordinary national legislation. In this sense we are in the process of acquiring a limited sort of Bill of Rights through decisions of the courts, and especially of the Court of Justice of the European Community, as these interpret and apply the Treaties to particular situations.

To illustrate—one field where some of these decisions has been of great importance concerns the terms of employment and the pension rights of women. Now we in the UK have had our own anti-discrimination legislation for some years; indeed, under the Sex Discrimination Acts it has been unlawful to discriminate against women (or men) with regard to ordinary employment contracts for over twenty years. But the UK legislation does not go so far as Community law in several important respects, and in the past few years many important decisions of the European Court have insisted on the paramountcy of Community law where there is such a divergence. For example, the Treaties allowed member states to retain for a limited period (which has not yet expired) different retirement ages for men and women under their social security systems. This was a long-standing tradition and it was felt that change on this matter could not be suddenly required—though the change will come eventually. But many countries, including the UK, understood the special exemption for social security laws to apply also to company pension schemes, and these schemes accordingly were allowed by the Sex Discrimination Act to treat men and women differently too. A few years ago the European Court held that this was a mistake: there was no exemption in the Treaties for private pension plans, and in so far as the British Sex Discrimination Act permitted it, the Act was invalid. This decision had enormous financial implications because it meant that women were now entitled to have the same pension rights as men, and for some years it remained unclear precisely how far back this went. Did it mean, for instance, that women were entitled to count their service with their employers ever since the UK joined the Community as giving them these new pension rights? The potential costs of doing this were estimated to be many billions of pounds, and the most extreme results of this were only avoided by an amendment to the main Community Treaties inserted into the Maastricht Treaty in 1992.

Another significant decision of the European Court recently invalidated the limits on the amounts of compensation which under the British Act could be awarded for acts of sex-discrimination. The British legislation had always limited the amounts which could be awarded for such acts, partly at least because the jurisdiction over complaints of sex- or race-discrimination is conferred on Industrial Tribunals rather than the ordinary courts, and it was felt inappropriate that these relatively humble Tribunals should have power to award unlimited sums as compensation. Now all these limits have been swept away, because the European Court has held that there must be full compensation without any artificial monetary limits for any violation of Community rights.

A third major decision was handed down in 1994. Under the British Act, many rights granted to employees are denied to part-time workers. But the House of Lords has now held that these provisions are contrary to Community law, and hence invalid, because the great majority of part-time workers are women, so the Act is in effect discriminatory.

In all these ways, therefore, Community rights are like fundamental rights, in the sense that they cannot be attacked or limited by UK legislation. But within the Community legal system itself, it must be appreciated that these rights themselves have their own hierarchy. Some, like the right not to be discriminated against on grounds of sex, are in the Treaties themselves, and could only be altered by amendment of the Treaties, that is, with the consent of all member states. These are like true constitutional rights. Other Community rights derive from Directives or other types of Community law. These are more like federal than constitutional laws: they take precedence over UK laws, but are themselves amendable relatively easily within the Community's own legal system.

But as indicated above, the Community protection of fundamental rights is still confined to a few relatively small areas of life and activity. There is nothing in the Community laws remotely like the broad, general guarantees of the American Bill of Rights. There is, for instance, nothing about rights of fair trial; nothing about a free press; nothing about racial (as opposed to sexual) discrimination; nothing about the protection of family life. But that does not mean that none of these matters could be protected under Community law. For example, because a citizen of a member state has the right to move freely around the Community, he has the right to have his family living with him, without which his own right of movement would be hollow. Similarly, because of the general ban on restraints of commercial activity in the Community, it would not be possible to ban or censor a newspaper if the newspaper circulated in the rest of the Community without restraint. As time goes on it is quite possible that the European Court will gradually enlarge the fundamental rights which are protected under Community law. In particular, the Treaties now expressly recognize that the Court is entitled to rely on the general jurisprudence of another court—namely the European Court of Human Rights. This is quite a different court, which also plays an important part in modern times in the protection of fundamental rights, and it is to this Court we must now turn.

The European Convention on Human Rights is a Treaty to which most European countries now subscribe. It contains explicit guarantees which the members undertake to observe with respect to a wide range of basic human rights—the right to a fair trial on a criminal charge, for instance; the right of free speech and a free press; limits on the kinds of punishments that can be handed down by courts or other authorities; and so on. This Treaty differs from the European Community Treaties in that its provisions are not incorporated directly in our own national law, so the rights protected by the Convention cannot be vindicated in British courts. On the other hand, the Convention also differs from many other international treaties in two important respects. First, the Convention has its own court whose task it is to hear complaints and decide whether the Convention has been violated. And secondly, individuals (and not just governments) have the right to challenge states under the Convention before the court. So a British citizen who believes his rights have been violated by the British government can take the government to the court for a ruling. The court is a slow-moving institution, and its procedure is long-winded and cumbersome, though moves are afoot to abbreviate them somewhat. But it has, all the same, been quite effective in the last twenty or thirty years. A string of cases has been taken to the court (often called the Strasbourg Court after its place of sitting), and in many of them our government has been found to have been in breach of the Convention. It has had, therefore, to pay compensation to the individuals concerned, and also to amend the law for the future. For instance, the law relating to contempt of court was found by the court to be too restrictive of the rights of a free press, and it has subsequently been relaxed. More controversially, the court decided some years ago that corporal punishment in public schools was a degrading form of punishment and was in breach of the Convention. In this instance, it was possible for the government to ban such punishment without actually passing any new law, simply by giving instructions to local education authorities. The large number of cases in which our laws have been found to violate the Convention has somewhat dented the rather complacent view which tended to prevail before, that we were such a freedom-loving nation that constitutional guarantees were unnecessary.

All these fundamental rights which are open to some kind of judicial protection raise difficult and controversial questions about 'government by judges'. Whenever judges have the power to override legislative bodies and governments, there is likely to be opposition to the idea that this is an appropriate power for judges.

Some of this stems from party politicians, who naturally dislike the idea that their powers may be limited when they are in office, and are willing to accept the unlimited power of the opposite party when that is in office as part of the price they have to pay for the present system. The opposition of the main political parties to such a loss of power is only to be expected and is, indeed, part of the very reason why a Bill of Rights may be needed; so this is not a serious argument against the proposal, though the organized and systematic opposition of the politicians might in practice make it difficult to carry through.

A second argument against the proposal is simply that it is un-democratic. The elected Parliament represents the people, so it is reasoned, and ought therefore to be legally able to pass any laws it wishes. But this argument begs too many questions: it assumes that Parliament 'represents' the people, which it only does in a very limited sense, and (frequently) only for a very short time after it has been elected. It also assumes that a majority of the people are entitled to do anything they like, at the expense of a minority, which is one of the very ideas denied by the supporters of a Bill of Rights. It may also be suggested—though this is doubtless highly controversial—that pure, undiluted democracy is a dangerous and unacceptable form of government if it means that every decision that has to be taken by governments (let alone by courts) must be in accordance with the popular will. Even in relatively educated soci-eties, with relatively sophisticated electorates, the government and legislature can come under enormous pressure from an inflammat-ory, prejudiced, and often ignorant media. The media may claim to represent the views of the ordinary man (and woman) in the street, but if they do, this may suggest that the man in the street would not be a fit person to have in charge of a government. The truth is that democracy requires the views of the man in the street to be expressed at elections from time to time, but it does not necessarily mean that a majority is entitled to have unrestricted power over the community as a whole. Indeed, it may be suggested that as the Western democratic ideal comes to be increasingly triumphant throughout the world, the next major task for many democracies is to decide how to limit and control their newly empowered majorit-ies. A Bill of Rights, restricting the powers of majorities by protect-ing the rights of the people, is one way of doing this.

But there is a third argument against a Bill of Rights which is a much more serious one. It may be conceded that there ought to be some limits to political power and legislative power in the interests of the rights of the people as against the government and Parliament. But it may be argued that the real question is who is to determine what these limits are. The present situation leaves the decision to be made by the *self-restraint* of Parliament. The only feasible alternat-ive is to hand the power over to the judges, and make it a matter of formal law. A Bill of Rights which is formally entrenched in the constitution would mean that the judges would become the ultimate arbiters of the powers of Parliament. A long historical tradition has rendered this acceptable to the people of the United States, but it is often argued that it would be less acceptable in this country. Here the people do not trust the judges with political-type decision-making; they would not accept the legitimacy of constitutional adjudication by the judges. Moreover, it is also said, with some truth, that American judges have become used to interpreting the broad declarations of their Bill of Rights in ways which differ significantly from the narrow and literal methods of interpretation commonly used by English judges in interpreting ordinary Acts of Parliament. If a Bill of Rights were ever entrenched in this country, there is no doubt that the result could be disastrous unless the judges were persuaded to alter their traditional methods of interpretation. For traditional and crabbed methods of interpretation could often lead to the invalidation of legislation which is absolutely necessary to keep pace with changing values or conditions; huge tensions would then build up in the legal and political system, and general discredit could be thrown on the law.

Finally, it is said by many, especially those on the political left, that the interpretation of a Bill of Rights would frequently involve decisions of a political character, and even if there were no objections of principle to handing these decisions to judges, the fact is that judges in this country tend to be politically conservative, and to be upholders of traditionally conservative, or perhaps liberal, ideologies.

So the argument against a Bill of Rights is basically an argument in favour of trusting Parliament, and relying on elections as the only real way of controlling Parliament. To people brought up under a different tradition, this is an inadequate protection. Americans who hear that Britain has no Bill of Rights are often aghast. What is to stop Parliament from doing the most heinous and iniquitous things, they ask? But it is not always certain that judges can be relied upon to stop heinous and iniquitous acts better than legislatures. This is a problem especially when there is honest and violent disagreement about what is heinous or iniquitous. Many people disagree, for instance, with the Strasbourg Court's decision that corporal punishment in school is degrading and should not be permitted. It is far from certain that a bill to prohibit this would actually pass in the House of Commons. Is there any reason to think that this sort of decision is better made by judges than by governments and parliaments? Many people would argue that this is not really a question of law for judges but a question of policy for politicians.

One argument for leaving this kind of decision to judges is that the procedure of courts is more likely to lead to calm and reasonably dispassionate analysis of the issues. Judges are, of course, as liable to be influenced by their cultural predispositions as politicians, but they do tend to be less strongly passionate or partisan on issues of this nature. The nature of their profession also imposes a greater obligation to be consistent in the application of their principles, or at least to aim for consistency. If we would all agree that degrading punishments should not be permitted in our society (and our signature to the Convention suggests we do agree at least on that), we must recognize that the question of what is a degrading punishment is likely to be controversial, but at least a court comprising judges of many European countries is likely to strive for a broad European-cultured answer to the question. If it turns out that most of these judges do think that corporal punishment in schools is degrading, perhaps those who think differently should re-examine their own beliefs rather than criticize the court for making 'policy' decisions.

All the same, there are serious worries about leaving issues of this kind to judges rather than to elected politicians, and the experience of the United States shows that in the long run a judiciary which does not exercise great self-restraint in wielding these powers is likely to become seriously politicized. The powers of the United States Supreme Court on matters of this kind are so great that everyone recognizes and believes that their decision-making is largely political, even though judicial language remains couched in legal terms. But the more political the court's function has come to be, the more political the appointment process for judges tends to become. In England, and most of Europe, judges are appointed for recognized professional skill and competence as lawyers. But judges of the United States Supreme Court are appointed primarily for their allegiance to the President's political ideology, though appointments have to be confirmed by the Senate. In recent years, as the Senate has come increasingly to appreciate the immense political powers of the Supreme Court, their confirmation hearings have themselves become increasingly political, and so, for instance, senators may even question nominees about how they will decide cases raising this or that issue. Sensible nominees try to avoid answering the questions, but they are often placed in difficulties by statements they may have made, as judges, in earlier cases. English lawyers and politicians find this kind of thing very distasteful, and tend to think it does no good to the reputation of the judiciary for impartiality. But the more politically controversial decisions the judges are asked to make, the more we shall run the risk of politicizing the judiciary.

For many of these reasons, politicians in Britain have tended to be opposed to the idea of entrenching a Bill of Rights in our constitution. At one time, indeed, the Labour party was intensely hostile to the whole idea, thinking that the judiciary was politically rather conservative, and that a Bill of Rights would enable them to stifle a radical Labour government's programme. But now that we have begun to see fundamental rights protected by the Court of the European Community, and also the European Court of Human Rights, more people are beginning to ask why the European Convention should not be incorporated into our own laws. It seems strange that Parliament is willing to have foreign judges tell it what it may not do, but denies the same power to English judges. Besides, the present situation is an absurdity. Too often we have seen recent battles about fundamental rights taken all the way through our own legal system, with the House of Lords deciding against the complainant on the basis of English law, and the case then proceeding to Strasbourg where, perhaps three years later, and after enormous additional legal costs have been incurred, the British government is told that our laws violate the Convention. The complainant then has to be compensated and the law changed. It would be a great deal simpler, many people now argue, if English judges could in the first instance take account of the Convention, thus obviating the need for many of these cases to go to the Strasbourg Court. If this were attempted there might be technical legal difficulty in providing some way for

English judges to declare Acts of Parliament void, but the *Factortame* decision is a precedent which shows that this can now be done. At the same time, it would have to be recognized that the long-run effects of doing this would be increasingly to politicize the judiciary, and probably therefore to make it the more essential to revise the current procedures for making judicial appointments.

The rejection of legitimacy

In modern times there are not lacking theorists who would press the positivist tradition to the extent of denying that the concept of legitimacy has any real meaning at all. To these theorists, all law is simply a manifestation of power. The possession of political power is, indeed, no different in essence from the possession of power by a gunman. Politicians who govern a country are just more successful power-grabbers than their opponents, and have succeeded in brain-washing the people to think that the power they wield is legitim-ate. This brainwashing is part of a deliberate propaganda exercise designed to make it easier for the politicians to retain power.

Further, to those of this persuasion, there are no natural or moral rights other than those which derive from the law itself. People may have *claims* against each other and against the State which are of a moral or political character, and the function of the law is to decide which of these claims should be recognized and converted into legal rights. It is not incompatible with such a theory to hold that the law or the State is in some sense mistaken in recognizing or refusing to recognize this or that claim: one can thus argue that there are grounds on which some claims should be recognized and others denied; but basically these grounds must all derive from the fundamental premisses of those who wield power. So one can argue that if those who hold power believe that their function is (say) to advance the public welfare, then it becomes intelligible to argue that individual claims of this or that nature should be recognized, because this is indeed the best way to forward the public welfare. But if those who hold political power simply reject the aims of others, talk of legiti-macy is idle. Thus, in the South African context it was (on this view) pointless to argue over the legitimacy of the government's apartheid policies. One could only protest that black and coloured people had *claims* against white people and against the State which, in the bad old days, the South African government refused to recognize, but one could not argue that the government was refusing to recognize their moral or political *rights*.

Put in this way, this sort of theory may sound unattractive. Few people involved in legal or political discourse are prepared to give away the idea that there are certain *rights* which ought to be respected by governments and law. But theories of this nature do at least show that, in the absence of any generally agreed way of deciding what *are* the fundamental rights which the law should recognize, the distinction between claims and rights may be largely verbal.

6 The making of law

The changing law

In modern times the law changes a great deal all the time. One way of measuring the mass of legal change is to look at volumes in which the law is recorded. Each year one or two volumes of statute law are added to the statute book, though a good proportion of this is often in replacement of earlier legislation, which is thereupon repealed. In addition, there are usually two or three large volumes of statutory instruments made every year, though here again much of this is in replacement of earlier instruments. Then there is case law which is recorded in the law reports. Each year there are added to the semi-official law reports one (sometimes two) large volumes of reports from the Queen's Bench cases (including cases decided in the Court of Appeal on appeal from the Queen's Bench Division); in addition there are usually two (somewhat smaller) volumes containing cases from the Chancery Division and the Family Division of the High Court (and Court of Appeal appeals from those divisions). Then there is the Appeal Cases volume which contains only appeals to the House of Lords and Privy Council; the latter are not usually appeals from English courts at all but from various Commonwealth courts, but since the law they deal with is often the same as English law, and since the judges who sit in the Privy Council are usually law lords, it is clear that Privy Council decisions may be important precedents in English law. There are also other decisions of the courts which may be of a specialized nature and do not get published in the semi-official law reports but which may be included in one of a number of series of specialized law reports such as reports of road-traffic cases, commercial cases, tax cases, and so on. There is much duplication between the sets of reports, but probably all the new reported cases in each year would fill some six volumes of reports.

On top of all this English law, we now have to cope with the changing European Community law too. Although the annual output of European law has actually declined recently, there is still a huge mass of legislation coming from the Council of Ministers, and new regulations and decisions coming from the Commission. In addition, the European Court is adding its own formidable case law to the law reports, so that another volume or two of annual reports have to be added, devoted exclusively to Community legal cases.

The extent of legal change is now a serious problem, not only for lawyers but also for businessmen and other professional people whose work involves some contact with the law, such as accountants (who need to keep up to date with the tax laws), architects and builders (who need to know about planning laws and building regulations), and all employers of labour (who need to keep up to date with safety requirements and a whole host of other laws as to the rights of employees and the obligations of employers). For lawyers themselves, the business of keeping up to date is costly and time-consuming. Many legal publications are produced solely to help lawyers track down the latest legal developments in this or that area; legal authors have to produce new editions of their books even on standard subjects every four or five years, and in some cases almost annually, if they are to be up to date.

This hectic pace of legal change is a relatively modern phenomenon. Until the latter part of the eighteenth century the law changed much more slowly. Statutory change was very limited in its general effect until well into the nineteenth century. Most of the Acts of Parliament passed in the eighteenth century were not really designed to change the general law at all: they were private and local Acts usually designed to authorize some land- or building-development which involved some adjustments to private rights, and could therefore only be carried out (in the absence of general agreement) by the authority of Parliament. And although the common law developed in the eighteenth century as it still does today, judgments were generally much shorter then than they are now, and reports were often shorter still. The usual four-man common law court would quite often dispose of an important point in two or three pages of print, with each judge saying (or anyhow reported as saying) only enough to fill perhaps two or three paragraphs. Modern judgments are much longer than this and are usually reported in full where they are reported at all. So the report of an important and complex case can easily run to thirty or forty pages of fairly small print.

Given that the present speed of change causes so much trouble, why does it happen? One trite answer is to say that all this change is needed to keep pace with social and economic change; and of course there is some truth in this. When motor vehicles were invented, the resulting changes in the law were as important and as far-reaching for the law, as the social changes were for our way of life, and as the physical changes were for the shape of our roads and our cities. The motor vehicle has brought in its wake great developments of the criminal law and of the civil law in their concern with the duties of motorists. The changes in the civil law have brought, in their turn, developments in insurance law and practice as new problems have arisen and needed solution in connection with the compensation of those injured in road accidents, as well as those whose own vehicles are damaged. Then the vehicles themselves are the subject of regulations designed to protect the public, and similarly the road system has brought vast changes in the law—laws needed to regulate motorway traffic, traffic signals, parking, and so on.

So it is clear enough that technological changes of this character have led to a demand for much legal change. And this certainly explains some of the changes that are still constantly being made. The computer brings new dangers about private information being disseminated to all and sundry, so demands for legal regulation arise; the hovercraft, being neither ship nor aircraft, brings a need for a new form of legal regulation; the widespread availability of private tape-recorders brings the need for changes in copyright laws concerning rights in broadcast music; and so on. But it is also clear that changes of this character are very far from explaining the need for all the legal change which is now occurring. A number of other relevant factors may well be more important than technological change in explaining what is happening to the law.

Naturally, also, the European Community produces the need for much legal change to implement the very purposes the Community is designed to serve. Much press attention focuses on unfortunate examples of bureaucratic excesses emanating from Europe, though the worst examples usually turn out, on examination, to be mythical. But actually a large amount of the legislation, and also the case law, of the Community is related to the creation of the very structure and laws which the Treaties are designed to serve. Because everything is still so new, there are many unsolved problems which require legal solutions. For example, the right of a European citizen to live and work in any part of the Community brings in its wake many problems. What is to happen, for instance, to social security entitlements? Suppose a doctor or lawyer wishes to work in another member state, will his qualifications be recognized? Can a member state ban or regulate the sale of foodstuffs coming from another member state, not on the open ground that the goods are being imported (which would plainly be unlawful under Community law) but on the different ground that (say) the goods contain some chemical component which the equivalent home-produced foods do not contain? The attempt to create a single market, and ensure the free flow of goods and services across the Community, brings in its wake huge numbers of new problems to which legal answers are required.

So it is obvious enough that these new political, social, and economic conditions generate a need for much new law, though it is perhaps unfortunate how little attention is sometimes paid to their cost before they are implemented. But there are other broad considerations which are relevant too. The most basic factor is probably one that was alluded to in Chapter 4, namely, the fact that much law is nowadays avowedly seen as an instrument of political or social or economic change. This means that whenever there is a change of goals among those in charge of the country, a change of laws is likely to be inevitable. A change of government must bring new changes in the law because a new government wants to aim in different directions. It wants to increase (or decrease) the power of the unions, to increase (or decrease) taxes, and so on. Similarly, if less dramatically, the precise type of instrumentality needed may change even if the goals themselves do not, and this may happen just because of a change of political ideology; for instance, one party wishes to stimulate industry by freeing it from regulation, while another party wishes to stimulate industry by introducing new import controls or the like. Further, given the extent to which governments these days have become involved in management of the economy, and their general lack of success at this management, it is not surprising to find that they frequently wish to change the precise methods of management while still retaining the same ultimate goal.

Because of the rather volatile political climate in which we have recently been living, changes of this character are apt to be frequent and often frustrating, if not stultifying, for those not closely involved in the political process itself. But there are also other causes of change in the law which are more deep-seated and which lead to changes over a broad front which are not nearly so reversible, at any rate in the short term. In particular, change in society's value system, in the sense of justice itself, is and has been for centuries a cause of legal change which is both widespread and deep. It is worth devoting consideration to some examples of change in attitudes, in moral beliefs. First, and perhaps greatest of all, has been the growing strength of the egalitarian ideal over the last 150 or 200 years. In earlier times this led to obvious legal changes such as the gradual emancipation of married women, and the spread of the franchise; in modern times it has led to the democratization of the jury, and the prohibition of certain types of discrimination based on race or sex. But it has also led to more subtle changes in the law and in the practice of the law. For example, it has led to pressure for greater conformity of judicial practice in relation to sentencing as well as in the award of damages. It has often led to, or helped, the gradual expansion of various forms of common law liability, because a feature of the step-by-step process of common law development is the way in which each case is often felt to be morally indistinguishable from an earlier one; hence the argument for like treatment is overpowering if one moves one step at a time. But eventually it becomes clearer that the last step leads to a result which is quite different from the first step.

Another way in which the ideal of equality has profoundly altered moral and legal attitudes lies perhaps deeper still in our social and economic system and in the law. This concerns attitudes to risk. In the early days of the Industrial Revolution there is evidence that one of the functions of the socio-economic and legal system was thought to be that of allocating risks: risks of loss and risks also of gain. So a bargain, a transaction, a co-operative venture of some kind might lead to great losses for some and great profits for others, and the result was morally and legally acceptable. Today, it seems much less acceptable. The ideal which today underlies many forms of risk is that risks should be shared, more or less equally, among those concerned rather than allocated to one or other party. This sort of change in belief has, of course, led to profound shifts in political ideology and hence to changes in the law as a mere instrumentality of the politicians. But it has also led to many changes in the law administered by judges, although this is only now coming to be perceived.

A second major change in moral values and beliefs which has had tremendous repercussions for the law concerns ideas of responsibility. The law is obviously very much concerned with questions of legal responsibility—who is responsible for this or that event, for this or that loss or injury, is a question of profound importance for the law of obligations as well as the criminal law. But notions of legal responsibility are inevitably closely bound up with notions of moral responsibility, and as these have changed, so the law has imperceptibly followed suit. Some of the changes are fairly obvious: a much greater willingness to impute responsibility for some situation to the State, for instance, leads to laws providing for social security, or the homeless. Similarly, belief that certain types of antisocial activity (over-extending oneself with hire-purchase commitments, for instance, leading to non-payment of instalments) are not 'really' the responsibility of the debtor but are the result of 'social pressures', leads to laws which protect the defaulting debtor to a greater or lesser degree. Other changes in concepts of moral and legal responsibility are more subtle. For instance, there is a growing willingness to treat someone as responsible for an accident which he has *failed to prevent*, even though another person is more immediately and directly concerned. A workman who falls off dangerous scaffolding because he has refused to wear safety harness, for instance, may today be able to persuade a court that his employer is 'really' responsible, because he failed to order or cajole the workman into wearing the harness. A hundred years ago such an argument would have been unsustainable; today it could succeed. Similarly, there is increasing willingness today to hold a landowner liable for injuries caused by serious dangers on his land even to trespassers, especially child or 'technical' trespassers. Here the changes in moral attitudes are better recognized perhaps, but then there are again other less obvious cases, as where, for instance, a danger arises on a person's land which he did not himself create. A hundred years ago judges would probably have said that a landowner was not generally liable for dangers on his land not created by him (or anyhow his workmen); today a court is more likely to say that landownership carries responsibilities as well as rights, and it is the landowner's responsibility to remove dangers from his land even if he did not create them.

A third major change in values which has had dramatic effects on the law concerns marriage, divorce, and sexual behaviour generally. The gradual liberalization of divorce laws has, of course, been going on for a long time; but in the past twenty-five years or so the changes in the law have been very fast, and have reflected the social revolution which has taken place. The introduction of what is, to a large degree, a 'no-fault' system of divorce reflects modern ideas that the breakdown of a marriage is rarely the fault of one party alone, and that ideas of fault are anyhow out of place in personal relations of this kind. Here we see how changing notions of individual responsibility have combined with changing values about sexual behaviour to affect the law. Adultery is no longer the heinous social and legal offence it once was: it is merely a matter of a change in sexual taste, so (for instance) the party who has committed adultery is no longer deprived of rights to custody of children, nor of rights to maintenance from the other spouse. Changing concepts of property rights have also combined with changing values about marriage and marital relationships to produce major changes in the law in the very practical issue of housing. It is now not uncommon for a wife to obtain an order from a court ejecting her husband from the matrimonial home (even though it is his house), on the ground that she and her children have a stronger claim to remain there because their need is greater.

Other major changes in legal attitudes and in the law itself have taken place with regard to the position of cohabitees. At one time unmarried parties living together would have been regarded by courts as beyond the pale, and outside the protection of the legal system. Arrangements between such couples were formerly (indeed, within living memory) stigmatized as 'illegal' (though not necessarily criminal), and contracts involving such cohabitation were not enforceable. Today the courts have virtually forgotten this old law, and have even begun the process of protecting the rights of those involved when such a relationship breaks down.

A fourth area in which changing attitudes have led to major shifts in the law concerns the employment relationship. Putting on one side altogether the highly controversial questions of strikes, picketing, and other industrial action, it can hardly be denied that the relationship between the individual employee and his employer has today been revolutionized by law. Much of this is due to statute law, creating new rights for the employee, for instance, the right to demand compensation for 'unfair dismissal', rights to redundancy payments, rights to trade-union membership, and so forth. But even the common law rights of employees have been improved as a result of changing judicial attitudes in various respects. For example, the sort of behaviour which would formerly have been held to justify instant dismissal without notice would today often be held not to have that effect (such an issue can still arise as a matter of ordinary contract law, or under the 'unfair dismissal' legislation). Again, actions for damages for personal injuries brought by employees against their employers are generally treated much more sympathetically today by judges, even as a matter of ordinary common law. For instance, many judges are reluctant to find that an employee has been guilty of 'contributory negligence' where his conduct, though perhaps strictly blameworthy, has been a momentary act of thoughtlessness in the stress of factory work. Cases in the last century on such matters are no longer safe precedents because of these changes in judicial attitude.

These are just four examples of the way in which changes in moral and social beliefs can have a profound effect on the law. There are, of course, many others. Changes of this character are often obscured in the law because they may take place without an overt change in the rules of law themselves. When the law is formulated in rather general terms—such as, for instance, rules of negligence requiring 'reasonable care' to be taken—ideas of what is reasonable care can change because values change; but the law itself does not give the appearance of having changed. Similarly, if the case concerns dismissal of an employee, the (common) law remains much the same as it was fifty years ago: wilful disobedience to a serious order may justify dismissal. But what is 'wilful' and what is a 'serious order' are matters on which opinion may shift. Lawyers are particularly prone to hide many of the changes which take place in this way, because it remains part of the 'official' theory that judges are not generally supposed to change the law. So it is often deliberate judicial policy to maintain the appearance of unbroken continuity in the law, and this may obscure the real extent of change.

A third reason for change in the law—though this affects mainly legislation and not the common law—is simply that, like any other institution, the law is in constant need of maintenance and repair. A considerable portion of our statute law today deals with large chunks of law like the law of landlord and tenant, tax law, or road-traffic law. These large bodies of law require periodical attention from the legislature. Things go wrong, there are unforeseen developments, cases which throw up hidden ambiguities or difficulties, there is a need to make minor adjustments arising from *other* legal or institutional change, and so forth. So there is a good deal of legislation of a relatively technical character—usually much of it is non-political —going through Parliament all the time, simply designed to keep the machine operating at acceptable levels of efficiency.

These are probably the three major reasons for most of the legal change which takes place. We are now in a position to examine the actual machinery of change: how are laws made?

European Community law

We must today begin with European Community law. It is true that a student could still study the English legal system, and learn a great deal of law, and a great deal about how laws are made without any reference to Community law. But because Community law is now similar to constitutional and federal law in a federal state, and takes precedence over English law in cases of conflict, it really makes more sense to start with Community law.

Community law starts with the Community Treaties because these are the central documents establishing the Community by agreement of all the member states, which provide the skeleton of a federal Europe, although (as we have already pointed out) there is nothing inevitable about the move towards a federal Europe. There are now many relevant Treaties, but the most important are the Treaty of Rome which established the Community in the first instance and for which legal effect was given, when the UK joined the Community, by the European Communities Act 1972; the Treaty known as the Single European Act (which is not itself an Act of the UK Parliament), to which legal effect was given by the European Communities (Amendment) Act 1986; and the Maastricht Treaty of 1992, which was given legal effect by the European Communities (Amendment) Act 1993. The founding Treaty of Rome, together with the later changes, is now reproduced in the 1993 Act, so that Act incorporates all the necessary law, so far as the Treaties themselves are concerned.

Unfortunately, the result of the Maastricht Treaty is to produce a confusing system of law-making for the new Europe, rather than a simple legislative structure. In a book of this kind it would be pointless to attempt to describe this in great detail. Essentially, a triangular arrangement still exists between the Commission, the Council, and the European Parliament. The Parliament, it must first be grasped, is not a general legislature for Europe. Its powers are still extremely limited. Most law-making is done by the Council, on the recommendations of the Commission, after consulting the Parliament. This law-making generally takes the form of Directives, which are addressed to the member states, and have to be implemented by the member states passing them into law through their own internal procedures. But Directives can also have *direct effect* where they are precise enough to operate without further implementation, though only as against governments themselves. However, there are now also European Regulations, which are a sort of general law of the Community, binding on everybody and on all the member states without further implementation. The procedure for the making of Regulations is more cumbersome and long-winded than that for Directives, which can still be made in some cases without even consultation with the Parliament.

The role of the Parliament varies with the kind of law in question. In some cases the Parliament is effectively given a right of veto over Commission proposals, rather than an initiating power, or even an amending power. The Parliament is, however, trying to work out a process by which it may threaten to veto a proposed new law, unless the Council agrees to incorporate amendments which the Parliament wishes to see introduced. In other cases the Parliament has a more substantial 'co-operation power'—at present this applies especially to law-making relating to the social provisions (from which the UK has opted out) and some monetary and economic provisions. Under this procedure, Commission proposals are laid before the Council and the Parliament in the first instance. The Parliament may then communicate its views to the Council, which has to take account of them before formulating its final proposals. These proposals are then returned to the Parliament which has a second chance of making its views felt. From then on, the procedures become more and more complex if there is disagreement between the Community's three main arms, as attempts must be made to secure agreement between them.

It is all exceedingly complex and cumbersome, and opens the door to challenges before the Court on the ground that the correct procedure has not been followed in any particular instance. It seems improbable that these legislative procedures can be maintained for long, and some simplification and streamlining must surely be aimed at when the Treaties next fall to be reconsidered at the intergovernmental conference in 1996.

Apart from Community legislation, decisions of the European Court are a major source of law for Community purposes. It has already been seen that these decisions can today involve the overriding of national legislation, so court decisions are now assuming within the Community the same importance that they have in federal constitutions where it is for the courts to decide upon conflicts of authority between the various political organs involved. Again, it is impossible to discuss this complex matter in great detail in a book of this nature, but it must be realized that, as in most federal legal systems, many of the central texts which constitute the agreed charter of the legal system are drawn up in broad, general language. The Treaty of Rome (and its subsequent amendments) is certainly much longer than the federal constitution of the United States, but it is still much less detailed than normal English legislation. For example, Article 119 of the Treaty of Rome, in three short paragraphs containing eleven lines of print, enshrines the entire principle of equality for men and women. This can be compared with the Sex Discrimination Act 1975 which introduced this principle into English law for the first time, and occupies eighty-seven sections and six schedules, and runs to some forty or more pages of print. What this means is that the detailed effect of Article 119 of the Treaty of Rome has to be worked out through decisions of the European Court, rather than through the legislation itself.

In this way case law becomes a far more important source of law in this kind of legal system than it is even in a system such as that of the UK where the system of precedent is well-established. Because much of it is of a constitutional character, the relationship of this case law to ordinary legislation is also very different. Ordinary English case law has in the past been easily reversible by Parliament where the results prove unsatisfactory for one reason or another. Decisions of the European Court on the interpretation of the Treaties may not be reversible by ordinary national legislation or even ordinary Community legislation. They may only be amendable by amendments to the Treaties themselves, which is a bit like amending a federal constitution. Amending federal constitutions is usually made rather difficult, because the whole point of a constitution is that it is designed to be the fundamental arrangement concerning the distribution of legal and political power, which is necessarily the result of compromise among the various contending groups. So a constitution cannot normally be amended by ordinary legislation; constitutional amendment usually requires a more complex procedure, frequently involving three-quarter majorities in legislative assemblies and, in federal states, requiring the concurrence of the federal authorities and a large proportion of the state authorities as well. But amending the Community Treaties is even more difficult than this; it actually requires unanimity among all the member states, and it is obviously not easy to reverse or amend a European Court decision in this way, especially as the number of member states grows. But it has been done in one case. The decision of the European Court in the *Barber* case, holding that Article 119 of the Treaty of Rome banned all sex-discrimination in company pension plans, had potentially immensely serious financial implications. The retrospective effect of the decision was therefore limited by a clause in the Maastricht Treaty.

There is no doubt that the Community legal system is at present a very *messy* legal system, and it must be undertood that objections to a messy legal system are not simply based on an aesthetic desire for tidiness. A messy legal system generates great uncertainties, as well as great costs. Many legal problems now require research into two entirely different legal systems before the law can be ascertained. Even lawyers will find it very difficult in many cases to say what the law is when much depends on the case law of the European Court. In the Sunday trading cases, referred to earlier, two successive cases had to be taken to the European Court before the Community legal position was established with any clarity; and taking a case to the European Court is a very lengthy and expensive procedure. Because the Community is still in process of being established, and the Treaties have so far been the subject of several major amending Treaties, the messiness and consequential uncertainties are at present greatly magnified. Even an ordinary and well-established federal legal system, like that of the United States or Australia, tends to generate more uncertainty in its law than a unitary system of law like that of England in pre-Community times. But the uncertainties in the Community legal system and their impact on the English legal system are much greater.

Another result of the messiness deriving from Community law is common to most federal systems. There is a sense in which any federal system tends to make the law less *rational*. This is because it is often not possible for politicians and governments to achieve their goals in the simplest and most direct way. The simplest and most direct route may be barred to them because of constitutional or, in our case, Community laws which deprive our government and

Parliament of the power to go down this route. They may still be able to achieve their goals by following a more tortuous route, however, so inevitably the law becomes less straightforward. What is even worse is that in following tortuous and indirect routes to their goals, governments and Parliament may have to accept that they do not have power to achieve *all* their goals by these means, so the laws they introduce may only apply to some of the cases they would like to cover. All this means that clean and straightforward reforms by neat legislative solutions become more difficult, and in many cases impossible in federal legal systems whose essential characteristics the Community legal order already possesses in this regard. In the very long run this may have the effect of making court decisions more important as a way of modernizing the law even than legislation, something that has already largely happened in the United States. But there are special features of the American system that other federal systems do not share, and it may be that the Community can avoid these extreme results.

UK legislation

It is almost a relief to turn from these complexities to the internal position of the law-making process in the UK, and especially in England which is our main concern. UK legislation consists of laws enacted by Parliament (which are known as Acts or Statutes, though individually modern Acts are almost invariably called Acts) and of subordinate legislation (known as statutory instruments) made under the authority of Parliament, usually by ministers, either individually or, more formally, sitting in the Privy Council, when the resulting law is known as an Order in Council.

Acts of Parliament are, of course, the most important types of law in the sense that major political and social change can only be implemented by such Acts. In modern times the great bulk of legislation passed by Parliament is government legislation introduced by ministers on behalf of the government, and passed by Parliament at the behest of the government. Government bills can be, and are, amended in the course of their passage through Parliament, but in normal times they are never rejected. Rejection of a government bill could only come about through a back-bench revolt which would probably entail the dissolution of Parliament, or as a result of a mis-calculation by the party whips about the number of their members actually in the House, and this very rarely happens. Of course the position of a minority government is somewhat different, and such a government may have to accept its inability to carry certain bills through Parliament. But except for some of the years 1974–9, we have not seen minority governments since 1931, and there does not appear to be any immediate likelihood that they are about to return as a regular feature of our political system.

Bills are introduced into either House of Parliament, though bills on more contentious matters usually originate in the Commons. A bill must be carried in both Houses, except in the case of finance bills which only need approval from the Commons; but since the Parliament Act 1911 it has been possible for the Commons to pass legislation on all topics without the concurrence of the Lords by the mere process of passing it more than once. Originally, such a bill had to be passed three times by the Commons over a two-year period, but since the Parliament Act 1949 it is enough for the Commons to pass a bill twice, over a one-year period. Procedure in the two Houses varies slightly, but in both Houses there are several stages to the passing of a bill, technically called 'readings', and a Committee Stage. In fact bills are not literally 'read' at 'readings'— which would be a very time-consuming and wasteful exercise. In the House of Commons there are three 'readings' and a Committee Stage, but the first reading is a pure formality. At the second reading the general principles of a bill are debated, and it is then passed to a Committee (which may confusingly be a Committee of the whole House) for detailed discussion and amendment. After the Committee has finished with a bill it is reported to the House, which then has a 'Report Stage', and this is followed by the third reading at which the bill as amended is put up for final debate and passed. It is then sent to the House of Lords where the process is repeated with minor variations; in the event of any amendments being made in the Lords, the bill is then returned to the Commons to obtain agreement to these amendments. If the amendments are not agreed, the bill re-turns to the House of Lords, and in theory it can be sent back and forth until its sponsors drop it. In practice, disagreement can only occur if the House of Lords insists on amendments to a bill which are against the government's wishes. Usually, indeed almost invariably, the Lords give way after some huffing and puffing, and the bill is passed in the form the government wants.

All this may suggest that legislation is 'made' by Parliament. But appearances are deceiving. Parliament has to pass the final version of the bill if it is to become an Act, though it sometimes does so with great reluctance. But Parliament does not draft bills, and even its powers of amendment are in practice modest in the extreme. The great majority of amendments made to bills are actually the government's own amendments. Many of these stem from second thoughts on the part of the draftsman or the minister or his department; many of them will be the result of consultations and representations (quite often from other government departments) after the bill is first published and introduced into Parliament, which arise from points previously overlooked; some of them, it is true, will be a result of the minister making a concession to his back-benchers, and occasionally even to the Opposition, or the House as a whole. But concessions of this kind are not common. In a study of legislation in the period 1967–71 Professor John Griffith found that while government amendments to bills were always carried, only about 10 per cent of back-bench amendments and fewer than 5 per cent of Opposition amendments were passed. It is also rare for a concession to be made which involves any alteration in the fundamental basis on which a bill has already been drafted, though conversely it is not true that all concessions are purely cosmetic or trivial amendments. Even amendments made in the House of Lords are predominantly government amendments, so the common claim that the Lords do a good job as a 'revising' second Chamber is at best misleading. If this was the only or best argument for a second Chamber, its function could be just as efficiently performed by the Commons adding a fourth reading to its handling of a bill, perhaps after a prescribed interval of a month or two, to enable final tidying-up to be done.

The time spent by Parliament on most of the bills it passes is also quite small. Professor Griffith, in the study previously referred to, found that the average time spent on a bill totalled between sixteen and twenty-three hours; but no fewer than 74 out of 183 bills were dispatched in under five hours all told.

It is clear that in practice bills are not seriously 'made' by Parliament. They are actually made, hammered out in principle and in detail, by a number of groups usually working closely together; these consist of, first, the politicians, secondly, the departmental policy-makers, thirdly, the departmental lawyers, and fourthly, the draftsmen. The politicians are, of course, ultimately responsible for the main goals which a bill sets out to achieve. In cases of major political legislation the outlines of a bill may have been thrashed out by shadow ministers and their party advisers while in Opposition; they may even have been agreed by the Shadow Cabinet and the bill may have been mentioned in the election manifesto. A good deal of hard work may go into preparing the main structure of a bill in this way before it is even considered by the civil service, but press talk suggesting that a new government sometimes takes office with draft bills already prepared is almost invariably erroneous; and a party which does prepare draft bills in Opposition is usually wasting its time. As we shall see later, it has always been a firm rule, adhered to by all governments, that government bills must be drafted by Parliamentary Counsel.

Of course, not all bills originate with the politicians. Many bills originate in the civil service itself. Those responsible for administering a large body of law or previously established policy usually become expert at it and they learn when the law or policy is not functioning well. Over a period of time these difficulties come to be noted by officials, and they frequently lead to departmental committees (or, in more important cases, interdepartmental committees) which take a fairly technical and narrow view of the position, and go over the existing law to see what amendments are needed. This is normally done where the main structure of the law is not being seriously questioned, but nevertheless substantial reforms may be made within the existing structure. Sometimes it will be apparent that a broader review of the whole structure of the law may be required, but such a review is likely to be a major operation taking perhaps several years, and in the meantime it is desirable to make such immediate reforms as can be done. An example of this process is to be found in the Hire-Purchase Act 1964, which was in fact quite a substantial reforming measure, but was largely departmental in origin, and mostly non-political. In the process of preparing the legislation it became apparent that there was a body of opinion among lawyers which favoured a much more basic restructuring of the law, but it was also clear that a serious examination of the issues raised would take several years. So the Hire-Purchase bill was passed and became the Act of 1964. Later, in 1968, the government set up a committee to examine the whole structure of the law of consumer credit, and this committee reported in 1973 after a wide-ranging review. Then in 1974 a new bill was introduced and passed through Parliament, the Consumer Credit Act 1974, though much of this Act could not be brought into force immediately, and indeed parts of it remained inoperative for several years.

To return to the actual process of preparing bills, once the initial decision has been taken to start work on a bill, whether the impetus comes from the politicians or the civil service, a great deal of work will be done by departmental policy-makers, that is, civil servants. Usually a team will work on a project of this kind, consisting of one or more senior civil servants, such as an under-secretary, a middle-rank assistant secretary, and a principal, the most junior grade in the administrative hierarchy. Most of the spade-work will devolve on the principal, though he will have constant consultations with his assistant secretary, and probably regular meetings with the under-secretary and perhaps others. From time to time ministers will be brought in, but, unless the bill has major political implications, ministers will normally only be consulted where important decisions of principle are to be taken which will thereafter control the direction in which further work proceeds. Unless there is a particular need for confidentiality, there will often be consultation with outside interests, and in technical legislation this will be frequent or even continuous. There will often also be consultation with other government departments which may have an indirect interest in, or responsibility for, areas of administration on which the bill may impinge.

All this effort will, in principle, be devoted to working out the details of the policy implications of a change in the law. But it is usually impossible to separate the basic decisions of policy which set out the goals to be achieved from the subsidiary decisions which concern the means to be adopted. In practice, goals and means are usually very closely entwined.

At a fairly early date—depending very much on the kind of subject-matter the bill is to deal with—the departmental lawyers will be brought into the exercise. All large government departments have legal (sub-)departments headed by a 'Solicitor' (who may in fact be a barrister) and smaller departments are serviced by the Treasury Solicitor's department. These lawyers act very much in the manner that a private firm of solicitors acts; in particular, it is the Solicitor's department which briefs counsel where the client (that is, the policy-makers and politicians) needs the services of a barrister. And since all government bills are drafted by counsel, it is the Solicitor's department which must instruct counsel before a bill is drafted. In fact, lawyers from the departmental Solicitor's office quite often play a much larger role than merely to act as intermediaries between the policy-makers and the draftsman. Frequently they will be consulted on a regular basis, and sometimes will play a significant part in the formulation of policy. For, as lawyers all know, it is in practice impossible to separate the policy-making function from the legal-instrumental function. The policy-maker will constantly need advice on the side implications of his policy goals; and the lawyer will often have experience and skills which will help to decide whether the policy-maker is pursuing goals which may in fact be unattainable, or only attainable at great inconvenience or cost.

There will then be a good deal of consultation and mutual planning within the government department concerned before the policy-maker is even able to give the Solicitor's department the go-ahead for instructing the draftsman. Once this is given, the lawyers will settle down to prepare a fairly elaborate document (depending again on the complexity and magnitude of the proposals as well as the time available) in the form of 'Instructions to Counsel' to draft a bill. At this stage, if this has not already been done, much thought needs to be given to the precise way in which the new bill is to be fitted into the existing framework of the law. Every new bill of any complexity will be contiguous in a hundred different places to the remainder of the vast body of the law which will be unchanged.

Each of these points of contact has to be thought through, and a decision made as to the way in which the two bits of law are to be cemented together. There will also be a need for a number of more-or-less technical questions to be considered, such as transitional provisions to govern the actual change-over period: for instance, what is to happen to cases which arise before the bill is passed but only come to court afterwards?

Instructions to counsel to draft a bill of any complexity may themselves run to thirty or more pages; indeed, in the case of a really complex bill (assuming there is time, which there often is not), the instructions could extend to 100 pages. Before the instructions are sent to the draftsman, approval is required from the appropriate Committee of the Cabinet; this is a necessary precaution because the draftsman's office is small and very busy, and some order of priority must be imposed on departmental demands for the services of the draftsman.

The actual drafting of all government bills is today done by Parliamentary Counsel, a small office of barristers (of very high technical skill and proficiency) which is ultimately responsible to the Lord Chancellor in so far as it is under a political head at all. In fact the office of Parliamentary Counsel has been able to maintain a very high degree of independence from all political control, and to use this independence to maintain an iron grip on the shape and form of the statute book. Even Lord Chancellors and other departmental ministers have sometimes had to admit defeat at the hands of the Parliamentary Counsel, both in relation to the way a particular bill should be drafted and more generally in relation to the work of the Office and the shape of statute law. The strange power of this Office (largely unknown outside the Whitehall machine) derives chiefly from two simple facts: first, it is very small, comprising no more than about twenty to thirty draftsmen, many of whom are at any one time regarded as learning the trade, and therefore not capable of being given full responsibility for a bill; and secondly, the Office has hitherto had a monopoly on the drafting of government legislation which so far no government has been courageous enough to break. This is now changing, for in 1994 and 1995 the government insisted on putting out to tender the job of drafting a number of technical bills. This could have major implications for the way bills are drafted, because until now Parliamentary Counsel have been largely responsible for the whole style and shape of our statute law. Indeed, they have been responsible for much of the substance as well; for, as we have previously seen, it is in practice impossible to separate the formulation of basic policy goals from the implementation of those goals through law, and the draftsman, no less than the departmental lawyer, may have a significant influence on the particular way the law is used as an instrument for pursuing the chosen goals.

Of course the draftsman is not free to draft without constraints. Apart from the obvious fact that in the last analysis he must produce a bill which substantially complies with his instructions, he must bear in mind a number of other important factors. First, the draftsman today has to be sure that his bill will not conflict with European Community law, though (if the experience of federal legal systems is anything to go by) there may be occasions on which ministers insist on going ahead with a bill which the draftsman thinks will be held invalid on this ground. Secondly, the draftsman has to draft a bill which aims at different readers—on the one hand, Members of Parliament, and on the other hand, the ultimate users, lawyers, professional men, even perhaps citizens. What is needed by one class of user is not necessarily the most suitable thing for another. Thirdly, the draftsman has to bear in mind a number of facets of parliamentary procedures—for example, that in committee debates, at the end of the proceedings on proposed amendments to every clause, there is a separate motion put: 'That clause —— do stand part of the bill', and that is a motion which can be debated, and voted on. So governments prefer fewer and longer clauses in their bills, while readers might prefer more and shorter sections in their Acts. It might have been thought that the obvious answer to this problem would be an amendment to parliamentary procedure to enable several clauses to be debated together; but amending parliamentary procedure is even more difficult than amending the law.

At all events, and whatever the causes, the ultimate style and shape of much legislation is today increasingly unsatisfactory. Many statutes emerge from the parliamentary process obscure, turgid, and quite literally unintelligible without a guide or commentary. They are also drafted in a detailed way which attempts to anticipate every contingency, and this in turn adds to their unintelligibility. This last feature is partly a product of the process—there is a sort of Parkinson's Law in which too many lawyers are employed to find flaws or weaknesses in each succeeding draft produced by Parliamentary Counsel—and partly a product of history. In the last century a narrow and crabbed method of statutory interpretation was often adopted by judges, seemingly (as was jokingly said) on the principle that Parliament usually changed the law for the worse and that it was the business of the judges to keep the mischief within the narrowest bounds. This in turn led the draftsman to spell out his bills in such detail as would prevent the judges from frustrating his aims; and this, in turn, reinforced the determination of the judges to interpret legislation in the most literal fashion possible.

While judges today are unlikely seriously to attempt to sabotage an Act by narrow interpretation, the tradition of literal interpretation remains paramount with lawyers and the courts. An Act of Parliament is law in its very words. The courts regard it as their duty to give effect to the words chosen, not to the spirit of the Act. Indeed, they will sometimes interpret the words in a way which is almost certainly contrary to what Parliament intended, on the ground that it is their duty to give effect to what Parliament has said, and not to what it *intended to say*. There is some justification for this approach. It is often unclear what Parliament intended, and where this is the case, it is reasonable for judges to say that the citizen is entitled to rely on what an Act appears to mean, read objectively by the citizen, doubtless with the assistance of his professional advisers. Anybody who is obliged to obey the orders of a superior is entitled to say that his superior has not made his intention clear, and that he has therefore simply adhered to the letter of the instructions. But where the intention is clear, where any reasonable man of common sense (and perhaps of good faith) must see that a literal interpretation of an Act does not lead to the result which Parliament must have intended, it is surely legitimate to question a slavish adherence to the literal text. In fact, judges today often pay lip-service to the notion that they should adopt a 'purposive' approach to interpretation, and from time to time they do so. Indeed, in 1993 the House of Lords reversed a very ancient rule of statutory interpretation, and held that in certain cases it would be legitimate to look at *Hansard* to see if the actual intention of Parliament could be identified by the words of a minister, where the statutory text is unclear. This decision gives rise to many difficulties, not least that it will substantially add to the cost of legal research, because lawyers trying to understand a statute will in future have to read the debates in *Hansard,* but so far it has not had much impact on the everyday process of statutory construction in ordinary cases. Adherence to the literal style of interpretation is still the most widely used technique, reinforced as it is by the style of drafting favoured by Parliamentary Counsel.

One of the curious paradoxes concerning the drafting and interpretation of statutes is that the present system in use in this country gives very little leeway to judges, little discretion to them to use their initiative and even common sense in helping to breathe life into the words of an Act. Yet in other respects (as previously suggested) the trend of modern law is increasingly to give ever wider discretionary powers to judges. Moreover, less literal styles of interpretation are more commonly used on the Continent, where judges do not generally enjoy such a high status as they do in England. As time goes by, Community law will familiarize English lawyers with different legislative styles, and it will then be interesting to see how far they retain a preference for the detailed, literal drafting style traditional in England.

It is the style of drafting and interpreting Acts which makes it impossible for lawyers to meet the layman's demand for simple, clear codes of law which are set out in short propositions intelligible to any reasonably competent professional person, not to speak of other citizens. In 1965, when the Law Commission was established by Parliament with the duty of keeping the law under review and making proposals for reform and simplification, there were some hopes that it might be possible to codify branches of the law in simple, clear language such as is used by many Continental codes. But thirty years on the Law Commission has virtually given up hope of making any progress along these lines in the foreseeable future. The blame for this state of affairs must be placed on the style of parliamentary drafting and those responsible for perpetuating it.

Delegated legislation

As previously mentioned, a very large amount of law is made every year by statutory instruments under the authority of Acts of Parliament. Many Acts delegate power to ministers (and occasionally other persons or bodies) to make such statutory instruments within limits. There are traditionally a number of important limitations which are almost invariably observed. For example, if a minister is to be given power to create criminal offences the maximum penalties will almost always be contained in the original Act. A tradition even more stringently observed is that Parliament does not delegate the power to levy taxes. It is also very rare for an authorizing Act to give power to make statutory instruments which themselves amend or repeal other Acts, except in the context of Community law. But within these and other limits expressly laid down in the relevant Act, ministers do often have great and extensive law-making powers. It is true, of course, that these powers must always be exercised within a general framework of law settled in the main Act, but it is not wholly accurate to say that delegated legislation only concerns matters of detail.

The fact that parliamentary debate and amendment play a relatively small part in the enactment of Acts is illustrated by the way in which statutory instruments are made, because essentially such instruments are made in the same way that Acts of Parliament are made, *with the omission of the parliamentary side of the proceedings*. They are, that is to say, largely the product of civil servants, subject to the over-riding political control of ministers, but usually with a good deal of consultation with interested bodies and groups. Yet the omission of the parliamentary side of the proceedings makes little difference to the ultimate product: a statutory instrument looks very much like an Act of Parliament, after due allowance is made for the essential differences between them. There are, it is true, other differences in the process. Statutory instruments are not drafted by Parliamentary Counsel but by departmental lawyers; therefore no formal instructions will be given for their preparation. But the informal comments, interchanges, and criticisms of drafts which occur in the drafting of bills will also occur in the preparation of statutory instruments of any complexity and importance.

To say that the parliamentary side of the proceedings is omitted in the case of statutory instruments is to over-simplify slightly. Most statutory instruments are made without any parliamentary proceedings at all, but statutory instruments are required to be laid before Parliament, and are then subject to what is called the 'negative resolution procedure'. This means that either House can pass a resolution to annul the instrument, which thereupon is effectively repealed, though not retrospectively. Naturally such resolutions are hardly ever passed when the government has a majority in both Houses, and it is very rare even for such a resolution to be debated in either House. A few more important statutory instruments are subject to a different sort of procedure which requires the instrument to be laid before Parliament *in draft* before it is made. Then each House must pass an affirmative resolution before the instrument is made. Neither the negative nor the affirmative procedure enables amendments to be formally made to a statutory instrument, nor are the proceedings of the Houses as protracted as the proceedings on a bill, even where a resolution is tabled and debated. For practical purposes statutory instruments are an example of law made by civil servants subject to ministerial control, in much the same way that Acts of Parliament are laws largely made by civil servants subject to parliamentary control.

Judicial law-making

As we have previously seen, a large part of the law of England does not derive from legislation at all, but from case law. Most of the law of contract and tort, virtually all of the law of trusts, and most of our modern administrative law, for instance, derive from decisions of the courts. In addition, many of the underlying principles of the criminal law and the law of property remain embedded in the case law, even though nearly all the criminal law, and a large part of property law, are now in statutory form. Furthermore, even where the basis of the law is to be found in Acts of Parliament (plus, where relevant, statutory instruments), the interpretation of the legislation is a matter for the courts. So here too case law may play a significant role and much-litigated statutes often become, after a few years, an intricate network of statutory provisions and case law, with cases interpreting and qualifying the Act and, often enough, amending Acts qualifying and altering some effects of the case law. So it is plain that decisions of the courts are an important part of the law, and in order to understand how the law is made, it is necessary to understand how the case law system works.

It is of course quite clear that law-making by the courts is a different sort of process from law-making by Act of Parliament. Apart from the totally different procedures involved, and the differing characteristics of the persons who make the law in the two processes, even the most fervent admirer of judicial law-making will admit that it differs from parliamentary legislation in important respects. First, it is subordinate law-making. Parliament can override judicial decisions, while the judges cannot override what Parliament does. A court can declare a statutory instrument void on the ground that it was not within the authority delegated by Parliament, but (subject to the doubts discussed above concerning Scotland) no court can declare an Act of Parliament void, except on the ground that it conflicts with European Community law. And that means, in effect, that it is void, not because the judge himself is in any sense superior to Parliament, but because parliamentary enactments are now subject to the European Treaties, as a result of Parliament's own decision to join the Community in 1972. Secondly, Parliament can legislate of its own initiative, while the court can only make law when an appropriate case is brought before it, raising the relevant issues. Thirdly, Parliament's law-making powers are vastly more extensive than those of the courts. Parliament can create new institutions (such as the Commission for Racial Equality), or new posts (such as the Director-General of Fair Trading), which courts could clearly not do. Parliament can wholly rebuild great bodies of law (for example, the law relating to landlord and tenant), and furthermore it can do it in one fell swoop. Courts move slowly; their law-making powers can only be exercised step by step, case by case. They are largely confined to filling in gaps in the law, or developing existing principles in new directions. The courts move one step at a time, like a pawn, while the legislative queen can sweep from one end of the board to the other in one move. But (as every chess-player knows) pawns matter; they can get to the other side of the board in the end, and they can even destroy a queen. And so too case law, if left to develop by itself, can, over many years, build great new legal principles. The modern law of contract and of tort, both almost entirely creations of the courts, have taken several hundred years to get where they are now, but it is unlikely that these parts of the law would have been improved by large-scale parliamentary intervention in the last century or two.

In all these respects it is quite clear that law-making by judges differs significantly from law-making by Parliament. A much more controversial question concerns the reasons for which law is made by the two sorts of institutions. On one view, judges are legislative delegates who, when obliged to make law because no settled rule appears to decide the case before them, must make law *as though they were legislators*. On this view, judges must examine the policy issues involved in cases before them, weigh up the private rights of the parties and the public interest as best they can, and then decide what they think is best, just as a legislator might. The judge then is in a similar position to a minister who makes a statutory instrument. He is in effect authorized by the legal system to make law where no law is already clearly established, but he does so as a minister might fill in details in a statutory framework set by Parliament.

An alternative approach, however, entirely rejects this idea of the judge as a sort of delegated legislator. On this view judges are concerned with rights, not policy. Matters of public interest, and broad policy questions relating to the community welfare are pre-eminently matters for Parliament and not courts; courts are concerned with enforcing private rights, and they are not well equipped for deciding major policy issues. Of course many lawyers will insist that judges have nothing to do with policy, and that their only duty is to apply the law; but we have already seen that this is too limited and facile a view of the judicial role. The problem is that cases frequently arise, especially in appeal courts, where there simply is no clear law for the judges to apply; where this happens the judges must make the law before they can apply it, and the whole question is, how do they make the law? What factors influence the judges to make it one way rather than another way? Are the judges confined to questions of private right (and hence largely moral arguments about justice) or ought they to take account of the public interest, the welfare of the community?

The reality is rather more complex than this simple statement of polarized issues might suggest. It is worth noting first of all that the legislative process itself is really quite a complex one. Legislators do not, individually, have the practical ability to make the law just as they think it ought to be. There are many legislators, not one; there is a party system which restricts the freedom of Members of Parliament to vote just as they please; there is the way in which bills are prepared by civil servants; and there is also the fundamental problem that nobody is ever in the position of redesigning the universe from scratch. Legislators operate within the constraint of many other laws and institutions and facts. A legislator may quite intelligently say, for instance, that he dislikes an Act of Parliament previously passed and would like to see it repealed, but given that the Act is there, he will vote for an amendment which will in his opinion improve it.

So the fact that the judge is constrained as to the options available to him does not of itself mean that his position differs basically from that of a legislator. True, the constraints operating on judges are more obvious and sometimes more tight than those operating on legislators. But even that is not always the case. Judges, for instance, never operate under a three-line whip as Members of Parliament sometimes do. So there are occasions on which a judge is actually more free to do what he thinks right than a Member of Parliament may be. On the other hand, it is true that legislators can often take into account a broader set of considerations than a judge can. It is not true that judges cannot take account of questions of the public interest. Indeed they habitually do so. But it is true that judicial procedure is often ill-adapted to enable the judge to make a satisfactory decision on public-interest grounds. The simple fact is that the judge is often not well informed about the public interest, and nobody represents the public before the bar of the court. Parliament has the whole machinery of the government and the civil service to adduce facts which bear on the public interest; courts do not. Judges, and judicial procedure, are also not well placed to make decisions of a 'polycentric' nature, that is to say, decisions in which one of a wide range of possible options must be chosen—for example, how much tax should be levied by the State, and on what activities it should be levied. Courts are much better adapted to making decisions of an adversary nature, where two parties (or anyhow not many more than two) oppose each other with a limited number of contentions or claims.

It is also true that what is an acceptable reason for a judge to give in support of a particular decision will differ in important ways from what is an acceptable reason which a Member of Parliament may give for voting in a particular way on a legislative bill. But even this difference can be exaggerated. A Member of Parliament may, for instance, welcome a bill on the ground that it will be good for his constituents; but it would seem odd if he added that he would therefore vote for the bill even though he thought it would be disastrous for the country and so utterly contrary to the public interest. When the rhetoric of political debate is stripped away, it will be found that many of the sorts of reasons given for legislative decisions by legislators are not essentially different from those given by judges. Fairness, justice, the rights of individuals, the public interest—all these enter significantly into political as well as judicial law-making. Of course, the answers that come out will often be different, because reasonable people will differ on the weight to attach to conflicting factors. And, as suggested in Chapter 4, there may well be something of a bias in the judicial process which tends to favour individual rights as opposed to the collective welfare. But, making all due allowance for these differences, it remains true that much judicial law-making shares at least some of the characteristics of legislative law-making.

The doctrine of precedent

There are, of course, rules about law-making by courts, rules laid down by the courts themselves. Not everything said by a judge makes law. In the first place, decisions on pure questions of fact clearly do not create precedents. The fact that X shot Y may make him guilty of murder but is of no relevance to another case in which Z is the accused. Even evaluative decisions, such as a decision that a certain piece of conduct constitutes negligence, are not regarded as decisions on points of law which can constitute precedents. To take a simple example, if a judge says that a defendant in a civil action was driving his car at 80 m.p.h. in a public street, and that he was therefore guilty of negligence, that is no precedent for holding that it is negligence for another driver in a subsequent case to have driven at the same speed (even on the same road). This is partly because (as is commonly said) evaluative decisions like this must depend on all the circumstances of the case, and so it is impossible to be sure that the relevant facts in the first decision were in all respects the same as in the second. But it also seems pretty clear that one reason why decisions of this kind are not treated as precedents is simply that the courts do not want to make their every decision suffocated under the weight of previous cases. If every case of this kind became a precedent the volume of case law would become enormous, the argument of simple cases would become inordinately complicated, as each side would support its case with a mountainous pile of precedents, and judges would find it increasingly difficult to explain why and how decision Z was consistent with decisions A, B, C . . . in favour of one side, and not inconsistent with decisions M, N, O . . . in favour of the other side. So judicial decisions would inevitably appear inconsistent, and this is disliked by judges. Decisions on discretionary matters are also not decisions which can constitute precedents, although the guiding principles on which discretions are to be exercised are treated as questions of law.

The doctrine of precedent, then, is largely concerned with pure questions of law. A decision on a point of law constitutes a precedent which can in principle bind other courts to follow it. But before we can say that a decision constitutes a binding precedent two further qualifications need to be made. First, it must indeed be a decision, and not merely an *obiter dictum*, that is, a statement made by the way, an aside. In principle, the distinction between the binding part of the decision (the *ratio decidendi*) and an *obiter dictum* is clear, but in practice it is not always easy to distinguish between them.

Sometimes judges give several reasons for a decision: are they all binding, or is there one binding reason, the others being merely *dicta*? Or again, there may be several different judgments given in an appeal court, and the reasons given by all the judges may not wholly coincide, so what is the *ratio decidendi* then? In any event, the question of *ratio* or *dictum* may be less important than the weight of the remarks in their context, and the tribunal from which they emanate. Fully considered *dicta* in the House of Lords are usually treated as more weighty than the *ratio* of a judge at first instance in the High Court. So the whole distinction is more blurred than might seem. Further, the distinction often does not matter at all. It does not matter basically when the second court agrees with the decision (or *dicta*) in the previous case, and would arrive at the same conclusion anyhow; it does not matter even when the second court might, if it were to go into the issue in depth, have doubts about the first decision (or *dicta*) but feels disinclined to reopen the issue for any one of a number of possible reasons. Nor does the distinction between *ratio* and *dicta* matter if the second court disagrees so strongly with what was said in the earlier case that it is not prepared to follow it, even if in theory some lawyers might regard the prior case as a binding precedent. Where this happens, the second court may 'distinguish' the first decision by finding some relevant fact to be decisive of the second case which was not present in the first. Every lawyer knows that fine distinctions are sometimes seized upon to justify departing from a prior decision without an apparent breach with the rules of binding precedent.

The second qualification that needs to be made to the binding nature of the doctrine of precedent is that the strictly binding feature of the doctrine depends on the relative status of the courts concerned. Decisions of the House of Lords bind all lower courts, and are normally treated as binding by the House itself, though in European Community matters they are of course subject to the ultimate authority of the European Court. Since 1966 the House has claimed the right to overrule previous decisions in exceptional cases, but it has so far been sparing in its willingness to exercise this power. Decisions of the Court of Appeal bind lower courts, and also in principle bind the Court of Appeal itself. But there is much controversy on this and practice varies. When Lord Denning presided over the Court of Appeal as Master of the Rolls (from 1962 to 1982) he frequently expressed his belief that that court ought to have the same freedom to depart from its own prior decisions as the House of Lords claimed in 1966; some of his colleagues appeared to agree with him, but a majority did not. Furthermore, while most of those who agreed with Lord Denning were generally prepared to accept the majority view that the Court of Appeal should remain bound by its own decisions, Lord Denning himself (and occasionally, it would seem, one or two others) were not. There are, in any event, a number of established exceptions to the rule that that court is bound by its own decisions, but their limits are somewhat ill-defined, so in practice it is really quite rare that the court must seriously face the question whether it is absolutely bound by one of its own decisions.

Decisions of Divisional Courts bind all lower courts, and even decisions of a single high court judge are treated as binding on magistrates and tribunals, and generally by lawyers in the public service. Decisions of judges below the level of the High Court are not regarded as binding on anyone, and there is no systematic method of reporting such decisions.

The above account of the doctrine of precedent may well give a misleading impression of the importance of single binding decisions. Undoubtedly there are some situations where such decisions settle the law on a clear, simple point. In the interpretation of a statute, for instance, a simple ambiguity may be found which gives two alternative meanings to a section: the choice may be stark and straightforward, even though the resolution of the ambiguity may be quite difficult. In such a case a single decision may settle the issue, particularly if it is in the Court of Appeal or the House of Lords. But much more commonly it is clusters of decisions which are important for the development of the law. Usually it is found that areas of doubt and uncertainty in the law, as well as newly developing areas, give rise to more litigation than other areas: this occurs for the obvious reason that lawyers are unable to advise their clients with the same degree of confidence in these areas, and the prospects of successful appeals may well be higher in such cases. So it quite often happens that a whole series of new cases arises in a relatively short period of time. When this happens, it also often becomes clear that new vistas are opening up, and perhaps, that new problems, hitherto unsuspected, have been thrown up. Such a cluster of cases may well trigger off academic writing, which in turn may influence counsel in arguing subsequent cases. After a while matters may settle down again, and a new bit of law is, as it were, digested by the law and lawyers. This sort of development does not necessarily raise serious issues about the binding force of particular precedents, though such a development is occasionally triggered off by a loosening-up of the effect of an earlier series of precedents.

One illustration of this process, of some general interest, concerns the liability of barristers and solicitors for negligence in handling their clients' affairs. Until the early 1960s the law was taken to be settled that (1) a solicitor was liable for negligence on the same footing as any other professional adviser, but (2) that a barrister was not so liable because a barrister did not have a direct contract with his client—the client being compelled to approach the barrister through the solicitor with whom he contracted. Then in 1964 the House of Lords decided the famous *Hedley Byrne* case [1964] AC 465 which had nothing at all to do with the liability of barristers or solicitors, but which recognized for the first time that liability for negligent professional advice might arise *in tort*, that is, even between parties not in a contractual relationship. Barristers, of course, were quick to appreciate that their own traditional immunities might now be called in question, and in two subsequent decisions the House of Lords began to explore this possibility. These two decisions have laid down a new framework of law, much of which remains to be filled in by later decisions. Barristers remain immune from negligence liability in respect of the actual conduct of a case in court and in respect of advisory work which is so closely connected with the conduct of the case that it is in effect preparatory work for the trial, but they are no longer immune in respect of purely advisory work. Further, although none of these cases actually involved the liability of a solicitor, it was pretty clear from *dicta* in them that a solicitor's liability would now be equated with a barrister's, and that he would share the barrister's immunity in respect of the actual conduct of a case in court, and indeed, this view was later confirmed by the

Courts and Legal Services Act 1990 which enabled solicitors to obtain rights of audience in the higher courts. What is now likely to happen is that there will be a number of cases defining somewhat more clearly the line between purely advisory work and preparation for actual litigation.

This series of cases (and I have omitted some of the less significant) illustrates the way in which the common law can still develop, step by step, almost as though it were an organic growth. We now have a number of judgments in several cases, each of which offers arguments and opinions in favour of this or that development. Hypothetical examples may also be given, some of the arguments in one judgment may be rebutted in another judgment, and so on. Then, for a while, the issues may move into the public domain, particularly where, as in this case, there is a public interest in the legal rules being developed. There may be academic articles and notes, media discussion, perhaps anecdotal evidence of past injustices, and possibly even a parliamentary debate. All this may indirectly feed into the next round of developments, and so the process continues.

Bad law

Now that we have made some attempt to understand how law is made we are perhaps in a position to attempt some answer to a question which laymen constantly level at lawyers: why is so much of the law so bad? Of course one common (and partially correct) answer is simply to deny the allegation. Most of our law is really quite good, but inevitably the bits and pieces that the layman hears most about (or reads most about in the popular press) are those which show the law to be, at least apparently, an ass. Another common reaction is to pass the buck: if the law is bad it is all Parliament's fault. But it is already clear enough that the buck-passing explanation of bad law is only a partial exoneration for the legal profession. Much of the law has been made by judges, not Parliament, anyhow: even the law made by Parliament needs interpretation by judges, and bad interpretation rather than bad legislation may be the cause of bad law. But the layman's question (and to be fair, many lawyers ask themselves the same question) is a serious one, and deserves an attempt at a serious answer.

We need first to distinguish two different kinds of 'badness' about law. Laws may be bad because they are 'technically' bad; for instance, because they are obscure, ambiguous, internally inconsistent, difficult to discover, or hard to apply to a variety of circumstances. And secondly, laws may be substantively 'bad' simply in the sense that they produce unacceptable results—injustice or plain idiocy, or less extremely, because they are inefficient and expensive, or produce inconsistency or anomaly between like cases. Let us look at each of these in turn.

Technically bad laws arise primarily from the way laws are made. Acts of Parliament are often obscure and even unintelligible, and we have seen something of the reasons for this: a tradition of narrow methods of interpretation which has led to a narrow style of drafting, which has in turn reinforced the same methods of interpretation; in addition, the need to cater for the ultimate user of statute law and for the Member of Parliament who is to vote for it, is a part contributor to the trouble. Some of these difficulties could be overcome if the political will was there. If Parliament was willing to pass Acts drafted in a broader style altogether, the judges might well respond by adopting new methods of interpretation—indeed, they could even be authorized to do so by Act of Parliament, although it is very difficult to change ways of thought and ways of work in this way. But in order to achieve these results the government will have to find lawyers able to draft their bills outside the Parliamentary Counsel's office which at present is virtually in charge of the way statute laws are produced.

Perhaps, as suggested earlier, increasing familiarity with the European style of drafting will gradually enable changes to be introduced. At the same time, it must be said that the English drafting style has many advantages. It may be more difficult to read and understand, especially for the layman, than some European legislation of a similar kind. This is, for instance, probably true of the UK Unfair Contract Terms Act 1977 and the EC Directive on Unfair Terms in Consumer Contracts 1993. But the English style is not mainly designed for the layman, but for the lawyer, and it aims for legal precision. So although the Unfair Contract Terms Act may be difficult to read in a general way, its legal effects tend to be more precise, and a careful study of the text, together with the previous case law, usually enables the lawyer to work out how it is intended to operate. This cannot be said of the European Directive on Unfair Contract Terms, which leaves very much more to be worked out by the courts in the course of future litigation, and therefore leaves the law in a state of much greater uncertainty.

More generally, it has to be said that much European Community legislation is technically bad law because its law-making procedures are so unsatisfactory. Far too much is left to the officials of the Commission, who work with a minimum of political accountability, and whose main task is often to balance the known views of different governments. The Commission's drafts are then submitted to the Council, whose ministers will have a chance to study the comments of their own civil servants on the drafts, but when debate is taken up in the Council there simply is not time, nor expertise, to handle verbal minutiae which are often so critical to technically good law. Whether the European Parliament will be able to add much of value in cases where it is consulted by the Council or the Commission seems doubtful. This Parliament, unlike our own (or indeed, other European national parliaments) is not, it must be remembered, filled with ministers who have civil servants and other expert advisers at their call. And, as we have previously pointed out, a Parliament which conducts its business in eleven languages is hardly a suitable body to scrutinize the wording of proposed legislation in any great detail. So technical proficiency in the drafting of laws is hardly to be expected from the European Parliament.

Technically bad case law is perhaps more difficult to deal with. It arises usually from the very nature of case law—a decision leaves the law uncertain on this or that point, and there is no way of resolving the uncertainty unless and until another case turns up raising the same issues. Or uncertainty arises because different judges say different things in their judgments: there was at one time support for the view that single judgments in appeal courts would get rid of this difficulty, and in the House of Lords and the Privy Council (which hears appeals only from certain Commonwealth courts) this is now the general practice. But there are disadvantages in single judgments also. The common law does not develop best when authoritative statements of the law are handed down *ex cathedra* as though they were statutes. Some of our leading modern judges (notably Lord Reid) have expressed the view that single judgments ought not to be the rule, and some of the most disastrous modern decisions of the House of Lords have been cases in which only a single judgment was delivered.

European Court judgments have additional characteristics which sometimes make them unsatisfactory as sources of law. In the first place, they differ very much in style from traditional English judgments which tend to be full and detailed to the point of discursiveness. The European tradition, followed in this respect by the European Community judges, is one of laconic brevity. The judgments tend to be a summary of the points being decided, with little by way of explanation or reasoning. Opinions may differ among lawyers familiar with both styles as to which is the more technically helpful in providing the raw material for the law itself. Certainly the very full English judgments do sometimes simply overload the law with quantities of unnecessary material which must be read by lawyers. But the virtually total absence of reasoning from European Court judgments is difficult for an English lawyer to come to terms with. It was this absence of adequate reasoning, for instance, in the first case on the Sunday trading laws, which led to the necessity for a second decision by the same Court before lawyers could say what the first case meant.

A second major difficulty with European Court judgments as sources of technical law concerns retrospectivity. Because judges nowhere claim the right to change the law, but only to declare what it already is, it is usually treated as axiomatic that court decisions prima facie have retrospective effect. The law is not merely what the court says it is; it necessarily follows from a judicial decision that *the law has always been thus.* English judges stick rigidly to this principle, and if the results are too inconvenient—for example, because the court's decision was totally unexpected and upsets a long-established pattern of behaviour—then the remedy lies in amending legislation. But because the European Court has some characteristics of a constitutional court, it is not usually possible to deal with any consequent inconveniences by amending legislation. The European Court has had, therefore, like many other constitutional courts, to recognize that legal theory must here give way to practical realities. A court decision upsetting existing practices must, therefore, be recognized for what it is—a decision with retrospective effect. To avoid the most unreasonable and extreme consequences of this, the court has been compelled on occasion to limit the retrospective nature of its decisions by announcing that it only applies to parties who have (for instance) commenced proceedings before a certain date. But this by no means eliminates all problems, because it is sometimes extremely difficult to decide precisely how far retrospectivity should be allowed to extend, and several decisions may be needed before this problem can be sorted out. In the most serious case of this kind, the *Barber* case (dealing with the rights of women in private pension plans), to which reference has been made before, the consequences of retrospectivity were so alarming that they had to be restricted by an amendment to the Treaties themselves.

Other reasons why our own national case law is sometimes technically bad, that is, obscure, uncertain, or contradictory, arise from simple human limitations. Judges are under great pressure of work; in the Court of Appeal it is still the practice to deliver judgment at the end of oral argument, without time for reflection or research, except in cases of particular difficulty. This makes the court peculiarly dependent on the skill and imagination of counsel: if counsel fails to dig up relevant authorities or place before the court new lines of argument, the court is unlikely to do this itself. And naturally the practice of delivering extempore judgments means that logically fallacious arguments are sometimes advanced which, if there had been time for reflection, would probably have been rejected, though not necessarily so as to change the ultimate decision. So also, the extempore judgment easily leads to the second or third judgment containing remarks which differ somewhat from those in the first. On the whole these difficulties do not appear to be serious. There is little doubt that any attempt to get rid of them would require a different judicial style which would only purchase greater certainty at the expense of greater rigidity.

Probably when laymen complain about bad law they are thinking more of its substance than its technical characteristics. Obscurity and uncertainty in the law are more usually troublesome for lawyers than their clients; although in the long run the client may pay for these defects, he is not usually conscious of them in the first instance. So we need to ask why the laws are often bad in substance; why do judges often find themselves compelled to arrive at decisions which they (and others) would find to be unjust, or otherwise unsatisfactory? This is a very important question which has been surprisingly neglected by lawyers and theorists, so only some preliminary and sketchy suggestions can be offered here. The subject really deserves a much fuller analysis.

The first, and most obvious, factor is that we live in a pluralist society in which ideas of justice are very variable. So the fact that judges and newspaper readers may find a legal rule absurd or unjust does not mean that everybody else would find it unjust also. Sometimes laws are passed by Parliament (for example, the old laws designed to confer legal immunity on trade unions for actions done in the course or furtherance of a trade dispute) which are strongly partisan in their nature. Many people may find such laws very unjust, but they are the outcome of our democratic processes, and if these are indeed bad laws, the blame must rest with the government and Parliament.

Sometimes—though fortunately not very often—laws are passed by Parliament where some of these matters have simply not been thought through with sufficient care. Two examples of this caused widespread public concern in 1992–3. Both followed amendments made by the Criminal Justice Act 1991 to the laws relating to sentencing. One amendment had provided for a system of 'unit fines' so that all fines imposed by the courts were to be expressed in units, rather than in pounds. The units were then turned into pounds by multiplying them by a factor derived from the accused person's income. The idea of this was, of course, to try to ensure that fines bore some relationship to a person's income, since it seemed unfair that the same fine should be imposed for similar offences regardless of the accused's wealth. But within a few weeks of the new law's introduction the most absurd examples of its operation began to receive widespread publicity. However just the basic idea of the

1991 amendment might have seemed to Parliament, it was clear that the new law did not work well, and it was very rapidly abandoned in its turn, by section 65 of the Criminal Justice Act 1993. Much the same fate befell another change first introduced by the 1991 Act, which restricted the powers of the courts in sentencing offenders who had a long string of convictions. Those restrictions were based on the idea that it was unjust to keep punishing a person for the same crimes, over and over again. Once he had been punished for an offence, the argument ran, courts should not in general take account of his previous convictions in passing sentence for new convictions. Once again, this law had scarcely come into force when press publicity began to focus on cases where it did not seem to be working sensibly. Again, policy was very quickly reversed, and further changes to the law were made by section 66 of the Criminal Justice Act 1993.

In these cases what seemed just to ministers and Parliament in 1991 began to seem very unjust in 1993, and the only credible explanation really is that the early changes were just not properly thought out. Although this kind of thing is, of course, inevitable from time to time, it does not happen very often. The effect of proposed changes in the law is usually examined with great care in the civil service, and Parliament rarely allows such ill-considered amendments to the law to slip through, almost unnoticed. By and large, our own national law-making procedures are usually quite efficient.

A second cause of unjust decisions, or perhaps even bad laws, is that courts are often faced with the excruciatingly difficult question of resolving conflicts between two or more values, or principles. Most modern societies which have largely abandoned their religious faith and not replaced it with a single-minded acceptance of some alternative secular creed, such as Marxism, are riddled with principles and values which frequently conflict with each other. For example, we believe in free speech, but we also believe it is prima-facie wrong to cause harm to an innocent person. What happens, then, if our use of free speech causes harm to a person thereby defamed? Or again, we believe in the principles of due process—a person is not to be deprived of his property (say by taxation) without due process of law; but we also believe that citizens should bear a fair share of the costs of running the State. What happens, then, if some rich person finds it possible to arrange his affairs so that he pays very little tax and yet seemingly complies with the law? Or again, we believe (to some extent) in rewarding the skilful and hard-working and able; but we also believe in looking after those who are less capable of looking after themselves. What happens, then, when a bargain is made between two persons which produces a handsome profit to one, and a serious loss to the other? These are just a sample of some of the perennial problems of the law. Most people do not have to face these difficulties, because the ordinary person does not have to resolve a conflict between two principles or values except in relation to his own life; and then most of us act from instinct or intuition or emotion. Even if we try to rationalize what we are doing, and justify our decisions to ourselves, we act as judges in our own cause and have no need to offer impartial and public reasons for our decisions. Courts and judges, by contrast, are constantly having to do just this. So here too decisions which appear unjust, laws which appear unjust, to some, may not so appear to others.

It may be said that these examples are misleading because in these cases there will usually be controversy: some will find the decisions or the laws just, but the cases or laws which really need explanation are those which everybody (or almost everybody) would find wrong or unjust. But it is not quite as simple as that. Even in the case of laws or decisions which would be condemned as unjust by a great majority, it may often be the case that this same majority would normally subscribe quite cheerfully to a principle of law or morality which actually justifies the law or the decision in question. The great majority of the public, for instance, might well regard a law which permits a rich man to avoid his fair share of taxes as grossly unjust; but this same majority might also agree that due process of law is an important principle which should not be departed from. Courts, unlike the man in the street, actually have to decide which of these principles is to govern in the circumstances of a particular case.

So far we have been considering laws and legal decisions which are in substance defensible, even though some may find them very unjust. But it is true that there are bad laws which virtually nobody would today defend. How does that happen? Broadly, this occurs in one of two ways. First, it may happen because laws which were at one time acceptable have ceased to be acceptable. Laws which worked perfectly satisfactorily in one century may simply become out of date. As we have seen, this may happen through technological change, though it seems possible that changes in moral values are actually more important in making laws come to seem unjust. One striking example of this concerns the common law rule which for centuries declared that a man could not be guilty of raping his own wife on the ground that, by her marriage, she 'consented' to all acts of intercourse with her husband. Now even cases of this kind may be said to raise some of the conflicts of principle referred to above. For even where laws appear to have become manifestly out of date and produce results which are quite offensive to the moral sense of the community, there are conflicting principles which suggest that such laws should still be respected by courts and judges. First, it may be said that if laws are to be changed, this is Parliament's job and not that of the judges; indeed, many would argue that it is unjust (because it would be undemocratic) for judges to change the settled law. So one can get a simple conflict here, as before. Justice, in substance, pulls in one direction; but constitutional practice and custom (which are also designed to secure just results) pull in the opposite direction. It may be quite legitimate to complain that the judges are too conservative and too deferential to Parliament in their unwillingness to get rid of obsolete laws, to bring laws up to date, and so on. But for everyone who complains of this feature of the English judiciary there are others who would argue that the judges are themselves out of date in their value systems, and for these, it is presumably better that the judges should be circumspect about changing settled law. In the case of the marital exemption from rape, the House of Lords eventually took the bit between its teeth and abrogated the exemption itself in the case of *R.* v. *R.* in 1991. But even in this somewhat extreme case, there were arguments in favour of leaving the matter to Parliament. The Law Commission had already produced a report on the point (which did not in fact recommend simple abrogation of the immunity), and the matter was by no means free from all political controversy.

A second principle which tells against too ready a willingness to depart even from manifestly bad laws is that the public, or some members of it, may come to rely upon the laws as they are, however bad. Some people may take advice about the law, and adjust their affairs in reliance on the law, and these are not neessarily bad people taking advantage of a bad law: they may be ordinary people trying to make the best of a difficult situation. When such bad laws arise in the courts there is a need to be careful that those who have thus relied on the law are not unfairly treated by sudden changes. Legislation usually can take care of these difficulties. It gives due warning of change, and transitional provisions may be inserted to deal with previous conduct; but case law which departs from previous law does so retrospectively, since the courts do not openly claim the right to change the law, but only to declare that it was always thus.

The second broad way in which bad laws occur is simply by accident. Making laws is a very complex and difficult process indeed. Sometimes accidents occur so that results flow from decisions or statutes which have not been anticipated, and would have been provided for if the legislator had been sufficiently far-sighted. One very common situation is the general principle which works well enough in the majority of cases, but which produces injustice in rare and unforeseeable circumstances. All human experience stretching back over 2,000 years confirms that, no matter how much care is taken in the preparation of legislation, unforeseeable side-effects will occur. This problem is, of course, not confined to the law, since it affects much social and even scientific planning. Doctors, like lawyers, have problems with treatment which works well in most cases, but produces unfortunate side-effects in a few. There are various ways of alleviating the problem, for example, by greater and greater care, by more detailed provision for exceptional cases, and in the last resort, by substituting discretion for fixed rule. But each of these has its practical disadvantages, so that in the end one must resort to some sort of balance, knowing that the total elimination of bad results is impossible, and that (as with unforeseeable medical side-effects) we must simply put up with these injustices as part of the price we pay for the general system of law.

One other possible source of bad laws deserves mention, particularly as this is probably often the target of the layman's criticisms. Bad laws may arise from restrictive practices in the legal profession, which may lead to the self-interest of the profession becoming an obstacle to reform. Many might suspect that the present-day system of conveyancing in England is an instance of such bad laws. The legal profession still has the lion's share of all conveyancing work, and although its statutory monopoly has been broken by the 'licensed conveyancers', some critics believe that its self-interest has delayed the adoption of more up-to-date and cheaper methods of transferring land—for instance, by computerizing land titles. Without entering into the merits of this particular controversy, it is right to note that the lay critic of the law often feels at a disadvantage in matters of this kind. He often believes that lawyers retain a sufficient element of mystery about their profession to make it hard for informed discussion of such issues to be conducted in a way in which the layman can satisfactorily participate. It is true also that the legal profession has long been a very powerful political group which has in the past been able to defeat or at least defuse proposals for radical legal reform which some members of the profession might have seen as a serious threat to their interests. Their political power derives from a number of sources. First, there is nearly always a significant number of lawyers in the House of Commons—usually the largest single professional group in the House (except perhaps, today, teachers) have been lawyers. Secondly, the Lord Chancellor is usually a powerful political figure who has in the past often acted as an advocate for the legal profession within the government itself, although the present Lord Chancellor, Lord Mackay, is hardly an apologist for the profession. And thirdly, since law is itself the machinery by which social change is implemented, the professional lawyers may sometimes be able to use their expertise so as to influence the direction of social policy in ways which the lay politician may not wholly understnd. But it is easy to exaggerate the influence of the legal profession in matters of this kind. Naturally it is to be expected that professional opinion will play a significant role in the formulation and implementation of social policy (just as one would expect medical opinion to influence the shape of medical practice), but there are not wanting radical lawyers prepared to advocate plenty of radical reforms even to the detriment of their own professional interests.

The conclusion of this chapter may seem somewhat negative and even fatalistic. That there will always be bad laws and unjust laws is not a reassuring or attractive conclusion, but it is not intended to be an excuse for complacency. The law is an immensely complex social machine. It is continually in need of patching, repairing, and from time to time overhauling in this or that area. Much of this repairing and patching goes on all the time, and we have institutions within the bureaucratic process (such as the Law Commission) entrusted with this work. The work is unceasing, and we must not look for perfection or for finality.

7 Conclusions

This little book has involved us in a brief survey of the law and the legal institutions of modern England. On the way we have looked at a number of theoretical questions about the nature and purposes of law, and the legitimacy of the legal system as a whole. It is not easy to draw any conclusions from so rapid a survey, but it may be helpful to attempt to highlight some of the main themes.

We have, in the first place, seen that (whatever its origins) modern English law is very much a man-made institution. Indeed, in the last chapter we devoted a good deal of space to an account of how the law is made. The law in a modern complex state is a very bulky social instrument, and large parts of it are constantly being made and remade. All this is the work of men and women: legislators and judges in the front line, but many other supporting staff behind, civil servants, the Bar, and other members of the legal profession, not forgetting even the academic lawyer whose ideas may eventually exert some influence on those in the front line.

The fact that the law is being so constantly and visibly made and remade means that it has tended to lose its association with religion on the one side, and its mystery or magical significance on the other. Inevitably, this gives added point to a number of traditional questions: in particular, it raises problems about the legitimacy of the whole system, and the purposes of the laws which are thus being made. Legitimacy is not an issue which has raised serious practical questions in England for nearly three centuries, but the disappearance of the religious and 'mystery' elements in the legal process, the growing obviousness of the fact that law is a human institution, made by men and women for the government of men and women, must raise in a more serious form these traditional questions. Just *why* should we the people accept the laws made by those who claim the right to govern us? Further, the human nature of man-made laws makes it increasingly obvious that much modern law has purposes, that it aims (for instance) to make some members of the community better off at the expense of others. This raises a challenge to the old liberal ideal of the neutrality of law.

Traditional liberal theory held that the purpose of the law was simply to provide a framework within which human beings could pursue their own salvation, their own purposes in their own way. The concept of the Rule of Law, vague and indefinable though it tended to be, was an expression of this ideal of the neutrality of the law itself. Law was not expected to have any purposes other than to maintain law and order, and the framework within which the people lived and worked. What went on within this framework was supposed not to be the concern of the law. Since laws of property and of contract were part of the essential structure of this outer framework, liberal theory tended to take for granted the existing distribution of property, with all the inequalities that this involved. So the cards may appear to have been stacked, but this does not mean that the Rule of Law was ever a complete sham. It did carry with it the essential notion of equality before the law, and it did recognize that in some formal sense the law was neutral between different persons and members of different classes. To this central concept, the judges and the legal profession in England were completely faithful. They believed in individualism, in laws designed to protect individuals and to enforce individual rights through a legal system framed for these ends. They had less sympathy with collective aspirations, and with redistributive ideals which seemed to clash with the liberal ideal and with their concept of the Rule of Law.

Given these traditions, the fact that the judiciary and the Bar tended to reflect an individualist value system may not have been a serious problem in the last century when the liberal ideal was so widely shared, at least by those who were entitled to any voice in the political process. Similarly, the broad consensus over the liberal ideal and the Rule of Law meant that the undisputed sovereignty of Parliament raised few problems concerning the conflict between the rights of individuals and the rights of majorities, or of the State itself. Nobody felt the need for a Bill of Rights in the nineteenth-century constitution. Such problems as did exist (and they were sometimes serious enough) arose out of the relationship between the Lords and the Commons; but the very coexistence of the two Houses throughout the last century provided some sort of limitation on the extent of majority power.

In modern times, by contrast, many of these traditional questions have been posed in a different and more challenging context. On the one hand, the waning of the liberal ideal, the growth of redistributive pressures, and the increased quantity of laws designed to give effect to collective aspirations have all meant that the old idea of the neutrality of the law has sometimes seemed in great danger of disappearing altogether. This was a very worrying development because, as the ideal of the neutrality of law declines, the authority of the law must decline with it. Laws, we all know today, do have purposes behind them. Most of the statute law enacted by Parliament is designed to give effect to quite specific purposes, many of them highly controversial purposes, those of a majority in the House of Commons. But although individual laws are in this way often designed to help one group or another in society, this does not mean, and should never be taken to mean, that the laws as a whole have lost their neutrality. In this context, the traditional liberal ideology of much of the higher judiciary, and of much of the common law which they still administer, which occasionally began to look outdated and contrary to the spirit of the times a decade or two ago, actually seems more relevant and stronger today.

When the first edition of this book was written in 1982 the political climate led me to suggest that our legal system was coming under great strain. The two main political parties at that time, and for several years thereafter, were moving further and further apart in their basic ideologies. As the Conservative party moved further to the right, the Labour party appeared to be moving further to the left, and the country was faced with the possibility of extreme swings from one side to another. It also appeared to be faced with the possibility at least of a Labour government whose basic philosophy involved a radical departure from the broad liberal concensus under which our laws and our judiciary had traditionally operated.

Fortunately, conditions have now changed again, and our two main political parties are today coming much closer in their ideologies. This has eliminated some of the threats to our legal system, because it suggests that we can look forward to a period of greater stability in the political process, and this in turn could lead to less violent changes in the law, and a re-establishment of belief in the neutrality of the law, and a greater confidence in the judges. At the least, it could lead to a greater sense of general public identification with the law, a greater willingness, once again, to accept laws that appear against one's own interests, from a deep belief that laws are broadly designed in the general interests of all. As I suggested in the last edition, in the short run the law can be a stabilizing and unifying influence in a temporarily divided society; but in the long run, the law cannot be more stable or more cohesive than the political society from which it emerges.

At the same time, a greater concensus on some issues which have been so divisive over the past decades has highlighted some of the other major issues which can be expected to dominate our legal system in the first years of the next century.

Even as matters now stand, fundamental change is already afoot. I have stressed in Chapter 3 the revolutionary nature of the *Factortame* decision which has given our courts power to declare Acts of Parliament void. To some people this is a deplorable symptom of the surrender of sovereignty which our membership of the Community involves, though a surrender which has been carried through almost by stealth. But many lawyers and civil-liberty groups find much to welcome in the *Factortame* decision, not so much because it demonstrates the supremacy of Community law, but because it enables the courts to uphold fundamental individual rights when these are threatened by a temporary majority in the House of Commons. As we have also seen, the possibility of incorporating into our own domestic law the European Convention on Human Rights is today being seriously canvassed, and it is hard to believe that this change can be deferred indefinitely.

But looming on the horizon are larger questions still. The first of these is unquestionably the future of the European Community. As I suggested earlier, the Community at present has many of the characteristics of a federal legal system, and the foundations of a federal European state have been laid; but I also stressed that further moves to a federal Europe were by no means inevitable. Clearly, the political shape of Europe in the next few decades is going to be a very important and a very controversial question. The present mood of the country suggests that it is not ready for entry into a federal Europe, and the same may well be true of several other European Community countries as well. But if, as seems quite possible, Germany and France, and several of the smaller member states decide to press ahead with the formation of a federal European state, regardless of the views of the UK and other dissentients, we shall be faced with an appallingly difficult question. It is one thing to oppose the creation of a federal European state; it is another thing to opt out of such a state if it is going to be created anyhow. Obviously these problems and possibilities are in the first instance political issues rather than legal ones; but equally obviously, fundamental legal questions will turn on the ultimate decisions. The whole shape and nature of our legal system in the next century will depend on the decisions which are eventually taken on these questions.

Suggestions for further reading

Chapter 1

The central role of the courts in a legal system is discussed from a jurisprudential point of view in H. L. A. Hart's classic, *The Concept of Law*, first published 1961, 2nd edn. (Oxford, Oxford UP, 1994). However, Hart's suggestion that primitive legal systems do not have the same use for courts is challenged in A. J. Allott's *The Limits of Law* (London, Butterworth, 1980). The standard work on the history of English courts is volume 1 of Sir William Holdsworth's monumental *History of English Law*, revised edn. (London, Methuen, 1956); a much shorter history of the court system is to be found in H. G. Hanbury, *English Courts of Law*, 5th edn., by D. C. M. Yardley (Oxford, Oxford UP, 1979).

Modern accounts of the English legal system can be found in M. Zander, *Cases and Materials on the English Legal System*, 6th edn. (London, Butterworth, 1992) and Smith and Keenan's *English Law,* 8th edn. (London, Pitman, 1986).

The legal administration of the social security system, referred to in the text by way of illustration, is briefly discussed by Sir Robert Micklethwait (himself a former Chief Commissioner) in his Hamlyn Lectures, *The National Insurance Commissioners* (London, Stevens, 1976). A more comprehensive account is to be found in A. I. Ogus and E. Barendt, *The Law of Social Security*, 3rd edn. (London, Butterworth, 1988).

Some material on the present system of law reporting will be found in M. Zander, *The Law Making Process,* 4th edn. (London, Butterworth, 1994), ch. 5.

The theory of law as a prediction of what courts will do was first stated by O. W. Holmes in 'The Path of the Law', first published in 10 *Harvard Law Review* 61 (1897), reprinted in *Collected Legal Papers* (London, Constable, 1920), 173 ff. The theory is much criticized in Hart's *Concept of Law* (above).

On the judges, J. A. G. Griffith's polemical book, *The Politics of the Judiciary*, 4th edn. (London, Fontana, 1991) is easy reading. The book is critically reviewed by Lord Devlin in 41 *Modern Law Review* 501 (1978), and several of Lord Devlin's own addresses on the judicial role are collected in his book, *The Judge* (Oxford, Oxford UP, 1979). More-recent books on the judicial role are D. Pannick, *Judges* (Oxford, Oxford UP, 1987), and Simon Lee, *Judging Judges* (London, Faber, 1988). Alan Paterson, *The Law Lords* (London, Macmillan, 1982) is a close (but very readable) account of the judges of the House of Lords, and of their role as law-makers.

The independence of the judiciary is now the subject of a full-length study (largely historical) by Robert Stevens, *The Independence of the Judiciary* (Oxford, Oxford UP, 1993). Other contributions to the debate on the independence of the judiciary can be found in D. Oliver, 'The Independence of the Judiciary', 39 *Current Legal Problems* 177 (1982) and Sir N. Browne-Wilkinson, 'The Independence of the Judiciary in the 1980s' (1988) *Public Law*, 44. In 1992 justice (the British section of the International Commission of Jurists) published *The Judiciary in England and Wales* (London, 1992), which identifies a number of relevant problems in this field. On a generally increased willingness of the judges to criticize and overrule governmental decisions, see J. Rozenberg, *The Search for Justice: An Anatomy of the Law* (London, Hodder & Stoughton, 1994). The role of the jury receives considerable support from a survey of jurors themselves, conducted by the Royal Commission on Criminal Justice, chaired by Lord Runciman, whose *Report* was published in 1993 (Cm. 2263, London, HMSO).

The doctrine of precedent is dealt with in Cross and Harris, *Precedent in English Law*, 4th edn. (Oxford, Oxford UP, 1991). The law-making power of the judiciary is dealt with in Devlin's book, *The Judge* (above), ch. 1; in B. Cardozo's classic, *The Nature of the Judicial Process* (New Haven, Conn., Yale UP, 1921); and in Ronald Dworkin's *Law's Empire* (London, Fontana, 1986). A comparison of the role of the judges in England and the United States will be found in P. S. Atiyah and Robert Summers, *Form and Substance in Anglo-American Law* (Oxford, Oxford UP, 1987), chs. 10 and 12, and also in L. Jaffe, *English and American Judges as Lawmakers* (Oxford, Oxford UP, 1969).

The leading work on the jury is W. R. Cornish's (mainly historical), *The Jury* (London, Allen Lane, 1968). The jury's right to return a verdict of Not Guilty in defiance of the evidence is discussed in chapter 5 of Lord Devlin's *The Judge* (above). A modern survey of the utility and reliability of juries is to be found in A. Ashworth, *The Criminal Process: An Evaluative Survey* (Oxford, Oxford UP, 1994, 230–52). See also M. Findlay and P. Duff (eds.), *The Jury System Under Attack* (London, 1988). Another useful survey, with a valuable bibliography, is J. Baldwin and M. McConville's *Jury Trials* (Oxford, Oxford UP, 1979).

The leading modern study on the legal professions is R. Abel, *The Legal Profession in England and Wales* (Oxford, Blackwell, 1988). Less up-to-date, though still valuable, are the *Report of the Royal Commission on Legal Services* (Cmnd. 7648, London, HMSO, 1979) and M. Zander, *Lawyers and the Public Interest* (London, Weidenfeld & Nicolson, 1968), still of some value on the issue of fusion.

The evaluative nature of negligence decisions is discussed in *Atiyah's Accidents, Compensation and the Law*, 5th edn. by Peter Cane, (London, Butterworth, 1993), at 32–4. The cricket-ball problem first arose in the famous case of *Bolton* v. *Stone* [1951] AC 850, and see also *Miller* v. *Jackson* [1977] QB 966.

There is no single work on Due Process of Law in English law, but the standard works by De Smith and Wade and Forsyth (referred to below) deal with many issues of Due Process. Peter Cane, *An Introduction to Administrative Law*, 2nd edn. (Oxford, Oxford UP, 1992) is a shorter work which also discusses some aspects of due process. A useful introduction to the American concept of due process can be found in L. Tribe, *American Constitutional Law* (Mineola, NY, Foundation Press, 1978), at 501–63.

The standard works on the supervisory jurisdiction of the High Court are S. A. de Smith, *Judicial Review of Administrative Action*, 4th edn. by J. M. Evans (London, Sweet & Maxwell, 1982) and H. W. R. Wade and C. F. Forsyth, *Administrative Law*, 7th edn. (Oxford, Oxford UP, 1994).

The *locus classicus* on the function of the judge in the English accusatorial trial process is the judgment of Lord Denning in *Jones* v. *NCB* [1957] 2 QB 55. The problem of miscarriages of justice is discussed in Stockdale and Casale (eds.), *Criminal Justice under Stress* (London, Blackstone, 1992); the justice report, *Miscarriages of Justice* (London, 1989); M. Zander, *A Matter of Justice* (Oxford, 1989); Walker and Starmer (eds.), *Justice in Error* (London, Blackstone, 1993); and B. Woffinden, *Miscarriages of Justice* (London, Hodder & Stoughton, 1989).

Problems regarding legal aid are discussed in J. Rozenberg, *The Search for Justice* (above). Lord Taylor, the Lord Chief Justice, also criticizes the tightened means test for legal aid in his Dimbleby Lecture (1992). See also the Legal Action Group, *A Strategy for Justice: Publicly Funded Legal Services in the 1990s* (London, LAG Education & Service Trust, 1992).

Chapter 2

On the nature of law as an 'institutional fact' see D. N. McCormick, in 90 *Law Quarterly Review* 102 (1974); J. Raz, *The Authority of Law* (Oxford, Oxford UP, 1979), ch. 6. The need for sanctions and the nature of the 'sanction' of nullity are discussed in Hart, *The Concept of Law*, above, and, in the context of international law, by Glanville Williams in an essay first published in 22 *British Yearbook of International Law* 146 (1945) and reprinted in *Philosophy, Politics and Society* (ed. Laslett), 1st series (Oxford, Blackwell, 1975), 134 ff.

The classic work on the element of mystique in law is Max Weber, on *Law in Economy and Society*, ed. Max Rheinstein (Cambridge, Mass., Harvard UP, 1954). On the social changes which have resulted from the American Supreme Court's decision in the school desegregation cases, see Charles L. Black, *Decision According to Law* (New York, Norton & Co., 1981).

On the poll tax saga, see David Butler, Andrew Adonis, and Tony Travers, *Failure in British Government* (Oxford, Oxford UP, 1994); particular aspects of the story are covered in A. Bloch, *The Community Charge in England: Local Authority Experience: Ten Case Studies* (York, Joseph Rowntree Foundation, 1990).

Chapter 3

Dicey's *Law of the Constitution* can now be best consulted in the 10th edn. by E. C. S. Wade (London, Macmillan, 1964). Dicey's views on conventions were vigorously attacked by Sir Ivor Jennings, *The Law and the Constitution*, 5th edn. (London, University of London Press, 1964) but (to some extent) defended by G. Marshall, *Constitutional Theory* (Oxford, Oxford UP, 1971), 7–12. The queries about the sovereignty of Parliament over Scotland are raised by D. N. McCormick in his article 'Does the U.K. have a Constitution?', in 29 *Northern Ireland Law Quarterly* 1 (1978).

On the essentials of European Community law, see T. C. Hartley, *Foundations of European Community Law*, 3rd edn. (Oxford, Oxford UP, 1994); S. A. Budd and A. Jones, *The European Community: A Guide to the Maze*, 4th edn. (London, Kogan Page, 1991); J. Shaw, *European Community Law* (London, Macmillan, 1993).

The structure of the Community's institutions is explained in a publication by the European Commission itself, *The Institutions of the European Community* (Office for Official Publications, Brussels, Luxembourg, 1993).

Dicey's well-known discussion of the Rule of Law is to be found in his *Law of the Constitution* (above). More modern treatment of this subject can be found in L. Fuller, *The Morality of Law* (New Haven, Conn., Yale UP, 1964) and J. Raz, *The Authority of Law* (above), ch. 11.

On police discretion with regard to criminal activity, see L. Lustgarten, *The Governance of Police* (London, Sweet & Maxwell, 1986).

Chapter 4

An introduction to the Marxist theory of law can be found in Hugh Collins, *Marxism and Law* (Oxford, Oxford UP, 1984).

A curious, but most interesting expression of profound belief in the Rule of Law by a well-known Marxist can be found in E. P. Thompson, *Whigs and Hunters* (London, Allen Lane, 1975, paperback edn. 1977), 258–69.

The notion of law as an instrument of policy is especially associated with the works of the American jurist Roscoe Pound, whose *Introduction to the Philosophy of Law* (New Haven, Conn., Yale UP, 1922, repr. 1961) remains readable and relevant. For a critical view of what he calls 'naive instrumentalism', see R. S. Summers' paper in *Law, Morality and Society*, ed. Hacker and Raz (Oxford, Oxford UP, 1977), 119 ff. The historical association between the law and 19th-century ideology is dealt with at length by the present writer in Part II of *The Rise and Fall of Freedom of Contract* (Oxford, Oxford UP, 1979). The idea that economic efficiency is the principal goal of the law has often been argued by the American, Professor (now judge) R. A. Posner: see especially his *Economic Analysis of Law*, 2nd edn. (Boston and Toronto, Little Brown, 1977). It was much criticized in a symposium published in 9 *Journal of Legal Studies* (1980), 189 ff.

The relationship between general rules and particular decisions is discussed by the present writer in *From Principles to Pragmatism* (Oxford, 1978); cf., for a contrary view, J. Stone, 97 *Law Quarterly Review* 224 (1981). In the historical context the powers of persuasion of the law are discussed by Douglas Hay in a well-known essay, 'Property, Authority and the Criminal Law', in *Albion's Fatal Tree*, ed. Hay and others (London, Allen Lane, 1975). In the modern context, some problems are discussed by the author in his article 'Judges and Policy' in 15 *Israel Law Review* 346. On the role of Bentham in demystifying the law, see H. L. A. Hart, 36 *Modern Law Review* 2 (1973).

Chapter 5

The legitimacy question is one which has been discussed by political theorists from the time of Plato onwards. A short general overview will be found in J. Plamenatz, *Consent, Freedom and Political Obligation* (Oxford, Oxford UP, 1968). Well-known American attempts to answer the legitimacy question (in very different ways) are those of J. Rawls, *A Theory of Justice* (Oxford, Oxford UP, 1972) and R. Nozick, *Anarchy, State and Utopia* (New York, Basic Books, 1974). John Griffith offers a spirited rejection of legitimacy in 42 *Modern Law Review* 1 (1979).

Hans Kelsen's theory of law is developed in two well-known books, *The General Theory of Law and State* (New York, Russell, 1961) and *The Pure Theory of Law* (Berkeley, Univ. Calif. Press, 1967). The foundations of positivism are to be found in Bentham's *Introduction to the Principles of*

Morals and Legislation, ed. Burns and Hart (Athlone Press, 1970) and J. Austin, *The Province of Jurisprudence Determined*, ed. Hart (Oxford, 1954). The most serious critique of positivism in modern times is to be found in the works of Ronald Dworkin: see especially his *Taking Rights Seriously* (London, Duckworth, 2nd impression, 1978) and his *Law's Empire* (above). John Finnis is another critic of positivism, writing from a 'natural law' perspective, see his *Natural Law and Natural Rights* (Oxford, Oxford UP, 1980).

A short account of the American decisions in the reapportionment cases is to be found in A. Cox, *The Role of the Supreme Court in Government* (Oxford, Oxford UP, 1976).

The principal decision of the European Court invalidating sex discrimination in private pension plans is *Barber* v. *Guardian Royal Exchange Assurance Group* [1991] 1 QB 344.

On civil liberties generally the leading work is now David Feldman, *Civil Liberties and Human Rights* (Oxford, Oxford UP, 1993). On the desirability of a bill of rights, see H. Fenwick, *Civil Liberties* (London, Cavendish, 1994); G. Robertson, *Freedom, the Individual and the Law*, 6th edn. (Harmondsworth, Penguin, 1989), ch. 12; M. Zander, *A Bill of Rights?* 3rd edn. (London, Sweet & Maxwell, 1985). See also the article by Sir Thomas Bingham, Master of the Rolls, advocating the incorporation of the European Convention into English law, 109 *Law Quarterly Review* 390 (1993). The European Convention on Human Rights is expounded in F. Jacobs, *The European Convention on Human Rights* (Oxford, Oxford UP, 1975), though this is now seriously out of date. Also somewhat out of date is J. E. S. Fawcett, *Application of the European Convention on Human Rights* (Oxford, Oxford UP, 1987). A more up-to-date book, covering a wider area, is McCrudden and Chambers (eds.), *Individual Rights and the Law in Britain* (Oxford, Oxford UP, 1994).

Chapter 6

The best general work on the whole subject of law-making is now Zander, *The Law Making Process* (above). On legislation as a source of law, see F. A. R. Bennion, *Statute Law*, 3rd edn. (London, Oyez, 1990). On the system of precedent, see Cross and Harris, *Precedent in English Law* (above).

The influence of egalitarian ideology on the law is discussed by the present writer in *The Rise and Fall of Freedom of Contract* (above), 631–49.

The liberalization of modern marriage and divorce laws is documented and discussed by Tony Honoré, *Sex Law* (London, Duckworth, 1978).

For criticisms of modern methods of statutory drafting, see Sir David

Renton, *The Preparation of Legislation* (Report of the Renton Committee, Cmnd. 6053, London, HMSO, 1975); *The Interpretation of Statutes* (Law Com. No. 21, London, HMSO, 1969).

There is a considerable literature on the concept of the *ratio decidendi* of a case, most of which is discussed in Cross and Harris, *Precedent in English Law* (above). Well-known articles are those by Goodhart, 'The *Ratio Decidendi* of a Case', published in his *Essays in Jurisprudence and the Common Law* (Cambridge, Cambridge UP, 1931) and Julius Stone, 'The *Ratio* of the *Ratio Decidendi*', in 22 *Modern Law Review* 597 (1959).

The functions and work of the Law Commission are discussed in J. H. Farrar, *Law Reform and the Law Commission* (London, Sweet & Maxwell, 1974).

Index